IT HAPPENED IN ITALY

Untold Stories of How the People of Italy Defied the Horrors of the Holocaust

ELIZABETH BETTINA

THOMAS NELSON
Since 1798

NASHVILLE   DALLAS   MEXICO CITY   RIO DE JANEIRO   BEIJING

Published in Nashville, Tennessee, by Thomas Nelson. Thomas Nelson is a registered trademark of Thomas Nelson, Inc.

Thomas Nelson, Inc., titles may be purchased in bulk for educational, business, fund-raising, or sales promotional use. For information, please e-mail SpecialMarkets@ ThomasNelson.com.

Pictures marked © "Fondazione Museo Internazionale della Memoria Ferramonti di Tarsia" have been used with permission specifically given to Thomas Nelson Publishers and Elizabeth Bettina and are for use only in this book, *It Happened in Italy*.

Library of Congress Control Number: 2009923243

ISBN: 978-1-59555-102-3

Printed in the United States of America

09 10 11 12 13 QW 5 4 3 2 1

To my grandmothers, Bessie and Tina, whose immense
influence is felt to this day . . .

. . . and to all who have the courage to care and are not
indifferent to the plight of innocent people.

He who saves one life saves them all.
(Talmud)

Love thy neighbor as thyself.
(Matthew 19:19 NKJV)

Contents

Author's Note: Some of the names of people mentioned in this book have been changed to protect their privacy, but it doesn't change the story, or what happened.

Preface

THE DACHAU LIBERATOR—EARLY FALL 2008

I f you hadn't shown me these photos, I wouldn't believe it. It's truly unbelievable."

Jimmy Gentry pored over rare pictures and kept shaking his head. As one of the American soldiers who liberated Dachau, the infamous German concentration camp, on April 29, 1945, he reminded me of many World War II soldiers who came home—strong, stoic, and sad. Today he was looking at something he'd never imagined: pictures of *Italian* concentration camps full of Jewish people who survived the Holocaust. He simply could not believe the difference between what he witnessed in Dachau and what he was seeing in these pictures of the Italian camps.

"The first thing I notice about these people is that they're not wearing rags of striped clothes; the clothes these people are wearing are nice, like clothes the men wore back home in Franklin at the time. They're well-dressed—jackets, ties. Not what I saw in Dachau, no ma'am." Jimmy shook his head before continuing.

"These people are fleshy, not like the walking dead I saw

in Dachau. They look well-kept. Nothing like the ones I saw in Germany—with those eyes—people with haunting eyes."

As we sat in a sunny garden house on Jimmy's Tennessee farm that crisp fall day, Jimmy paused at his memory of the haunting eyes, and a shadow crossed his face. He continued to look at my photos of an Italy he still could not imagine.

"I see children here," he said, pointing. "There were no children in Dachau. These children look well-cared for and look, here, they were in school? A piano and a concert? No, nothing like this in Dachau."

I asked him if he'd known there were Jews interned in Italy during the war.

"I didn't," he replied, "and I don't know why I haven't heard about it. I can't believe Italy treated the Jews in their internment camps so well. It doesn't make any sense, because Italy and Mussolini were allied with Hitler for most of the war."

The fact that someone like Jimmy wasn't aware of this didn't make sense to me either, and that's why I've been researching the story since the day I first discovered it. For forty years Jimmy had not been able to speak about his World War II experience of walking into the German concentration camp and seeing the human tragedy there. But twenty years ago he looked into the eyes of a Dachau survivor who asked Jimmy to share his story with others. "When you die," explained the man, "nobody will know anything about what happened." Jimmy understood. "After that, I had to tell others," he said. So in 1986 he began speaking about his experiences and has continued ever since.

In October 2007, Jimmy traveled back to Dachau and recalled the unforgettable horrors he saw upon entering the camp: the skeletal figures that had been human beings; the filth; the death and destruction. His recent visit to Dachau made the contrast he was seeing in these pictures all the more poignant.

On that fall day in 2008, Jimmy looked directly into my eyes and said, "Tell this story. It is a story of goodness amidst evil. You must tell this story. If you don't, who will?"

Introduction

If you travel to New York City and visit the Museum of Jewish Heritage, you eventually come upon a large plasma television screen that displays a scrolling map of Europe. It depicts Europe before and after World War II. Each country's map shows two sets of numbers: one set reveals the number of Jews in that country before the war, and another, the number murdered during the war. What numbers appear for Italy? There are no numbers at all. The museum, like most history books, does not even mention that Italy had Jews, either before or after the war, let alone that any survived. Next to Denmark, Italy had the highest survival rate of any Nazi-occupied country in Europe. I've met some of these survivors and their children and grandchildren, and I've heard their amazing first-hand stories of escape from certain death by the Nazis.

This book tells the incredible story of the discoveries that unfolded as I traveled along an unexpected road, including my personal encounters with people who lived during that time —witnesses to little-known history—and their vivid recollections. My journey took me to tiny villages throughout Italy that I had never heard of and eventually inside the Vatican to meet with the Pope. It is an intricate web of information, seemingly disconnected pieces of a vast puzzle that overlap and continue to surprise—the complete picture of which we may never know. Wondering why almost no one really knows what happened—even those who live in the areas in Italy where these events occurred—compelled me to tell this story.

I wanted to provide a glimpse into the impassioned lives of a different kind of Holocaust survivor. You will hear their gratitude to Italy and to the Italians who so many years ago risked their lives to save people whose only crime was being of another religion. After speaking with many of the Italian survivors, I learned that they only survived because someone— an average citizen, police officer, town official, or local priest or nun—helped them during their time in Italy. Not that everyone in Italy helped the Jews during this time—many Jews were deported and many perished. Jews still suffered. But many survived, and what follows tells those stories.

The Italian-run internment camps where these survivors were sent were not work camps or death camps; they were more like "detainment" camps for displaced persons, where Jews were generally treated with dignity and respect. They were even able to practice their religion—the reason they were exiled to these camps in the first place.

Spending time with these survivors has changed me. Because of them, I view the world in a different way and realize that things might not always be as they seem on the surface. The truth is often far more powerful than we can ever imagine.

A TALE OF TWO CAMPS

I always told Fred that he had a picnic in Italy. I said to him, 'You complained that sometimes you had too much soup, while I was lucky to get a few spoons of some dirty water,'" recalled Edith Moskovich Birns. Edith is a survivor of Auschwitz, while the man who would become her husband, Alfred (Fred) Birns, survived the Holocaust in Italy.

Edith, a tall, slender, elegant woman, reminds me of an older Grace Kelly. She is in her eighties, is always fashionably dressed, and carries herself with an air of confidence. To see her today, you would never guess that at one time she was beaten simply for being a young Jewish woman. And you could not imagine, unless she told you, that during World War II, she was held in Auschwitz and other German camps.

Edith was born into a Jewish family in 1925 in Konus, Czechoslovakia, which was then part of Hungary, near Ungvar. Her father was an accountant, and they led a nice upper-middle-class life until the day it was abruptly ripped from them by the Nazis. On April 10, 1944, the family—Edith, the eldest at eighteen; her two sisters, ages six and eleven; two brothers, ages seventeen and fourteen; and her parents—and their Jewish neighbors were rounded up and taken to a ghetto in Unvbar where they remained for about two months. From there, a cattle car took them to Auschwitz, the notorious Nazi death camp.

"I remember being taken out of my home in Hungary with my family. None of our neighbors tried to help us. No one warned us of what was going to happen," said Edith with a faraway look in her eyes. "In Italy, Fred and his friend Walter [Wolff] were helped by the Italians and warned when the Nazis were coming—even by the police. Fred was able to survive because the Italians did not assist the Nazis. They [the Italians] hindered the Nazi efforts and helped the Jews. That did not happen to us. The Hungarians cooperated with the Nazis.

"In fact, as we were being taken away, one of our neighbors asked us which of our cows gave the most milk. Can you imagine? That is what they asked us as we were being taken away. I will *never* forget that! From the truck, I saw them entering our home and taking our belongings.

"After a few months in the ghetto, we were put on trains, in cattle cars. It was terrible. There was no place to sit. We all stood. It was hot. There was no place to go to the bathroom. We were locked in the dark with no light and no air for days.

"Then the doors opened. We stumbled out and right away were sent in different directions. My little sisters were holding my hands, but I was forced to go into another line and had to let go of them. They went with my mother, and I never saw them again. They were taken straight to the showers and murdered."

Edith's voice cracked as she whispered, "I still have nightmares about that, and cannot forgive myself for not trying to save them. This was Auschwitz. You know what *that* means. Absolute horror. The guards would make fun of us and beat us if they saw us praying. They worked us to death, and we barely had enough to eat. If I found the core of an apple in the field, I picked it up and sucked it. That little juice helped me survive one more day, but if a soldier found me picking the apple up, he would have shot me immediately." She continued. "What was happening to us? I asked. *Why* was this happening to us? *What did we do?*

"Toward the end of the war, I was transferred to Ravensbrück, near Berlin. When the Nazis realized the Allies were closing in, they sent us on the famous Death March. As the war was ending, the Nazis tried to murder the remaining survivors by forcing them to march away from the Soviet Army and die from the cold weather, exhaustion, and famine. I was liberated on May 5, 1945, by the Russians. That is what saved my life. There is so much more to tell you, but can I tell you another time?"

"Of course," I said.

We were both silent for a moment.

"You know," she said. "Fred and Walter, their experiences in Italy were so *so* different. *The Italians treated them like human beings.* Fred survived for six years in Italy. No one could ever have survived six years in German concentration camps. That was impossible."

"When did Fred arrive in Italy?" I asked.

"He went to Italy from Dresden with his mother and father around 1938. They didn't like what was going on in Germany and decided to leave."

Fred's family, like so many others, decided to leave Germany before the country's political situation worsened, and Italy was the only country that would let the Jews in without a visa. Life was good for Fred's family until the war; then they were sent to camps. Fred was sent to Campagna and his father to Ferramonti. At the time, their last name was Birnberg. (Later, when they immigrated to the United States, it was changed to Birns.) Then Fred made a *domanda*, kind of a "request," to join his father, and he, too, went to Ferramonti.

"As I said before," continued Edith, "the Italian camps were a picnic. Whenever Walter and Fred got together, they loved to speak Italian, and they both loved Italian people. They told stories like old friends do about their time together and what they did. You know what they did? They played cards! Can you imagine that? When I tell other survivors that my husband played cards in his concentration camp in Italy, *they don't believe me.* If Walter and Fred didn't have the pictures, I wouldn't believe it either. What kind of camp was that? Nothing like the ones that I was in.

"Eventually, when the Italians became enemies of the Germans, the Germans looked for Jews in Italy to take to their camps in Germany. Fred was able to get help from a priest who arranged fake papers for him. Fred became Mario Rossi. No one in Hungary helped my family get fake papers. No. Instead, they pointed the way to our house. That is the difference."

"What happened to your family?" I asked.

"My whole family except my brother and me were killed in Auschwitz. A family of seven—we became two."

And Fred's family?

"They all survived," she said. "They were in Italy. But Fred's relatives in Germany? They were all destroyed by the Nazis. Every one of them died."

✦

Edith's heart-wrenching story highlighted yet again the stark differences Jews experienced when they were interned in Italy, compared with the death camps elsewhere in Europe. I was months into my journey of discovery, and by now I'd heard many other survivors tell stories with the same theme: life in Italy, instead of death; kindness from strangers instead of cruelty; humanity instead of depravity. The unfolding tale had taken me across the world and through many turns and surprises, but it all started with a simple photo.

2

THE PHOTO—THE RABBI!

A picture changed my life.

The faded gray photo showed something that just didn't make sense. What was an Orthodox rabbi doing standing on the steps of the church where my Catholic grandparents were married? This was not the typical church in New York City with a synagogue around the corner. It was a church in the tiny Italian village of Campagna, a place practically invisible to the outside world, hidden in the folds of the rugged Apennine Mountains about an hour southeast of Naples.

Questions raced through my mind. *Since when did this village have a rabbi?* Just about everyone in Italy in the 1940s was Catholic. So how did this rabbi get there—especially during World War II? But there he was, surrounded by smiling people, including a bishop and a police officer. I didn't think police officers and rabbis got along anywhere in Europe in 1940.

I came to discover that this picture not only said a thousand words, but it also represented a thousand lives, and then some. It began a journey to discovering the true story of how

A rabbi, priest, and police officer on the steps of the Church of San Bartolomeo in Campagna, Italy. Dott. De Paoli (police officer in white uniform), Vescovo Giuseppe Maria Palatucci (priest), Rabbi David Wachsberger of Fiume.

thousands of Jews were spared almost certain death at the hands of the Nazis, simply because they were in Italy.

✦

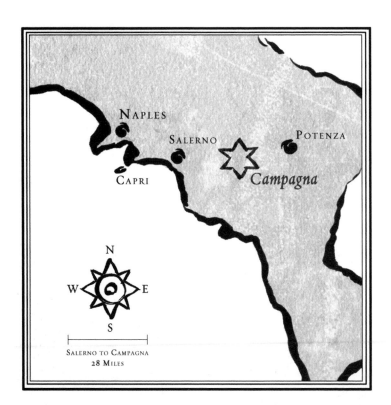

Like many other Italian-Americans, my grandparents moved to the United States for the many opportunities it offered. We still had family in Italy, so starting from the time I was ten years old, my grandmother, "Nanny," and I would spend our summers in Campagna. We visited almost every year until I graduated from high school, and it was a different world from the New York City suburbs I lived in the rest of the year.

Elizabeth Bettina as a young girl in Campagna. (left to right) Great Aunt Elvira Insalata, Cousin Paolo Granito, Elizabeth Bettina, Concetta Granito Insalata (Nanny).

No one in Campagna talked much about World War II. It was a difficult time, I was told, and my uncle Zio Pierino spent part of it in a German prisoner-of-war camp. At one point, the Americans accidentally bombed Campagna when they thought they saw Germans in the town. There were no Germans there—that day—but many townspeople had gathered for their daily ration of bread, and many of them were killed that day. Almost as an afterthought, I was told that few *Ebrei* (Jews) were hidden in the surrounding mountains. When

Germans did come through, searching for Jews to deport to Germany, my great-grandfather and others in Campagna hid some of the Jews from them. That was all they told me. No one ever elaborated.

So I knew of a *few* Jews hidden in the mountains, not the hundreds—or maybe even a thousand—who spent years in Campagna. The way I heard it, it sounded as if a handful of people, similar to Anne Frank's family, were hidden there. And no one ever mentioned a rabbi!

✦

Over four years ago, on a sizzling hot Sunday evening in August, my eighty-nine-and-a-half-year-old grandmother (she added the half back in) and I were enjoying brick-oven pizza with family and friends at *Ristorante/Hotel Avigliano*, a restaurant located high in the mountains of Campagna. This was the last night of a wonderful trip I'd planned as a complete surprise, an opportunity for Nanny to visit her family in the village where she and my grandfather were born. No one in Campagna knew we were coming, and were they ever surprised to see us! Little did I know that the surprise would be mine.

Campagna is a picturesque, quiet village that can only be reached by one narrow, winding road. If the road is blocked for any reason, the only way in is to climb the mountains. (Think *The Sound of Music*.) In many ways, time has stood still in Campagna. My friend David Parker visited Campagna a few years ago and nicknamed it Brigadoon, after the fictitious Scottish village that appears for only one day every hundred years. It fits. The streets are narrow, made for *i ciucci,* the donkeys. In some places you can stand in the middle of the street and touch the walls on both sides with your outstretched arms. Little old ladies dressed in black lean over balconies keeping watch or peer out of seemingly shuttered windows. I say "seemingly shuttered" because the ladies manage to look through the slats and see all that is going on. Nothing escapes their ever-watchful, inquisitive eyes. You'll find the men sitting around the town or playing cards at the local cafés, and no one ever seems to move very fast—even on a Monday morning.

Nanny was seventeen when she married my grandfather and moved to New York, and as they say, the rest is history. She maintained close ties with her family over the years through letters—the old-fashioned kind with airmail stamps that took weeks to arrive, and she kept them all these years in her dresser drawer.

When I first began going to Italy, Nanny's parents were still alive, and I got to know my great-grandparents. They were the *oldest* people I had ever seen—at the time they were *only* in their mid-eighties. My great-grandmother looked like the other elderly ladies in town: she was petite, wore long skirts, and kept her snow-white hair neatly rolled up in an old-fashioned bun. My great-grandfather was short and had a mustache accompanied by a stern look on his face. He never left the house without a hat on and his shotgun slung over his shoulder—like the other men his age.

One summer led to another, and after I graduated from high school, I continued to visit every few years. After all that time, I thought I knew *everything* about this village and its quiet, almost backward, ways.

That evening at *Ristorante Avigliano*, Zio Peppe, a distant relative in his mid-seventies (it seems everyone is a distant relative in Campagna) and the owner of the restaurant, gave me a copy of a doctoral thesis. It was written by a wonderful man from Campagna named Gianluca Petroni. The picture of the rabbi on the church steps was in the book, just one in a series. There were more pictures from Campagna in the 1940s—of a menorah, of Jewish men playing cards, and of Jewish men singing. How did they get there? And *why* were they there?

This book has since traveled with me all over the world, and continues to unlock mysteries. Little did I know that this discovery would change not only the course of my life, but many other lives.

Flying back to New York at thirty thousand feet over the Atlantic, I read in the thesis about Jews in Campagna during World War II and what their lives were like. Mostly, they were foreign Jews interned in Campagna in the former Convent of San Bartolomeo, located next to the Church of San Bartolomeo (at times referred to simply as the convent). They were allowed to practice their religion and could make *il matzo* (flat, cracker-like bread) for *Pesach* (Passover), a holiday Italians of the time referred to as the "Jewish Easter." Now, I cannot imagine *matzo* in Campagna—ever—let alone in a time and place where to be Jewish meant persecution and almost certain death. Did they allow Jews in Dachau or Auschwitz to make *il matzo*? I hardly think so.

© *Corbis*

Synagogue in the interment camp of San Bartolomeo attached to the Church of San Bartalomeo, Campagna.

I wanted to ask the pilot to turn the plane back so I could learn more. How could this have occurred in Campagna and no one ever talked about it? Gossip is the favorite pastime of people in this little village—in fact, in all the little villages in Italy. They could win a gold medal for gossip, if such an award existed. They know everything about everyone and are faster than any BlackBerry. Why didn't I learn about it from either the people of the town or from my history books in school? Why did the world not know? And how did my Jewish friends *not* know?

Many ask why I am so taken by this story. I grew up Italian-Catholic in a suburb of New York City that was predominantly Jewish, and I was aware of the Holocaust long before I learned about it in school. Even as a little girl I never understood why people—human beings—persecuted others just because of their religion. Some of my friends and neighbors had relatives who were survivors or, worse, were killed in the death camps.

Discovering Campagna's extensive connection to Jews during the Holocaust amazed me and began an extraordinary journey, one I could *never* have imagined but one it seems I was born to take. Looking back, I can now see that almost every facet of my life up to that point led me to this story. *Destino*, as the Italians would say.

I have an unbelievable desire—I could go as far as to say it is a calling—to connect the pieces of this intriguing puzzle. In searching for the pieces, I discovered that Campagna was not the only place where Jews were interned in Italy during World War II. Quietly, all over the boot of Italy—from small towns outside Torino, Milano, and Perugia to small towns in the regions of Abruzzi, Basilicata, and Calabria and many in between—Jews were helped by Italian people who risked their lives to keep them from the hands of the Nazis.

Jimmy Gentry was right. This story of goodness in a time of evil must be told.

Elizabeth with Concetta Granito Insalata (Nanny) in front of the Chiesa di San Bartolomeo (Church). This picture was taken a few days prior to Elizabeth discovering the story of the Jews in Campagna who were interned in the former convent. A piece of the convent door can be seen at the far left.

3

THE ITALIAN SCHINDLER

Giovanni Palatucci. Italians call him "The Italian Schindler." Oskar Schindler was the German factory owner who saved nearly twelve hundred Jews during the Holocaust by bringing them to work in his factories. The movie *Schindler's List* dramatizes his story.

So imagine this. It is the 1940s. An Italian police official working under Benito Mussolini (Hitler's primary ally in Italy) actively defied orders to implement Hitler's "Final Solution" of eliminating Jews from the face of the earth. In the process, he saved thousands of Jewish people from being deported to Nazi death camps. This extraordinary man was Giovanni Palatucci, and for his heroic efforts, he was killed at Dachau.

In 1990, Palatucci was honored by the Yad Vashem, the famed Holocaust museum in Israel, for his ultimate sacrifice. The Yad Vashem honors as "Righteous Among the Nations" Holocaust rescuers who, at great personal risk, saved Jews during the Holocaust. In 2002, Palatucci was also recognized for his sacrifice and was beatified—a step before sainthood—by the Vatican's Cardinal Camillo Ruini.

Palatucci was born in Montella, near Avellino (Naples

area), attended high school in Benevento, and was stationed in Fiume, now Rjeka, Croatia, in 1937. His role in Fiume was *Questore*, which can best be described as part police chief, part immigration officer, and part census officer. All foreign residents in Italy were required to register at the *Questore* office, and this gave Palatucci access to their documents and personal information, including their religion. As a result, he had a list of all foreign residents, many of whom were Jews who had come to Italy to escape unrest in their countries prior to the beginning of the war in 1940. Italy was also the only country that kept its borders open to Jews until the war began. Palatucci hid this list from the Nazis, because he knew that in the wrong hands, it was a map that led directly to a concentration camp and almost certain death for the Jews on the list.

Giovanni Palatucci enabled people to leave Italy by supplying false documents, and if they couldn't leave Italy, Palatucci arranged to send them to an official Italian government internment camp in Campagna, the former Convent of San Bartolomeo, where his uncle, Giuseppe Maria Palatucci, was the bishop. With his uncle watching over the Jews, Giovanni Palatucci knew they were safe—at least for a while. Italy eventually joined the Allies and, as far as Germany was concerned, the Italians were now "the enemy." Once the Nazis figured out what Giovanni Palatucci was doing, they sent him to Dachau, where, on February 10, 1945, he died the death from which he'd saved thousands of Jews (some estimates are as high as five thousand). Just two months later, on April 29, 1945, Dachau was liberated.

Why did this man risk his life to help others? Like most Italians, Giovanni Palatucci believed in one sentence: *Amare gli altri come te stesso.* Love thy neighbor as thyself. Both survivors and their saviors repeatedly describe their experiences using this simple sentence.

Giovanni Palatucci, along with many other Italians, could not understand why Jews were being persecuted just because they were of another religion, and he decided he would do whatever he could to help. In addition to his official role, Palatucci also had a personal interest in helping save Jews. His Jewish fiancée survived the Holocaust because he performed the selfless act of giving her his transit visa for Switzerland, even though he knew the Nazis were coming for him. She eventually made her way to Israel and died just a few years ago.

In a way, Palatucci symbolizes all the other unnamed "Giovanni Palatuccis" in Italy, people who risked their lives and their families' lives to help others simply because it was the right thing to do. As Walter Wolff said, "At least fifty people helped me, and if each one of them didn't do what they did at the *exact* moment they did, I wouldn't be here today." In honoring Giovanni Palatucci, all of those nameless people are honored as well.

The first Giovanni Palatucci Courageous Leadership Award was given in October 2007 to David Cohen, deputy commissioner of intelligence for the city of New York. In his speech

Cohen said, "Giovanni Palatucci didn't save five thousand Jews, he saved twenty-five or thirty thousand—or more. There are now four generations of what could be called 'Palatucci Survivors,' children, grandchildren, and great-grandchildren of his original protectees."

The people saved and their descendants are additional proof that Hitler failed at his "Final Solution." I always question what makes some people risk their lives to help others. What would I have done? What would *you* have done?

GIOVANNI PALATUCCI
(1909–1945)

4

BLESSINGS FROM
A CHILDHOOD FRIEND

I couldn't wait to show "the picture" to my childhood friend Ellen Barre Spiegel and get her reaction. She and her husband Bill were coming to New York for the Jewish holidays, and we were getting together for dinner while they were here.

Dinner was to be at a Chinese restaurant—where else would a nice Jewish girl and a nice Italian-Catholic girl go out to dinner in New York City? Ellen was looking forward to hearing about my trip to Campagna. After all, she had thrown me a "bon voyage" party when I went to Italy for the first time in elementary school. Over the years Ellen had heard many stories about my Italian friends and family, met some of the aunts and cousins, and felt she knew a bit about this small town hidden in a valley. Never in our wildest dreams did either of us think that thirty years later we'd be looking at a picture of a rabbi in Campagna.

After our meal it was time for the picture, and I took the book from my bag. She was as surprised as I was to see a rabbi in Campagna and hear that so many Jews were there during the war. Ellen had traveled to Italy many times and, as a practicing Jew interested in learning more about the

Italian Jewish community, had visited synagogues in Rome and Florence. I showed Ellen more pictures and documentation of the Jews and explained what I had learned.

After thinking it all over she said, "We always knew you were an honorary Jew. Now we know the reason you grew up in a Jewish neighborhood. Who else could understand the story of Jews and Campagna? You are the only person!"

Together we poured over the 272 Jewish names listed in the book, people who had been interned in Campagna. This list was of one particular day: September 16, 1940. Hundreds more Jews were interned in Campagna from 1940 to 1943, and so the list does not include people who came to Campagna after that date.

"Look," she said, "these are all New York Jewish names: Epstein, Hoffmann, Lehmann, Schwarz, Weinstein. This is amazing. You need to look into this, Elizabeth. You were born to do this."

And so the journey began. With the blessing of my Jewish childhood friend, I embarked on an unknown path, determined to find the answers to this fascinating story.

	Cognome	Nome	Paternità	Età	Professione	Cittadinanza
1.	Adler	Leo	Giacobbe	1887	orefice	germ.
2.	Barta	Maurizio	Simone	1881	commerc.	slov.
3.	Beder	Abramo	Szyja	1913	medico	pol.
4.	Berg	Rodolfo	Luigi	1890	albergatore	germ.
5.	Berger	Alberto	Maurizio	1914	tappezziere	apol.ex boemo
6.	Bestándig	Samuele	Leone	1902	pelliciaio	apol.ex pol.
7.	Blaufeld	Wolf	Markus	1904	rabbino	apol.ex pol.
8.	Blej	Giulio	Leone	1910	insegnante	rumeno
9.	Borensztajn	Lajbus	Mosè	1901	commerc.	pol.
10.	Brandweiner	Enrico	Salomone	1889	macellaio	germ.
11.	Buchsbaum	Maurizio	Pinkas	1906	commerc.	pol.
12.	Carenni	Giovanni	Nicola	1899	impiegato	apol.ex ital.
13.	Cingolani	Ruggero	Riccardo	1904	maniscalco	ital.
14.	Danzig	Giovanni	Bertoldo	1920	meccanico	boemo
15.	David	Sigfrido	Alberto	1908	prof.in filos.	germ.
16.	Degai	Alessandro	Nicola	1890	pittore	apol.ex russo
17.	Donath	Edoardo	Bernardo	1905	ingegnere	slov.
18.	Ehrmann	Giuseppe	Emanuele	1897	commerc.	pol.
19.	Eisen	Mosè	Chaim	1887	viaggiatore	germ.
20.	Elsner	Rodolfo	Bernardo	1900	impiegato	germ.
21.	Engel	Guglielmo	Giulio	1906	architetto	slov.
22.	Epstein	Bernardo	Mosè	1913	rabbino	slov.
23.	Ernst	Arturo	Massimiliano	1885	scrittore	germ.
24.	Fabbris	Girolamo	Francesco	1920	falegname	jugosl.
25.	Feith	Guglielmo	Michele	1899	avvocato	boemo
26.	Finkelstein	Mosè	Enrico	1897	commerc.	germ.
27.	Förster	Ugo	Ernesto	1915	chimico	germ.
28.	Fränkel	Bernardo	Saul	1889	commerc.	apol.ex pol.
29.	Freudmann	Massimil.	Carlo	1892	orologiaio	boemo
30.	Friedjung	Giovanni	Ernesto	1913	possidente	germ.
31.	Gaffiers	Walter Alb.	Alberto	1869	prof.giornal.	ingl.
32.	Gewürz	Szyja	Henoch	1895	libraio	pol.
33.	Grott	Bela	Giacobbe	1916	tipografo	slov.
34.	Grünfeld	Massimil.	Vojtech	1900	commerc.	slàv.
35.	Habib	Eliezer	Giuseppe	1903	commerc.	apol.ex turco
36.	Hammerschmidt	Daniele	Leopoldo	1884	commerc.	germ.
37.	Hammerschmidt	Guglielmo	Leopoldo	1889	commerc.	germ.
38.	Hauser	Maurizio	Ermanno	1898	commerc.	apol.ex pol.

*Elenco, composto di sette pagine, degli internati presenti a Campagna in data 16 settembre 1940.

This is the first page of the list of 272 names of internees living in Campagna on September 16, 1940. The complete list is located in Appendix A of this book.

5

AN UNEXPECTED CONNECTION

One of the reasons I decided to attend the cocktail party near my office in Manhattan was that I knew there would be tasty food. It's one thing you can count on at Italian cocktail parties.

If you were to stand next to me on the subway, by the time you reached your stop we likely would have shared our life stories. I'm like that—I love to make connections with people, to learn about their lives. My friends laugh at me because of this and call me "the connector." So I was in my element at the cocktail party when I began chatting with a woman named Consuelo Bandini. She'd recently moved to New York with her family when her husband was transferred from Italy. I shared that I had returned from Italy a few weeks earlier and had discovered the most amazing story about Jews in Campagna during World War II. By now I had grown accustomed to Italians not knowing about this, but to my surprise, Consuelo *did* know the story, and the stories of many other villages that helped Jews.

I couldn't believe it. We didn't have time to discuss the details, so Consuelo and I exchanged phone numbers and agreed to get together soon for coffee. Before we parted, I asked where her husband worked, assuming it was an international bank or Italian company. I did not expect to learn that she was the wife of the Italian consul general in New York!

The two of us did get together for coffee, and it was the beginning of a wonderful friendship, one I will always treasure, not just because she is delightful, but also because she was the first to verify my findings. After meeting Consuelo, I had a feeling there was significantly more to this story.

6

THE FIRST SURVIVOR

Eva Deutsch Costabel is the first person I met who actually survived the Holocaust under Italian rule. She is a spirited woman, filled with energy and passion. We met on January 27, 2003, at an event in New York City on *Giorno della Memoria*. This is an important date because it is the anniversary of the liberation of Auschwitz. The Italians began recognizing this date in 2001, and on November 1, 2005, the General Assembly of the United Nations designated January 27 as "an annual International Day of Commemoration in memory of the victims of the Holocaust."

Eva is originally from an upper-middle-class family in Yugoslavia. She escaped with her mother, her sister, and others from her town, Zagreb, to the Adriatic coast, which was occupied by the Italian military.

I was interned in the resort town of Crikvenica and then was taken to a concentration camp, Porto Re (Kraljevica). From there we were transferred to the Island of Raab. The Italian military did not want to deliver us to the Nazis or the Croation Ustacha, and they gave the Jewish leaders the right to administer the daily life of the camp, which gave us a fair amount of autonomy in our daily lives. In the camp we wore our own clothes and were not required to wear a Jewish star. We were never abused and [were] treated with respect. The camp was not a death camp. They didn't kill anybody in this camp. This was the difference.

This was a very different kind of camp than the ones I knew of.

"Why are you so interested in this story?" asked Eva.

I explained by taking out the book and showing her the picture, and we discussed why I found this story fascinating on so many levels.

The first is that Jews, both Italian and foreign who were in Italy during the war, were saved from the horrors of the Holocaust because they were in Italy—even though Mussolini was Hitler's prime ally. To me it is the most interesting paradox of World War II. In occupied Europe approximately 75–80 percent of the Jewish population was executed. Yet in Italy, a country that was Hitler's ally, approximately 75–80 percent of the Jewish population *survived*, and that may not include some foreign Jews who were already in Italy when the war began.

I also explained to Eva that I never heard these stories of survival in the predominantly Jewish community where I grew up, or in Italy. I wanted to know why a story of goodness was buried in scholarly documents and not known to the general public. My inquiring mind needed to know more.

Eva looked at me, her eyes intense, and said she felt this story was the most important story of the Holocaust. "You must write about this and let people know," she said. "The world needs to know what happened."

So now I was on a mission with Eva's encouragement added to that of Consuelo and Ellen. *If Eva had survived,* I thought, *there must be other Jewish people still alive who had escaped the brutality of the Nazis because of the Italians.*

It began to dawn on me that they marched to the beat of their own drums, the drum of their conscience. It wasn't only Giovanni Palatucci. Italians, in general, did not do what they were told to do or "follow the leader." After extensive research and interviews all over the boot of Italy, north to south, I came to understand that most Italians were going to do what *they* thought was *right*—and helping persecuted people was right.

7

UNEXPECTED JOURNEY

Meeting Walter Wolff was a bit of a miracle, for many reasons. First, he is a Holocaust survivor, and anyone who survived the Holocaust is, by definition, a miracle. Second, he was in Dachau and was released when virtually no other prisoners were. Finally, meeting Walter was a miracle because I actually opened my mail in a timely fashion! (I have been known to let what I call "extra mail" pile up on my desk.)

In this particular extra mail pile, there was an announcement from Queens College, which is located not too far from my home. A man who survived the Holocaust in southern Italy was going to speak at the college about his experience. *Perhaps,* I thought, *he might know something about Campagna—or know someone who was in the town.* Looking at the date, I was relieved. Good. It was the next week! I hadn't missed it.

Accompanied by Aunt Ida, Nanny's youngest sister, off I went to Queens College. Walter began his talk by describing his life in Germany before the war. At the time of his presentation, he was a very energetic, eighty-eight-year-old man, with twinkling eyes and a mustache, who reminded me a bit of my great-grandfather—but without the shotgun! Somehow, he had managed to save many personal documents and photographs from the war, and he showed a number of them in his slideshow.

His early life in Frankfurt, Germany, was one of solid middle class that included Walter, his brother Bruno, and his mother. Sadly, Walter's father had died of natural causes when Walter was a young boy. Life wasn't easy, but the little family managed, especially with the help of his grandparents. Walter attended a high school called Reform Real Gymnasium Philanthropins in Frankfurt and received an excellent education. It was a school that I would hear more about over the next few years. Walter was also a very good soccer player and loved music, and both helped him survive during the war. As he recounted his life story, the life so cruelly taken away from him by his fellow German citizens, he showed us pictures of the way things were.

For most Holocaust survivors, their pre-war lives are just a faded memory, but if they *are* lucky, as in Walter's case, they may have a photograph to remind them of what once was. It proved they didn't just invent a former life—a life I call "BH." Before Hitler.

Walter explained that he lived through ever-increasing anti-Semitism, and through *Kristallnacht* (kris'täl-näkht), the night of crystal. In German history, the night of November 9, 1938, was a night of violence against Jews and of destruction of businesses and other property belonging to them. The name is a reference to the huge amounts of broken glass that resulted from the destruction. That night, Storm Troopers, the SS, and the Hitler Youth killed ninety-one Jewish people and injured hundreds more. They destroyed at least seventy-five hundred businesses and hundreds of synagogues—burned them completely to the ground. The event marked the start of the deportation of Jews to German concentration camps and is considered the beginning of the Holocaust. Walter was arrested by the Germans and sent to Dachau on November 10, 1938, the day after *Kristallnacht.* His brother, Bruno, was sent to Buchenwald. Their crime: being Jewish.

In 1938, Germany appeared to be focused on having Jews leave the country rather than eliminating them completely. It did not matter where the Jewish people went, as long as they left Germany. Sounds simple, right? In reality, it was not. Without a visa, you could not enter another country, and during this time, almost every country in the world turned its back on the Jews.

Walter and Bruno should have been able to enter the United States on student visas, because they had been accepted to the Hebrew Theological College in Chicago. Walter's mother had the letters to prove it. She apparently was quite a lady with an enormous amount of *chutzpah,* and the letters she wrote to German officials on her sons' behalf must have been incredibly powerful. She asked that they be released from the camps because after their studies in Chicago, they would not return to Germany. She was successful in her quest, and her sons were released under the condition that they leave Germany within six months.

All they had to do was apply for visas at the United States Consulate in Germany. They did, but were rejected. The consulate believed that once Walter and Bruno were in the United States, there was no assurance they would leave after the three years of study—even though Walter explained they would then go to Palestine. "No" remained the answer. The United States did not offer assistance even when presented with legitimate documents.

Walter and Bruno faced a dilemma. They had been freed from Dachau but had no place to go. Italy was the only country allowing Jews to enter without visas, so naturally, with that six-month time clock ticking, Italy was where they went, with the thought to continue on to Shanghai, a city where many Jews found refuge during the war. They hoped to take a steamer for China from Genoa, but once in Italy decided to remain. Walter realized that learning to speak Italian was imperative to survival in Italy, as it would enable him to secure a job. Plus, it did not behoove a person to speak German in those days if he were trying to hide from German soldiers.

Then in June 1940, Walter was arrested in Genoa. His crime: being Jewish. It seemed as if the safe haven that Italy appeared to be was safe no longer. After all, Mussolini was Hitler's ally at the time, and now he was having Jews arrested and taken away, just as the Nazis did to Jews in Germany. Walter was terrified. He could not believe that he had been released from Dachau, only to be sent to another camp—this time in Italy.

"Wonderful—I exchanged one camp for another," Walter

said more than sixty-five years later. "Now I was back in the same boat, except the Italian camps were *nothing* like German camps. In comparison, it was like going to a hotel. There was no forced labor in the Italian camps. We could do whatever we wanted during the day, as long as we obeyed the simple rules of being present for roll call in the morning when the doors to the camp were opened, and in the evening when the doors to the camp were closed. The *carabinieri* (police officers) treated us well. In order to pass time, we played cards, took walks around the little village, read books, or played soccer at a field just outside town. We even had our own orchestra and performed for the local residents."

1940. Walter's string group in Campagna. Walter is second from the right. (From the book, Bad Times, Good People, *© 1999, Walter Wolff)*

1940. Part of the chorus practicing in Campagna. (From the book, Bad Times, Good People, © *1999, Walter Wolff)*

No one in the room could believe this. It certainly did not sound like any concentration camp we had heard of.

Walter then said, "Obviously this camp was not Dachau. It was in a small town, south of Naples—Campagna."

Campagna appeared on the screen! I couldn't believe Walter Wolff was in Campagna! Aunt Ida grasped my hand, and we looked at each other in disbelief. I had tears in my eyes, and my throat tightened. I had hoped that this man would have *some* information about Campagna, but I never dreamed he had *been in* Campagna.

I raised my hand. "Excuse me, Mr. Wolff, which camp were you in, the old Convent of San Bartolomeo or the old military barrack?"

Walter, in turn, could not believe that someone in the

audience knew of Campagna, or that I knew there were *two* camps at the time. "I was in San Bartolomeo," he said. "How do you know there were two camps?"

I told him my family was from Campagna, that, in fact, my great-grandparents' house is only a few feet away from the old convent *and* my grandparents were married at the church attached to the convent. Everyone in the room was stunned. What were the chances?

Walter continued his lecture and said several times that if it were not for the Italians who helped him and his family along the way, he would not be here today. In addition to treating the Jewish internees with decency, Italy had a policy of trying to keep families together during their internment. Walter explained that he spent about a year in Campagna and then was transferred to Ferramonti, the camp where his brother Bruno had been sent. Walter's mother was in the small town of Brienza, near Potenza, about an hour southeast of Campagna. She was also sent to Ferramonti, where the family was reunited.

Ferramonti is located near the town of Tarsia in the region of Calabria, the southernmost region of Italy before the island of Sicily. It was also the largest internment camp in Italy and was a true camp with barracks, housing anywhere from two to three thousand people during the 1940s. But the barrack-style housing was the only aspect of Ferramonti that was similar to a German camp. Like Giovanni Palatucci, Ferramonti appears numerous times in this story.

1941. Jewish internees in Ferramonti.

After the Wolffs were reunited in Ferramonti, they had the opportunity to be transferred to their choice of one of several towns. This was called *internato libero*, or internment that was free, meaning they could live in a town amongst the Italians. They only had to stay in the town, sign in at the police office daily, and seek permission from the *carabinieri*, the police, if they wanted to leave for the day. Walter and his family received a list of various approved places to live and—because it had an active Jewish community and a beautiful synagogue—they chose a small town in northern Italy called Casale Monferrato, near Torino and Milano.

My first question was why Walter went to northern Italy, toward Germany, during the war—closer to the enemy? Walter's answer: being Jewish in Italy before September 8, 1943, was not a safety concern. Only after September 8th, when northern Italy was under German occupation, did he fear for his safety.

Walter knew that if he was able to obtain false documents, he had a better chance of surviving, so he asked a priest in the town of San Giorgio Monferrato for help. This priest arranged for Walter to receive fake documents from a man who worked in *Comune* named Giuseppe. Just *mentioning* the priest's name was all Walter had to do. Giuseppe *in Comune* knew *exactly* what it was about. He issued Walter Wolff a series of papers that renamed him Valter Monti from the Province of Cosenza in southern Italy. (Note: Southern Italy was under Allied control by that time, and town records would be difficult to verify.)

"Even though Giuseppe and I encountered one another only twice in my lifetime, I owe him an immense debt of gratitude for risking his position as well as his life for providing me with the false identification papers," said Walter. "I also owe the priest. Without his word—well, nothing would have happened." Those documents helped save Walter's life because they said he was Italian. This was the first time I had heard of documents being issued in Italy—but certainly not the last.

After his presentation, I met with Walter and his friend Gerda Mammon. Gerda is also Jewish, from Germany, and as a young girl during the war escaped with her family to Holland, where she was part of the Dutch underground. Neither could believe someone in the audience actually knew of Campagna. Walter said he had told his story for almost twelve years all over the country, and this was the first time someone in the audience was familiar with Campagna. Aunt Ida and I were amazed that Walter had spent time a stone's throw away from where she grew up. Who would think that they would meet so many years later in New York?

While chatting with Walter and Gerda, my mouth got ahead of me—as it sometimes does. Walter said that it was a dream of his to return to Italy one of these days. *One of these days*, I thought. Walter was eighty-eight years old when I met him, and "one of these days" was not an option as far as I was concerned. It had to occur—now. And if Walter returned to Italy, I believed he needed to go as an honored guest. Anyone can buy an airline ticket, book a few hotel rooms, and show up, but that was not the way *this* visit was going to be. I would make sure that Walter was honored by Campagna and the people in Italy for his work in teaching others that even during bad times, there can be good people. That's the title of a book he wrote: *Bad Times, Good People*. It tells Walter's story in detail and includes copies of photos and documents that depict his experiences during that time.

I found myself telling these two lovely people that if they really wanted to go back to Italy, I would arrange it, and they would go back the way they should—honored. I had *no* idea *exactly* how I would accomplish this, but I knew that was the way it was going to happen.

The next day I called Rosario Mariani, a senior executive at

Eurofly, a European-based airline, and asked if Eurofly would sponsor tickets for this historic event that I was planning.

"Just let me know the dates," he said.

The Italian Tourism Board contacted a hotel in Rome, the Atlante Star, located near the Vatican. Thus began a lifelong friendship with the Mencucci family, who own this unique jewel of a hotel.

I now knew I could take Walter Wolff back to Italy.

What I did not know was that this trip would be the first of many in which other Holocaust survivors returned to Italy where they had once escaped the atrocities of the Nazi regime.

COMUNE DI SAN GIORGIO MONF.

Provincia di Alessandria

IL PODESTA'

Attesta che il militare *Monti Valter*

di *fu Guglielmo* e di *Rossi Francesca*

nato a *Cosenza*

il giorno *2. dicembre 1912*

già appartenente *Reparto Detramiles - 613*

P. M. 169 - residente in Cosenza

si è presentato a questo Ufficio in data odierna in ottemperanza al proclama emanato da Capo della della Provincia.

Lì *29 - aprile 1944.*

IL PODESTA'

1944. Walter's false identification papers provided by Guseppe (Municipality of San Giorgio Monf. Province of Alessandra).

(Translation)

THE MAYOR declares that the soldier Monti, Valter, son of the late Guglielmo and of Rossi Francesca born at Cosenza the day of : 2 december 1912 (not Walter's correct birthday) was a member of:Department Detramiles 613 P.M. 169—residence in Cosenza

REPORTED TODAY TO THIS OFFICE IN OBEDIENCE TO THE PROCLAMATION OF THE COUNTY EXECUTIVE

Date: 29 April 1944

THE MAYOR

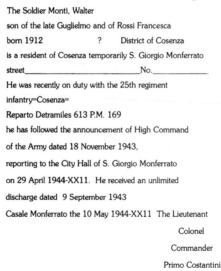

1944. Walter's "discharge" papers from the Italian Army.

(Translation)

COMMAND OF THE MILITARY DISTRICT OF CASALE MONFERRATO

Office for Mobilization and Discharge

The Soldier Monti, Walter

son of the late Guglielmo and of Rossi Francesca

born 1912 ? District of Cosenza

is a resident of Cosenza temporarily S. Giorgio Monferrato

street_____No._____

He was recently on duty with the 25th regiment

infantry=Cosenza=

Reparto Detramiles 613 P.M. 169

he has followed the announcement of High Command

of the Army dated 18 November 1943,

reporting to the City Hall of S. Giorgio Monferrato

on 29 April 1944-XX11. He received an unlimited

discharge dated 9 September 1943

Casale Monferrato the 10 May 1944-XX11 The Lieutenant

Colonel

Commander

Primo Costantini

8

PLANNING THE RETURN

I met Walter Wolff on a Monday, and on Thursday flew to Italy for business. I had arranged my trip so that I could spend the weekend in Campagna visiting my relatives and friends. I especially wanted to visit Zia Maria, an aunt who was all of four-feet-eight-inches tall and a bundle of energy, but it was not to be. Zia Maria died the week before the trip.

It remains a mystery why she never mentioned the hundreds of Jewish men, many young and handsome, who for years lived up the street. Not telling the story was completely out of character for her.

I was very sad about Zia Maria's passing and returned to Campagna with a heavy heart and many questions. Zia Maria would have been the perfect person to answer them. I am convinced that she must have known Walter Wolff.

Walter's book, *Bad Times, Good People,* and its many pictures of him in Campagna, came with me. I showed the book to Michele Aiello, president of the *Comitato Giovanni Palatucci*—the Giovanni Palatucci Association. Michele is a wonderful man in his early forties with dark hair and dark eyes, who has taken the Palatucci story to heart. The association's goal is to promote the good works of Giovanni Palatucci.

Michele was thrilled that I met Walter Wolff and was working on bringing him back to Italy the coming year. Naturally, he and his group were excited about the possibility of meeting Mr. Wolff.

✦

One thing I don't understand is why there has not been an effort to trace these survivors. With *Giorno Della Memoria* beginning in 2001, I would think that the locals would be curious to learn what happened to the interned Jews in the Italian villages. Indeed, some of the internees' names were listed in various government offices throughout Italy. Gianluca Petroni found a list in the government archives in Rome, and I would find other lists while researching. What I didn't know at the time was that I would soon meet many other "names" on the list—all with incredible tales to tell.

9

VINCE MARMORALE: 1+1=3

When I first met Vincent Marmorale, he reminded me of the lawyer in the movie *Erin Brockovich*. He is a bundle of energy, a retired high school history teacher and former adjunct professor at Long Island University, and a walking encyclopedia, or better yet, a human search engine regarding all aspects of the Holocaust. Frankly, Vince's knowledge is scary. Ask him anything about a document, treaty, or meeting during World War II, and he can tell you the exact date, who signed the document, and with what color pen. Vince and I have been to many lectures over the years by various experts in Holocaust studies, and they are amazed at the broad scope of Vince's knowledge, especially in lesser-known areas of the Holocaust.

Vince has always been interested in the Holocaust, even as a young boy. He grew up in Brooklyn, a neighborhood that was predominantly Italian and Jewish. As a ten-year-old, he asked his father why their friend Mr. Topal had a "tattoo" on his arm. His father kindly explained, "I have to tell you a story, a bad story. There were some people who wanted to hurt Mr. Topal and people like him—other Jewish people."

Mr. Topal's story began Vince's intense lifelong study of the Holocaust, which caused Vince's path to cross with mine so many years later.

Vince met Walter Wolff in 1995. At the time, Walter believed there was no story to tell about how he survived the Holocaust, because, as he said, he did not suffer much once he was in Italy. After two hours on the telephone, Vince assured Walter that he *did* have a story to tell—a story of goodness during one of history's darkest moments. The two men began a strong friendship.

For years afterward, Vince and Walter spoke at various events, synagogues, schools, Italian organizations, and the like. Their goal was to explain that during the Holocaust, some people did the right thing by helping their neighbors in need. Because many people risked their lives to help, Walter Wolff survived the Holocaust. When Walter spoke at Queens College on the day I met him, it was one of the few times Vince was not with him. As a result, Vince and I did not meet until Walter and Gerda introduced us in July, two months before the scheduled trip to Italy.

The bond that Vince and Walter had formed over the years was immediately apparent to me, and I knew that Vince should be part of this historic trip. Once again, I spoke before thinking things through, and I heard myself asking Vince to join us. Thank goodness when I called Rosario Mariani at Eurofly (again) and asked him for another ticket that night, he said yes. Rosario is an angel.

Together, Vince and I formed an unstoppable team—what I refer to from time to time as "1+1=3." When two elements combine, they are often more powerful together than on their own. Vince's heart and knowledge, combined with my passion and *chutzpah*, would lead us down paths that neither of us ever thought possible.

Gerda and Walter were right. Vince and I hit it off over one word: Paestum. Vince could not believe that I knew about Paestum. Located about thirty minutes from Campagna, Paestum has some of the best-preserved ancient Greek temples in the world. As a little girl, when spending summers in Italy with Nanny, I often stayed in Paestum with relatives. Until we met, Vince had not encountered another American who had heard of the place, let alone been there.

Vince's parents were from the Benevento area, about an hour north of Campagna. Now, in Gerda's kitchen, an ocean away on Long Island, Vince and I discussed Italy and the Holocaust and ancient Greek temples. I knew then that each of us had found a new and wonderful friend.

10

HOW TO GET TO THE VATICAN: CALL AMY

The train passed Naples. We were about an hour from Battipaglia, a town roughly twenty minutes from Campagna. We would be there at 8:30—the traditional time for *cena* (dinner) in Italy. After all the planning, it was actually happening. Walter Wolff was going back to Campagna, where he was once interned, as a free man.

Walter was excited and knew that his trip would be historic. It isn't often that someone who once was officially interned, albeit "Italian style," had the opportunity to thank the people there for helping to save his life. That Walter was enjoying this trip meant the world to me.

Arranging this trip was a minor miracle, but it was nothing compared with another miracle—later in the week we would meet with a cardinal in the Vatican. *That* required some special help.

◆

While walking to work in Manhattan one morning, I had a crazy thought. Giovanni Palatucci was a candidate for sainthood, so I thought it appropriate that Walter Wolff meet the cardinal who beatified Palatucci, Cardinal Camillo Ruini. I figured that it must take an extraordinary amount of documentation to propose someone for sainthood. Walter had a direct connection to the Palatucci story, as he was under the watchful eye of Giovanni's uncle, Vescovo Giuseppe Maria Palatucci, the bishop of Campagna. Walter could shed light on what happened at the time because he was there.

So, exactly how do you connect with popes and cardinals? Do you just dial 1-800-POPE and someone answers, and your call is put through?

Now *this* was a challenge.

I was determined to have Walter and Cardinal Ruini meet, but writing a cardinal felt a bit like writing to Santa at the North Pole. I knew in my heart that if Cardinal Ruini read the letter, he would want to meet Walter. But it was a matter of getting the letter read. Who did I know who could help deliver this letter to the right person in a timely fashion? I wracked my brain and contacted my friend Ed Reilly, whose close family friend is Cardinal Theodore McCarrick of Washington, DC. I also called the office of Bishop Murphy of Rockeville Centre, New York. Walter lived in Long Beach, within the diocese of Rockeville Centre.

It was already June, and time was of the essence. The trip was scheduled for the beginning of September, so to the untrained American mind, that gave us two months, July and August, to arrange schedules and make travel arrangements.

But in Italy, most of the country goes on vacation in August. Even the pope leaves Rome for the month! In the real world of the Italian calendar, we only had until the end of July, at best, to finish planning.

Cardinal McCarrick was traveling in the Middle East, but his assistant promised that she would have him review my request as soon as he returned. And although Bishop Murphy was going on vacation, his assistant assured me he would review the request when he returned.

I knew they would come through. This, after all, was a good story, a true story, but would it be soon enough? July was fast approaching, and we were going to Italy on Labor Day weekend. I decided to try one other option, the telephone, and set my alarm clock for 2:45 AM, so I could call the United States Embassy to the Holy See. The Holy See is what the Catholic church is referred to in diplomatic relations.

The Internet provided the embassy's phone number. Although I knew that Vatican City was considered a separate country within Italy, I was not up on my Vatican or United States politics and did not know exactly how the system worked. In fact, I thought that the United States Embassy to the Holy See was part of the United States Embassy to Italy. Little did I know that it's actually a separate embassy with its own ambassador, staff, and building. Thus, the United States has two embassies in Rome: one to Italy and another to the Holy See. The things one learns!

The alarm went off as scheduled, but, even under the best

of circumstances, I am not a morning person. Let's just say I desperately need a strong cup of coffee before I get going.

Coffee made, I dialed the number, and a woman's voice answered.

"Amy Roth speaking."

I asked if Amy had a few minutes to listen to a story that she would find of interest. She kindly said yes, and I wondered what she was thinking as I started. How many phone calls must she receive from people who request meetings with Vatican officials, especially those looking for a miracle?

I gave Amy a short version that explained how Walter Wolff was connected to Dachau, Campagna, and the Palatuccis. With a knot in my throat, I asked if we could possibly meet with Cardinal Ruini—and perhaps even the pope. I figured both Cardinal Ruini and Pope Benedict XVI would find the story of interest if they only knew about it: a German Jewish man traveling back to Italy to express his gratitude to the Italians for saving his life and the lives of other Jews from the hands of the Nazis.

And that is how it all began. And when I say all, I mean *all*. I sent Amy, who became our angel—a true bright light in this wonderful story—information via e-mail, fax, and overnight mail. She received photos of Campagna with Walter from two different books, and information about the town and both Palatuccis (the bishop and the *Questore*).

Amy and I corresponded via e-mail, and I knew she "got it" when she wrote that "time was of the essence." Yes, it was. It is for all of us, but many times we choose not to see it. However, time becomes very precious in situations involving elderly people.

Amy took charge and presented the story and letter to United States Ambassador Rooney. He, in turn, forwarded to Cardinal Ruini my letter requesting a visit with him. It seems that a letter from the United States Embassy to the Holy See has high priority.

Now I was in a waiting game. Cardinal Ruini would have to return to Rome before we received an answer. Patience is not one of my virtues, to understate things a bit, and this situation was testing what little patience I had. It was completely out of my hands. I had contacted everyone I could think of to move this along. Time would provide the answer.

Some of my colleagues at work knew I was planning a trip to Italy to take a Holocaust survivor back to the village that saved him, but very few knew that I was also trying to secure an appointment with a cardinal in the Vatican and maybe even the pope. After all, who was I to do something like this? I certainly was neither a head of state nor rich and famous, and I was definitely not Mother Teresa. I merely "connect dots" and have an unrelenting passion to bring people together—the sooner the better.

I reviewed our plans for the Vatican portion of the trip with Alicja, one of my coworkers. She looked up from her desk and said, "It will happen. God will make it happen."

I just stood there for a few seconds, speechless. I responded in a whisper, nodding my head. "God wasn't on my list of contacts. He doesn't have e-mail or a phone number."

We both laughed so hard that everyone else in the office turned around. Truly, of all the people on my list, God was not there. I had listed people whom I could contact "directly," through "normal" means. Asking God just hadn't occurred to me. But Alicja was right; God would see this and make it happen. I realized God did need to be on "the list," so I asked for a little help. Now there was nothing I could do but wait for Italy to return from its month-long vacation.

✦

My apartment is in Midtown, not the quietest of neighborhoods, but definitely convenient. I can walk to Central Park in five minutes, to Fifth Avenue in ten minutes, and to work in fifteen minutes. When I leave my apartment, I usually have my cell phone out of the big, black bag that is my pocketbook. Why they call these enormous things "pocket" books is beyond me. If the cell phone was in the "pocketbook," it would take me a few rings to fish it out, and inevitably I would miss the call, so it stays in my hand or jacket pocket.

It was now the end of August, and my cell phone rang just as I was ready to go out the door.

"Hello, is this Elizabeth?" asked a voice that sounded like one of my friends from college.

"Well, it depends who this is," I responded in a sarcastic voice.

"It is Amy. From Rome."

I took a deep breath, my mind racing. I couldn't believe I was so flip on the phone, and it was the nice angel from the United States Embassy to the Holy See—not my college friend. My heart was pounding. I was certain Amy must be calling with good news. We chatted a bit about how Rome was beginning to come alive again and how the trip planning was coming along. She finally said what I knew she was calling about. Cardinal Ruini had said yes to meeting Walter!

I started to cry. It was a deep, sobbing cry, the kind usually reserved for something extremely sad, yet this was a joyous occasion. I never knew that getting an appointment to meet a cardinal in Rome would have such a profound effect on me. The appointment was the "seal of approval" that this was significant—and the Vatican recognized it.

All I could say was, "Oh my. I don't believe it!" I guess Alicja was right. God was in this mix of contacts after all. I finally managed to string along a few words that formed a sentence. Amy was moved to hear the emotion in my voice; I was completely embarrassed.

Amy said she would review schedules and dates with me over the next few days. It was really happening!

I called Vince right away.

"Sit down," I said. "I have something to tell you, and trust me, you need to be seated."

I didn't know it at the time, but this would be the first of many calls beginning with "sit down, you aren't going to believe this." I told him that we had not one, but two, meetings in Rome with cardinals. (Amy also had arranged a meeting with Cardinal Kasper, president of the Pontifical Council for Promoting Christian Unity and the liaison for Vatican-Jewish relations. I didn't even know that post existed!)

Vince was speechless, something quite unusual for him. Never in his wildest dreams did he think he would go to the Vatican with his friend Walter. This was definitely different from the speeches they gave together on Long Island at the local synagogues and Italian community centers.

I walked to work in a fog. What incredible twists and turns life takes. Going to the Vatican certainly wasn't anywhere on my "to do" list a few months ago. At the office I walked straight to Alicja's desk.

She said, "It happened, Liz, didn't it?"

"How did you know?"

She started to laugh. "The look on your face says it all. See, I told you it would happen. God is making it happen."

Alicja was right. As this story progressed, I would see God's hand in the string of coincidences and the twists of fate that continued to come my way. In making plans for trips and the many survivors, never again did I leave God out of the mix. God's hand would eventually take us to other offices in the Vatican as well.

11

FINDING OUT
ABOUT CARDINAL RUINI

I t is wonderful that you are bringing Mr. Wolff here to Campagna," said my Italian cousin Antonio. "There have been talks in the town to have the Convent of San Bartolomeo turned into a museum, *ma, la burocrazia italiana . . . Elisabetta, non hai idea.*" Ah, he was saying, *but the Italian bureaucracy—you don't have any idea.* Italy is known for its complicated bureaucracy. This is a country that changes governments at the drop of a hat.

"Yes, I have an idea," I said with a smile, imagining all the *fogli,* pieces of paper, sitting in piles scattered in various government offices in Italy that all need special stamps. "I've also arranged a meeting with the cardinal who beatified Giovanni Palatucci, Cardinal Ruini."

"*Cosa?*" What? Antonio questioned.

"I made an appointment with Cardinal Ruini," I repeated, thinking he didn't hear me on the international phone line.

"*Ruini, ma Elisabetta come hai fatto?*" Ruini, how did you do that? "With Ruini, or someone in his office?" he asked.

"*Con il Cardinale Ruini.*" With Cardinal Ruini. I did not understand why this was such a big issue.

"*Elisabetta,* no one gets an appointment with Ruini. *È quasi impossibile.*" It is almost impossible. "It is harder for us to see Cardinal Ruini than it is the Pope!" said Antonio.

"*Cosa?*" I asked. "Why?"

"Ruini is, how do I explain this to you, he is like 'vice pope' for us. Think how everyone sees the president of the United States, and very rarely do you see the vice president. Ruini's official title is Vicar of Rome," he said. "*Ora capisci?*" Now do you understand?

"Oh," is all I could manage to say.

"*Come hai fatto?*" he questioned. How did you do this?

"I wrote a letter," I said, shaking my head.

I wrote to Cardinal Ruini because *he* was the person who signed the papers for Giovanni Palatucci's beatification. My theory was that papers relating to beatification were given to a cardinal who was from the same country that the person being considered for beatification was from. This way, those working on the beatification would have easier access to research papers and be able to read documents in the original language. If Giovanni Palatucci were, for instance, from Spain, it would be a Spanish cardinal; if he were French, it would be a French cardinal; and so on. It was obvious to me that Cardinal Ruini was given the Giovanni Palatucci papers because he was an Italian cardinal, and for no other reason. I was obviously wrong.

"*Sai,* he was the cardinal who officiated at the funeral mass for Pope John Paul II," he continued, trying to give me the *CliffsNotes* version of Who's Who in the Vatican.

I had watched the pope's funeral mass; in fact, I had been honored to see Pope John Paul II twice, once with my church group in high school at Madison Square Garden and at Midnight Mass at Saint Peter's during my junior year in college. There were so many cardinals participating at the funeral. I never thought I would meet one of them, let alone the Vicar of Rome.

As soon as I finished the conversation, I called Vince, who suggested I call the Italian Consul General Antonio Bandini. "He should know about this."

Consul Bandini had been very supportive of our project, and I always kept Consuelo and her husband informed. Vince was right. Meeting with Cardinal Ruini was more than just a meeting with a cardinal.

"How are your plans for the trip?" Consul Bandini asked.

"So far, so good. I'm calling to let you know that we have an appointment with Cardinal Ruini when we're in Rome," I said.

There was a moment of silence, and then Consul Bandini asked, "How did you arrange that?"

I gave him the short version and concluded, "Somehow an appointment was made."

"Unbelievable. Even if I wrote a letter as the consul general, it could take months for an appointment—if I were to receive an appointment. That is amazing."

A few minutes after we hung up, the phone rang; it was Consul Bandini calling back.

"Elizabeth, I just spoke to the rabbi of Rome, Riccardo Di Segni, and explained what you are doing. He is expecting your call. Here is his number; you can call him now. He knows about your trip and appointment with Cardinal Ruini."

A minute later I was speaking with the rabbi of Rome.

"Yes," he said. "I was expecting your call. I understand you will be in Rome with Mr. Wolff. What can I do for you?"

"Well, perhaps if your busy schedule permits, you could meet with Mr. Wolff. I am certain you would find his story quite informative. I could also use some help organizing Shabbat for him in Rome." Shabbat is the traditional weekly Jewish worship.

"When will you be here?" he asked.

"We will be in Rome twice. First at the beginning of the week, then we go to Campagna and return to Rome for the weekend."

"Call me when you arrive, at the beginning of your trip," he said.

And so I did.

12

ARRIVING IN ITALY

It took a lot of planning to get Walter to Italy. I worked with Michele Aiello of the *Comitato Giovanni Palatucci* in Campagna, Amy in Rome, and Rosario at Eurofly. We were set and ready to go, until Vince called at four PM the Friday before we were supposed to leave.

It was one of those "you need to sit down" phone calls. Now it was my turn.

"Your worst nightmare," he said. "Walter's in the hospital. He has an infection they want to watch."

Tears welled up as I put my head down on my desk and took a deep breath.

"I'm headed to the hospital now with Dorothy to find out exactly what's going on," he said.

Naturally our first concern was Walter's health, and that's why Dorothy, Vince's wife and an amazing OR nurse, went with Vince to the hospital. She was the extra set of eyes and ears needed to review what was going on. I shifted to my role as organizer and began the flurry of phone calls: Rosario, Consul General Bandini, the hotels, Walter's friends Giorgio and Adriana Ottolenghi (with whom he was planning to visit when he was in Italy), Michele, and Amy, to let them know our trip was on hold.

Vince and Dorothy arrived at the hospital and reviewed Walter's chart with the doctors. Everything seemed to be okay. Walter had a mild infection and was expected to be released in a few days. That's exactly what happened. Walter's doctor gave him permission to travel, and off to Italy we went—a few days later than planned.

13

EXPLORING ROME

After Walter visited his friends Giorgio and Adriana Ottolenghi in Casale Monferrato, where Walter was *internato libero*, we arrived in Rome. The next day was our meeting at the United States Embassy to the Holy See, when we would finally meet our angel: Amy.

Vince, Walter, Gerda, and I were tired but happy to be in Rome. Our cab brought us to our hotel, the Atlante Star, located one block from the Vatican. As the cab approached, the Cupola, the famous dome over Saint Peter's Basilica, came into view.

At the hotel, owner Roberta Mencucci greeted us warmly and accompanied us to our rooms. The next morning, we were off to the United States Embassy to the Holy See, found in a beautiful, peaceful part of Rome, not in the middle of the hustle and bustle of Via Veneto where the United States Embassy to Italy was located.

The cab ride to the embassy was breathtaking. In addition to traveling to our destination, we were having an unexpected tour of many famous monuments of Rome: the Vittorio Emanuele monument, nicknamed the "Wedding Cake"; the Coliseum; the Roman Forum; and more churches than I could count.

Finally, there was the United States flag. We had arrived. Naturally, we had to go through security, similar to an airport, and were ushered into a beautiful conference room. Then there was Amy. She was right out of central casting for her role as an expat working in the United States Embassy in Rome. She was very pretty, tall, and blonde. Being blonde in Italy, well, let's just say Italian men will notice you. Amy quickly made us feel at home and introduced us to the vice consul general. Walter began telling them his story of survival, and together we reviewed photographs and documents of that time.

"You must know," Walter explained, "the Italians treated me well, and they helped me until the war ended. If they hadn't, I would not be here today. I know I wouldn't have survived had I remained in Germany, in Dachau. We all know what happened there."

"Mr. Wolff, your story and the story of other Jews surviving in Italy is not well known. We're honored that you made this trip here, to give testimony to what happened," said Amy. "I was able to reschedule your appointment with Cardinal Ruini for Friday morning, and I thought perhaps Elizabeth and Vincent could meet with Cardinal Kasper, who is responsible for Christian/Jewish relations, on Saturday. It was the only day both the cardinal and your group is in town. I understand it is Shabbat, but Cardinal Kasper is not here during the week."

Walter thanked Amy for arranging the meetings and agreed that we should meet Cardinal Kasper on Saturday, so he could learn about Walter.

The next day, we took the train to Campagna. After more than sixty-five years, Walter Wolff, the former internee, was returning to the little hidden town.

Vice Consul Chris Sandrolini, Walter Wolff, and Amy Roth at the United States Embassy to the Holy See in Rome.

Gerda Mammon, Walter Wolff, Vince Marmorale, Giorgio Ottolenghi, at the Synagogue of Casale Monferrato, built in 1595.

14

WALTER WOLFF RETURNS A FREE MAN

S*ignorina, fra poco Campagna,*" Walter leaned over to tell me with excitement in his voice. He loved to speak Italian. In fact, all the survivors I interviewed who lived in Italy during the war love to speak Italian. Translation, "Miss, soon Campagna." But no sooner were his words spoken than the train stopped dead on the tracks. I hoped it was just a short delay.

No such luck. In true Italian form the train stopped for what seemed like an eternity. To make matters worse, we were only a few minutes from our destination. After an hour, the train started moving and finally pulled into Battipaglia.

Now for the fun part. We had to get two elderly people and all the baggage off the train in just a few minutes. Michele was waiting for us at the train station with the mayor of Campagna and a host of other people. Italians love ceremony and always want to *salutarti*, but there was no time for two kisses, one on each cheek, when trying to exit a train. I had a fearful image that because we were trying to be polite by greeting Michele and the mayor, the baggage, or—worse—

Walter and Gerda, somehow would be left on the train, which was headed for Sicily. So, not to be rude, I called Michele on his cell phone and said we would *salutare* after everyone and everything was off the train.

After almost five hours of what was supposed to be a three-hour trip, we were glad to disembark. From the window, I could see the Campagna delegation, including the mayor with a "Miss America" type sash designating him as mayor. It appears that wearing the sash somehow makes things official in Italy. Eventually, we all left the train and not a bag was lost. We were off to Campagna.

Unfortunately, it was evening and Walter could not see much of the area as we approached. The cars made their way to the town and the *Ristorante/Hotel Avigliano* where the staff was waiting for us with a lovely dinner. Walter's kosher diet meant he would be eating mostly vegetarian dishes—pasta with tomato sauce, salads, and eggs.

The next day was a busy one. We met with the mayor and others in town and visited the statue of Giovanni Palatucci, where Walter encountered a man, Antonio Paladino, who remembered him when he was not free. We then drove a small Fiat up Via San Bartolomeo to the convent. (How cars manage to fit through these narrow streets is beyond me.)

Walter climbed the same steps where, so many years earlier, photos were taken of Jewish internees with Italian police officers. The difference this time was that he *chose* to be there.

1940. Group picture of the Jewish internees in front of the concentration camp Campo di San Bartolomeo, which is also the front of the Church of San Bartolomeo, Campagna (Salerno). Walter Wolff is seated in the fifth row next to the man with the guitar. Please note that they are wearing their own clothes, not uniforms, and they are not wearing Jewish stars. (From Bad Times, Good People, *© 1999, Walter Wolff)*

As we entered the former convent, Sandro Scannapieco, a local trumpet player, began playing "Taps." Well, that was it for me. The tears came pouring down. Walter walked slowly through the convent, pointing to where they used to pray in the makeshift synagogue. It is amazing to think that, in a former convent attached to an active Catholic church, Jews could practice their religion while officially interned by the fascist Italian government.

Upstairs we saw what was once Walter's room, and he described how it was set up at the time. "I shared the room with others. There were comfortable beds, warm wool blankets, hooks for my clothes, room for my suitcase. Nothing like Dachau," he said. "Campagna was more like a hotel."

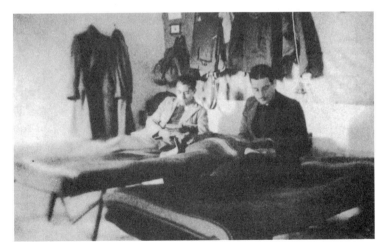

1940. Walter Wolff's bedroom in Campagna. Walter is on the right. (From the book, Bad Times, Good People, © *1999, Walter Wolff)*

We looked out the window toward where, in 1943, the Jews escaped into the mountains when the Germans marched into Campagna.

It was now time for lunch, and we headed back to the hotel. A group of people joined us, as they all wanted to get to know Walter better.

At four in the afternoon, we headed to *Comune*, town hall, where Walter and Vince would give the same presentation they'd delivered countless times. Only this time they were in Italy, where it all began. The *Comune* was packed with hundreds of people who came to hear Walter and Vince, including my friends Gilda Bassano, and Maurizio and Antonietta Cammerano, whom I have known since I was a young girl. We were delighted to have Padre Vanzan and Anna Foa attend from Rome. Padre Vanzan prepared many of the documents for Palatucci's beatification, and Anna Foa, who is Jewish and a professor at Sapienza, the University of Rome, worked with Padre Vanzan, the *Comitato Giovanni Palatucci*, and the *Comune di Campagna* in bringing to light the connection between Campagna and the Palatuccis.

Vince began. "We are honored to be here this evening. This is an historical event: Walter Wolff returning to Campagna a free man! What you also must remember is that if there was no Campagna, Walter may not have survived the war and be here today more than sixty-five years later."

Vince went on to review for the audience what was happening at the time in the world and, in contrast, what was happening in Campagna. Then it was time for Walter to speak.

"I am happy to be here—again!" said Walter. "I want to thank the people of Campagna for treating me and the other Jews here at the time with dignity and respect. It is nice to be here again, a free man. But frankly, I felt free even then, especially compared to my time in Dachau."

The room was packed with people who wanted to see Walter. One man in particular stood out: Remo Tagliaferri, a former police officer in the camp of San Bartolomeo.

"Tagliaferri" means "cut iron," and when you meet Remo Tagliaferri, who is ninety-two years old, you see that the name fits. One glance and you know you don't want to mess with him. He is strong, looks you directly in the eye, and has a full head of steely gray hair. It wasn't hard to imagine him in his former job as a police officer in charge of San Bartolomeo.

Today he was sitting with Walter Wolff, remembering their time in the camp; they could have been former college classmates attending a reunion. All of a sudden, Tagliaferri took out the whistle he used in roll call and blew it. Walter immediately came to attention. They laughed.

"*Ricordi*, Wolff, when we all would go to the soccer field, just outside of town. You were a good player, one of the best," Tagliaferri said.

Imagine a Jewish man returning to a place where he once was held against his will, laughing about old times with the police officer who controlled the camp. They embraced like long-lost friends. It is hard to fathom. But here we were in Italy, and Walter and Tagliaferri were together, smiling. Truth *is* stranger than fiction.

2006. Walter Wolff with former police officer Remo Tagliaferri.

The evening continued with speeches by various officials, as is customary in Italy. They really like to talk, especially while wearing those "Miss America" sashes.

Then I was asked to comment.

"This is an important event for Mr. Wolff, Campagna, and the world," I said. "People need to know what happened here and in other parts of Italy. It is even more significant now, in today's world, with terrorism on the rise. As a young girl, I heard about bombs falling in Campagna and other parts of Europe, but, to me, those were things of the past. I had not experienced bombs falling from the sky and thought that was something that could not happen in my lifetime in America, in New York. As we are all aware, I learned that I could see bombs in my peaceful, bright blue sky, bombs in the shape of airplanes filled with innocent passengers who killed innocent office workers—some of whom were my friends. Once again, the world was not the same. Man showed how evil and destructive he could be. Here, so long ago, Campagna showed how good and healing man could be."

Various medals were presented, and Walter received the key to the city. He was thrilled.

In turn, the people of Campagna were happy to have Mr. Wolff back in the town as a free man, a tourist. And we did play tourist together. Before heading back to Rome for our Vatican appointments, we went to Paestum to see the extraordinary Greek temples. Vince was delighted.

(left to right) Elizabeth Bettina, Walter Wolff, Gerda Mammon, and Vince Marmorale in the City Hall of Campagna in front of pictures taken in 1940.

15

VATICAN VISITS

S *ciopero.* A transportation strike in Italy—*what a surprise,* I thought, as I listened to the TV while lying in bed in the morning, too tired to move. The Italians love to strike, and they have this strange habit of letting people know when and where in advance.

I was glad we weren't going anywhere today that would require trains or planes. Somewhere, someone was striking, and it would not affect us one bit. And, if there was a strike today, then when we left on Sunday, the chance of another strike was greatly diminished, so, selfishly, I was happy. We had arrived in Rome from Campagna the night before, and the only events we had scheduled were interviews for Walter with journalists and, of course, our meeting with Cardinal Ruini.

"C'è sciopero generale di tutti i trasporti pubblici oggi a Roma." I shot up in bed and reached for the TV remote and my glasses. Did I hear correctly? Great! Here I was thinking this *sciopero,* this strike, was not my problem, but it was! All methods of public transportation were going on strike today, including taxis. How was I going to get Walter to Cardinal Ruini's office

on the other side of Rome? Put him on the back of a Vespa and have him hold on for dear life?

I called Vince in his room.

"What's up?" he asked.

"We need to get moving a bit earlier than expected," I said. "There's a strike of all public transportation, including taxis."

"You're kidding."

I laughed. "Do you think I could make this up? I thought we were safe with only a few more days. Remember I said a strike was one of my biggest nightmares in Italy?"

"What do you suggest?" he asked.

"Breakfast! We'll think about it over coffee, which I desperately need. I'm sure people from the hotel will have some ideas."

We all met in the dining room. Gerda laughed at the image of Walter strapped on the back of a Vespa. Walter laughed too. I'm certain his younger self would have loved that.

Fortunately, in a few minutes, the problem was solved. The hotel had a special taxi service that would take us to Cardinal Ruini's office. The day was beautiful, and we left half an hour early to be sure we got to our eleven o'clock appointment on time. Naturally, the traffic in Rome was awful.

We arrived at Piazza San Giovanni in Laterano, a big square, like so many in Rome, with a large *palazzo* building and an imposing church. Where was number six located? Technically, taxis weren't permitted in the square, but we entered anyway,

Italian style, which means "just pretend you didn't know it was off limits and see what happens." I thought I should ask someone where six was. It was probably better not to drive around aimlessly searching for the correct address.

Good. Two police officers, one more handsome than the next, were stationed in the center of the piazza. I could ask them where number six was. The taxi pulled over. In my hand on United States Embassy stationery were instructions for our appointment with Cardinal Ruini. Then it dawned on me.

"Vince, they might not know where it is," I said. "They might only be here for *bellezza,* for their good looks!" I said only half jokingly.

"Get out of here—of course they know where number six is," he said, thinking I was a bit crazy.

I leaned out of the window. "*Dove si trova il numero sei?*" Where is number six?

They looked at each other and simultaneously gave me the "shrug." An Italian shrug includes a slight tilting of the head to one angle and can be interpreted as "I don't have a clue," or "We'll see, who knows?" or, "Does any of this really matter?"

Vince laughed. "You were right. They don't know where it is."

"Stay here; I'll go look," I said as I got out of the car.

A few feet in front of the car was number six.

"Two police officers don't know where six is, and they were directly in front of it," I said.

"That is *why* I survived. I am *here* because things like that are not important to the police," said Walter with a smile.

I checked my watch. Even with the strike, we had arrived with time to spare. Entering the building, we saw to the left an office where we had to register. Our names were on a guest list, and we were told to go through a door, make a right, and take the elevator to the second floor.

We went through a beautiful courtyard and followed the directions. The elevator took us upstairs to a large corridor where we were ushered into an office. There we met Monsignor Filippi, Cardinal Ruini's secretary. He was about forty, quite tall, and wore black pants and a black shirt with a clerical collar. He smiled, and we chatted as he showed us into a sitting room.

Naturally, we were slightly nervous. None of us had ever met a cardinal before, let alone one who was on the short list to become the pope! That was another little fact we had just learned about Cardinal Ruini.

The door opened and a man who looked like a local parish priest walked in. He, too, wore the "priest clothes" of black pants and black shirt with a clerical collar. There were no big red velvet cardinal clothes in sight. Was this Cardinal Ruini, or another priest who had stopped by to say hello?

"*Buon giorno*. I am happy to meet you. You come very well recommended. In fact, today I received a letter about your visit from Cardinal McCarrick," said the man who was indeed Cardinal Ruini.

We asked which language he would prefer, and he said

either was fine, so we began in Italian—each of us with our different accents and dialects. Walter spoke perfect Italian with a German accent, I spoke Italian with a mix of Florentine and American accents, and Vince spoke a Neapolitan dialect.

"I was interned in Campagna, and we were treated very well in the Convent of San Bartolomeo and by the people of Campagna," explained Walter. "In fact, the people of Italy treated me and the other Jews with respect and dignity. If it weren't for the people of Italy, I would not have survived. I would not be here today."

Vince and I listened intently as a German Jewish man praised Italian Catholics, especially the contributions of Giovanni Palatucci, who might one day be a saint.

Walter continued, "It's important for people to know what happened in Italy. We've been surprised that the Italians do not know what happened in their own backyard. If it were not for the many 'Giovanni Palatuccis' of Italy, who chose to listen to their own hearts instead of following orders of people who were crazy . . . well, none of us would have survived, and I have many friends who survived because they were in Italy. If we had remained in Germany, we probably would not have lived."

"What the people of Italy did was amazing," said Cardinal Ruini, "especially given the circumstances. It's wonderful to hear you give testimony to what happened so long ago. Thank you." Walter gave a human face to Giovanni Palatucci's ultimate sacrifice.

The conversation continued, and I couldn't believe how comfortable I felt. Actually, we all felt at ease, not intimidated. We stayed for about an hour, and when we left, I felt we had found a friend.

We had to wait for the taxi to pick us up. It was now lunchtime in Italy, one o'clock, and most offices close at that time of day. Car after car left the Vatican offices, each filled with priests and nuns. I had never seen so many priests and nuns driving before.

Then, a car with one priest waved to us. Was that Cardinal Ruini driving? Yes, it was.

September 2006, Rome. Vince Marmorale, Cardinal Ruini, Walter Wolff, Elizabeth Bettina, and Gerda Mammon meeting regarding beatification of Giovanni Palatucci.

Later, in the evening before sundown, Vince and I accompanied Walter and Gerda to an Orthodox Jewish home in a residential area of Rome where they could celebrate Shabbat. We left Walter and Gerda there, knowing we would pick them up Saturday evening after sundown.

Amy, our guardian angel, joined us for dinner. As she had lived in Rome for a few years, she selected the restaurant. We ended up at a place called Café Trilusa, in Piazza Trilusa, located along the Tiber River, not far from the Jewish quarter. The area was hopping with people and reminded me of Greenwich Village in Manhattan. Street vendors, painters, and local craftsmen were selling their goods, and people were milling about. Given the warm September evening, we dined *al fresco*, outside.

"I chose this place because the food is amazing, typically *romana*," said Amy. "And I especially like this part of the piazza. It's just around the corner from all the hustle and bustle, so we can really talk. Finally!"

We agreed. Most of my conversations with Amy had been on the phone, and our meeting earlier in the week at the embassy was guided by protocol. Now we could let our hair down and enjoy a glass of wine.

"I have to tell you," she said, "this story and what you're doing is extraordinary. I get calls all the time from people who want to meet the pope, cardinals, members of the Vatican. Elizabeth, you had me within fifteen seconds. Your passion traveled thousands of miles over the phone, and I could feel it at my desk. Then you followed with emails, faxes, books. You left no stone unturned."

"Well, I've never done this before," I said. "I just knew it was a good story, and by showing you it was true and that I didn't make it up—I'm not that creative—I thought maybe we had a chance."

"You know," Vince added, "I've spoken with Walter all over, at synagogues, at Italian organizations, at consulates, and I felt we had done what we could in telling this story. Then we met Elizabeth, and she took it to a whole different level."

"She certainly did," said Amy, smiling. "So, how did your meeting with Cardinal Ruini go?"

"The *sciopero* didn't start the day off right, but after that, well, it was amazing," I said. "It was peaceful. I didn't expect that. There was no pomp and circumstance. In fact, we all thought Cardinal Ruini looked like a local parish priest. At first we weren't even sure it was him, but he made us feel comfortable right away."

"Then, we didn't know which language to speak, so we spoke our own versions of Italian," Vince said, laughing. "Imagine me speaking to a cardinal in my Neapolitan dialect!"

The Neapolitan dialect comes from the Naples area. It's more than an accent and can include a very different vocabulary.

Amy laughed. "You were a breath of fresh air. Most people are too uptight to enjoy the moment, and that didn't seem to be your case at all! By the way, your meeting might be cancelled with Cardinal Kasper tomorrow because of the way some of the pope's statements have been interpreted."

"What do you mean?" we asked. For the most part we'd been in a fog during this trip, and had heard very little news. Apparently the pope had given a lecture at the University of Regensburg in Germany a few days earlier and a statement he made had offended the Muslims. It sparked unrest, and newspapers all over the world were commenting.

"Cardinal Kasper might have to meet with people at the last minute to deal with this," she said.

"Should we still try to keep the appointment?" I asked.

"Yes, go and see what happens," she said.

16

AN INVITATION FROM A CARDINAL

The next day we went to Cardinal Kasper's office, only a few feet from Saint Peter's Square on Via della Conciliazione, and were brought to a sitting room. We could hear the phones ringing: the ambassador from Great Britain, a journalist from RAI (the Italian Public Broadcasting Network), and more. Vince and I looked at each other and knew Amy had been right.

"We're only going to get a few minutes of the cardinal's time with this going on, if we get any time at all," Vince whispered.

But a few minutes later, Cardinal Kasper appeared. He, too, was dressed in what I now call regular "priest clothes"— the black pants, shirt, and collar.

We explained that we were representing Mr. Wolff because, due to Shabbat, he could not travel to the cardinal's office. Cardinal Kasper understood, and Vince and I gave a summary of Walter's story and the Campagna and Giovanni Palatucci connections. Naturally, being responsible for Christian/Jewish relations, Cardinal Kasper knew how powerful these intertwining stories were. In fact, he was so intrigued that he asked when it might be possible to meet Walter.

"We leave tomorrow afternoon to go back to New York," said Vince. "Perhaps in the morning, before we go to the airport?"

"I am leaving for a trip tomorrow at eight o'clock in the morning," he said. "Maybe another time."

Vince looked at me and then turned to Cardinal Kasper.

"There might not be another time . . . Perhaps tonight, after Shabbat? Shabbat ends at eight twenty-two this evening."

Cardinal Kasper took out a piece of paper, wrote down an address and telephone number, and handed it to me.

"This is the address of my apartment and my telephone number. Please come to my home after Shabbat this evening. I would be honored to meet Mr. Wolff."

Did I hear correctly? Did Cardinal Kasper just invite us to his Vatican apartment on a Saturday night at the last minute? I took one look at Vince's face and knew that what I'd heard was right.

We said thank you and that we would be there about nine that evening.

✦

"Did you have your meeting with Cardinal Kasper?" asked Amy a few minutes later over the phone.

"Yes, we did, in between his calls regarding the pope's statement," I said. "In fact we met with him for about an hour."

"I'm surprised he kept the appointment, let alone spent an hour with you."

Something told me she would be *more* surprised about what I was going to tell her next.

"Cardinal Kasper really wants to meet Walter, so he invited us to his apartment tonight after Shabbat," I said.

"That's incredible. It just doesn't happen, Elizabeth. On the spur of the moment, a cardinal invites you to his home? Plus, with what's going on now, *everyone* has been trying to reach him. The pope's statement has everyone wanting to speak to the Vatican, especially Cardinal Kasper because he was there with the pope. Ambassadors can hardly reach him today, and here he is seeing you twice!"

"I thought that's what you were going to say," I said.

"Well, my dear, you must call me as soon as you finish tonight," Amy said. I could almost see her through the phone, shaking her head in disbelief.

"Don't worry, we'll call. You're our guardian angel."

At eight o'clock, Vince and I went to pick up Walter and Gerda on the other side of town. I was especially excited because Walter and Gerda had no idea what awaited them this Saturday night.

"Walter, we're off to something quite unusual tonight," said Vince. "An impromptu meeting with Cardinal Kasper—at his apartment."

"What?" said Gerda. "His apartment? Now?"

The cab wove its way through the Saturday evening Roman traffic and finally approached Saint Peter's. It made a right and stopped in front of an apartment building that had a police officer stationed in front.

We followed our instructions and rang the bell, then entered the building and took the elevator up to Cardinal Kasper's apartment. Besides the four of us, we had two small suitcases, ones that Walter and Gerda had taken with them for Shabbat.

When he answered the door, Cardinal Kasper looked confused. He had invited us to visit after dinner, not *stay* as his guests. As we entered the apartment, I explained that we had come directly from the other side of town, and I saw a look of relief on his face.

We followed the cardinal into his library, which looked like a typical library in anyone's home. The shelves were filled with books—mostly books on religion, all religions. There was a menorah on the credenza, and a painting of the Burning Bush.

Initially, Walter, Gerda and Cardinal Kasper spoke in German—then they switched to English. Walter explained how so many people throughout Italy helped him, many risking their lives in order to save his.

An hour later we left; it was almost ten. I was amazed again at how comfortable we all felt.

"*Buona sera*, Amy."

"What happened? Did you really visit Cardinal Kasper at his home?" she asked.

"*Si*. Yes, we did."

"Unbelievable," she said. "What did he say?"

"Walter told him his story, and they discussed how important it was for people to know there were good people during the war—people who risked all to help others. What was also important to both of them was that by telling this true story, perhaps it could help people in today's world."

The next day we left Rome and Italy behind, not really believing everything that had actually happened. All the dreaming and planning could never have prepared us for the unexpected surprises and new friendships. It made for quite a memorable trip.

Cardinal Kasper and Walter Wolff in the home of the cardinal.

17

MUSEUM OF MEMORY AND PEACE

When Walter Wolff heard that some people in Campagna were considering using the former Convent of San Bartolomeo for a purpose other than to commemorate its unique history—namely, potentially adding a section for modern art—he became extremely upset. Vince and I had consulted on plans for a museum honoring the memory of the Jews who were interned in that building, and we had discussed it with Walter, who had intense thoughts on the matter:

> It is still unbelievable to think that after all these years, I returned to Campagna, this time as a free person. To walk through the Convent of San Bartolomeo, where I was interned with hundreds of other Jews, was an incredible moment. So many memories came back, and I am so grateful for the *Campo di San Bartolomeo* and all it symbolizes for me and all Jews. It is a symbol of the respect and dignity that Italy, the Italians, especially the people of Campagna, showed us during a time when being Jewish meant certain death in the camps run by the Germans.
>
> The Italians were kind to us and were true examples of

the basic principle, *Love Thy Neighbor as Thyself*. Because of this, the Convent of San Bartolomeo is truly unique and *must* become a center or museum that honors the memory of the Jews who were there. I have seen the plans that Elizabeth worked on with Vince along with members of the *Comitato Giovanni Palatucci* and the architectural team, and I fully support them. In addition, it would honor Giovanni Palatucci and Bishop Palatucci, and all nameless Italians who helped us, especially the citizens of Campagna. It is a link with the past that can serve to teach future generations about this little known story, a story that the world must know. The saving of the Jews in Italy, especially Campagna, gives hope to all that during bad times, there can be good people.

It will focus on the Righteous people of that time, in a place where it *actually occurred*. The [former] convent must only be used to tell the history of Campagna, the history of the Holocaust, and the history of the Jews in Italy. If it is not used for this purpose, it will not be respecting history that transpired in its very walls, history that *must* be respected. There are few places in the *world* that can honor *goodness during the Holocaust*, actual places where hundreds of people were saved from the horrors of the German camps.

The Convent of San Bartolomeo symbolizes what was good at that time—and there was very little good at that time. Keeping the integrity of San Bartolomeo is an o*bligation* that Campagna and Italy have to honor history for future generations.

I'm happy to say that Walter's hopes did not go ignored by the planners in Campagna.

18

VINNIE D AND THE DOCUMENTARY

After we returned from Italy, Vince wanted to share our experience with his childhood friend Vince De Giaimo (affectionately known as "Vinnie D"). So, we met for dinner at my favorite place in New York City, Rockefeller Center. When I was a little girl, my grandmother would take me to visit the famous Christmas tree at Rockefeller Center, which, in its own way, is New York's answer to an Italian square.

Vinnie D recognized the significance of Walter's story and the stories of others who survived in Italy and offered to finance the professional filming of the survivors, so their words would be preserved for future generations. This is the foundation of a documentary focusing on our developing story of the Jews in Italy. What did we know about making a documentary? Not as much as we needed, so Vince and I went to the experts at Engel Entertainment to guide us through the process. We are forever grateful for Vinnie D's contribution.

Vince and I reviewed the list of Jews we knew who had lived in Italy during World War II and survived. Walter Wolff had a group of friends from Italy who lived in the United States and had participated in various conferences with him and Vince.

This group included Horst Stein, Max Kempin, Herta Pollak, and Marina Lowi Zinn, all of whom you will meet in this book. Unfortunately, just a few months earlier, Alfred Birns, Edith's husband, who had also been in Campagna, passed away. Luckily, Vince had already interviewed him, so I came to know him via film. We began interviewing each of the survivors separately in their homes and eventually brought them together at a round-table meeting. And so, another part of the journey began.

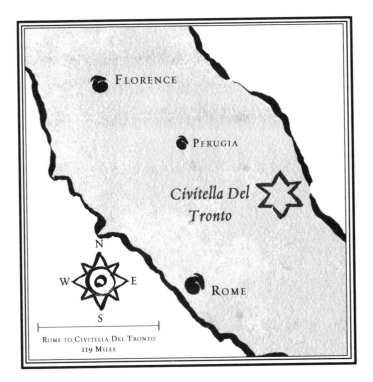

19

I AM EIGHTY-SIX YEARS OLD
THANKS TO ITALY

I first met Horst Stein on the telephone. Like Walter, Horst is German and from Frankfurt. In fact, they knew each other when they were in high school. They attended Philantropins, and although Horst was a few years younger than Walter, they played soccer together.

Horst was expecting my call, and when he answered the phone, the first thing I noticed was his authoritative, booming voice.

"How can I begin to tell you how grateful I am to Italy and the Italians? I would not be here today if it were not for them," he said.

"That's what Walter says all the time."

"I'm glad you and Vince are going to film us so that the world will *know* what happened. People need to know, and they need to know from us, the people who were there. Otherwise I am afraid people will not believe it really took place," he added passionately.

"Can I ask you some questions?"

"Absolutely," he said.

"Then let's start from the beginning, from Germany. Tell me how you got to Italy, and we'll go from there."

And so he began. "I was born in Germany in 1920, an only child. We lived a comfortable life in Frankfurt. My father was a traveling salesman who sold fabric. Believe it or not, much of what he sold was the black cloth that Catholic priests wore. One day my father made a political remark that was contrary to the Nazi regime, and the remark was reported to the Gestapo. It was 1935, there was already anti-Semitism in Germany, and the Gestapo came to our home looking for my father. Fortunately, he was still traveling and had called my mother as he usually did once or twice a week to check in. That call saved his life. If the Gestapo was looking for you in 1935, you didn't come home if you wanted to live. We knew that even then."

"So, what did your father do?" I asked.

"To enter other European countries, you needed a visa. The only country that did not require a visa was Italy, so that is where my father went. He went to Milano, and six months later my mother and I followed."

"What did he do for work during that time?"

"He was sort of in the same business. He sold fur pieces that could be made into fur coats. In fact, he knew Herta Pollak's father, who was also in the same business."

"Did either of you speak Italian?"

"Not in the beginning. No. But we learned," he said. "My mother spoke the least of all of us. I spent hours in the movie theaters learning the language—a language I love and speak to this day."

"So, what was life like in Milano?" I asked, trying to imagine the city in the late 1930s.

"Until World War II began, June 1940, we lived a nice life. Initially I worked as an office employee and then became a salesman, of all things, for a German company. The company needed someone who spoke both German and Italian. We had friends, both Italian and Jewish. We would meet our Jewish friends at a café in Piazzale Susa in the evenings and on weekends. My family got together with Herta's family and Marina Lowi's family. Marina was another girl we knew in Italy. And I met Max Kempin. What can I tell you? Life was normal.

"Then the war began, and it all changed. Foreign Jews were placed in internment camps. I refuse to use the term 'concentration camp' for any place in Italy because in concentration camps, people were killed, and almost no one was harmed in Italy.

"One day, while walking in Milano, a few of us were arrested and taken to the San Vittore prison. When I entered the jail, I saw a familiar face—Herta's father. My father was not taken that day; his time would come a few months later. I was held in that prison for thirty-three days and then transferred to a camp in the Abruzzi region, in the province of Teramo. The first camp was in Tossicia, and after a few months, our group was transferred to a camp, a *libero internamento* camp, in the very small town of Civitella del Tronto. Both camps were situated in the village itself, and we had contact with the local people, who were extremely cordial, helpful, and respectful, as were the *carabinieri*, the police," he said.

"Where was your mother during this time?"

"For some reason—I do not know why—my mother was not taken to a camp. Neither was Herta or her mother," said Horst.

"Where did she stay?"

Horst Stein with his dog Tossi in Tossicia (Abruzzi).

"She stayed with Italian friends, both in Milano and in a little town in the countryside. Then, as I mentioned, my father was arrested, and he was sent to Ferramonti. I made a *domanda,* an official request, and after a few months, he was transferred to Civitella to be with me, where we spent the rest of our time as internees. At first we lived in an apartment, and then in an old hospital. We lived in the town, amongst the people."

Horst Stein in "Campo di Concentramento" Tossicia (Abruzzi): 1. Hain
2. David 3. Alexander 4. Werner Weil 5. Herschberg 6. Pressburger
7. Nadelberg 8. Warmund 9. Kirsch 10. Winkler 11. Kort 12. Hersing
13. Thiersfeld 14. Evi Weil 15. Mrs. Rector 16. Kurt Deutsch 17. Fischler
18. Mr. Rector 19. Signora Weil 20. Mr. Weil.

"What did you do with your time?"

"I read, played cards, taught English, played the saxophone, and played with my dog Tossi, who was named for my time in Tossicia. At one point my father wasn't feeling very well, and he was sent to a spa, San Pellegrino."

1942. San Pellegrino. Horst's parents at the spa of San Pellegrino, paid for by the Italian government.

"What?" I said. "I can't imagine any internee being sent to a spa."

"Well, it's true. It wasn't like the German camps where if you weren't feeling well, it was over."

Then he saved the best for last.

"Not only that, my mother was invited to join him at San Pellegrino during his stay."

"You're kidding, right?" I said.

"It's the honest truth—and I have pictures."

If I didn't know better, I might think he was making this

up. But given everything I had heard from Walter and seen in his old black-and-white pictures, I believed him. Truth really was turning out to be stranger than fiction.

"What was being interned like?" I asked.

"Sometimes it was difficult to know that you were not free, and your spirits would get down," he continued. "The people who gave us the most hope were representatives from the Vatican. They visited us in Civitella. They kept our spirits up. In fact, many times I have been asked about what the church did. I know that they visited me and helped us. I also know that the Swiss guards and their swords were definitely no match to Hitler and his military machine. Remember, it took the two world powers at the time, England and the United States, along with the rest of the world, almost five years to beat Hitler and Germany, a country the size of Pennsylvania. And they almost lost."

1942. Easter in Civitella del Tronto (Abruzzi). Front Row: Mrs. Hein and Mrs. Stein. Back row: Mrs. Rosenzweig, Morris Rosenthal, Mr. Hein, Mr Stein, Horst Stein, Mr. Rosenzweig and Sigfried Kort.

"Did you ever feel you were in any danger while you were in Civitella del Tronto?" I asked.

"No. not in the begining. It's difficult to comprehend that during the time Mussolini controlled Italy, I felt safe and lived as normal a life as I could, given the circumstances," he said. "There was a war going on, and times were difficult for everyone in Italy, not just the Jews. We had what they had, the same rations. Before September 8, 1943, we were safe. After that it changed."

Horst Stein and other internees in Civitella del Tronto (Abruzzi). Left to right: I. Szenkir, Fredl Waxberger, Raffaele Rosenblatt, Mr. Goldman and Horst Stein.

"How?"

"Well, Italy became Germany's enemy. We had to hide, and the people of Abruzzi helped us hide. I have so many more stories to tell you when we meet in person, but I want to leave you with one more thought," he said. "Not too long ago I enjoyed my eighty-sixth birthday with my family, and as always, I received various gifts. But lately I have recognized that the best and most significant gift I ever received and have not given thanks for was the open arms of Italy. Italy saved my parents and me. Without Italy I would not have been able to enjoy the last sixty-plus years, my marriage, my children, and my grandchildren."

Wow. After I hung up the phone, I knew one thing: I could not wait to meet Horst Stein in person.

2002. Horst Stein's family.

20

WALTER WOLFF'S FUNERAL

The phone call I dreaded came. I knew I would receive this call sooner than later. How could I not? I met my new friend when he was already eighty-eight years old.

Walter Wolff had grown quite frail in the last month or two. On his last birthday, only a few weeks before he died, he spoke at Hofstra University about his experience during the Holocaust, and I was delighted to spend the day with him and Vince and Gerda. During his speech, his voice was weak but filled with passion, and it was evident that he wanted to contribute his wisdom and ninety years of experience to the students. The professor even had a cupcake with a candle for Walter, and we all sang "Happy Birthday."

Gerda called me at work at around four fifteen on a Thursday and left a message asking me to call her back. I knew it wasn't going to be good news. Walter had been in the hospital for a few days. I picked up the phone already knowing what she was going to say: Walter was gone. Gerda's voice was slow as she explained that Walter's kidneys had failed.

Vince was in Alaska on a cruise with his wife and friends, planned over a year before. He could not return in time for the funeral, scheduled for the next day, as is the custom in the Jewish religion. It would be at ten AM. Vince was devastated.

Attending Walter's funeral was sad, as all funerals are. I went with Vince's son Michael and sat with Gerda. Here I was, this Catholic girl in an Orthodox synagogue, listening to Walter's eulogy. The rabbi gave a wonderful tribute and mentioned that when Walter retired, he didn't choose to take it easy. Instead, Walter's time was filled with activities, and one, his passion of telling his story, began to consume more and more time. Soon, Walter was speaking all over the country about his experiences in World War II. The rabbi even mentioned that Walter had recently traveled to Italy.

I contacted the Italian consul general, the Vatican, and the United States Embassy, and they all wrote letters of condolence to Walter's family.

Calling Horst Stein to tell him the news was difficult. How do you tell someone that his friend of sixty-plus years has passed on? But Horst brought everything into perspective for me when, at the end of our conversation, he said, "We lost one. Let's not lose another before we finish our work."

How true those words were, I thought, and they gave me a strong incentive as I struggled with my sadness. Given the ages of the survivors, there was no time to waste. A friend once said, "No one knows how much time we have, but we can choose what to do with our time." I had already decided that my time would be devoted to piecing together the puzzle we had found. Horst did not need to worry. We would finish our work.

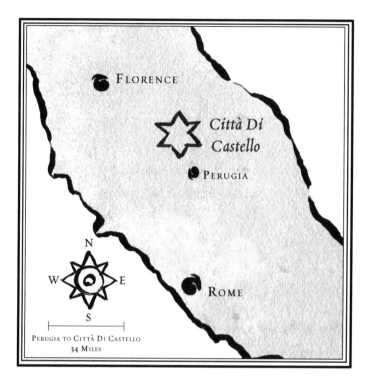

PERUGIA TO CITTÀ DI CASTELLO
34 MILES

21

URSULA, THE PRIEST, AND THE NUNS

W hen I met Ursula Korn Selig, I couldn't believe she was a Holocaust survivor. A feisty, stylishly dressed, petite blonde woman answered the door. Not many women in their eighties look fantastic in a miniskirt. A far cry from my Italian-born grandmother!

A few days earlier, Vince and I had attended a memorial that took place one month after Walter's death, as is the custom in the Jewish tradition. Vince saw Karen Sutton, a woman he knew through his speaking engagements with Walter.

"You must meet my friend Ursula," said Karen. "She was in Italy during the war."

Ursula was born in 1925 in Breslau, Germany, which is now Wroclaw, Poland. Her parents were both from wealthy families and owned a department store, D. Korn and Company.

"In Germany, I lived a very privileged life. We had cooks, butlers, housekeepers, and nannies," she said, a faraway look in her eyes.

"Things were beginning to change in Germany, and in 1935 my mother decided to join her parents, her sister, and her family in Alassio, a resort town on the Italian Riviera. My grandparents had bought a hotel, so they could get some of their money out of Germany."

In 1938, the Italian racial laws forbade Jewish families from owning property in Italy, so Ursula's family sold their possessions. Her life would never be the same.

"My dad remained in Breslau to run the department store. He thought, like most German Jews who had been in the German army in the First World War, that he would be okay— exempt from the anti-Semitism that was sweeping Germany. It couldn't get as bad as people were saying. They were pessimists, he thought. He remained there until 1939, when even he realized that this was not a good situation." Ursula's father then joined his family in Italy, a haven in the turmoil of Europe. It would not last long.

When Italy declared war, Ursula's father and uncle were arrested because they were foreign Jews. They were taken to internment camps as part of Mussolini's way of going along— to a point—with Hitler's ideas.

Ursula and her mother were arrested a few days later, along with her mother's sister, Erna Frank, and her cousin, Inge. Ursula's grandmother had died in Alassio in 1938 and her grandfather remarried a German Jewish woman and lived in Genoa for most of the war. Ursula does not know why they were not interned. After a few days, the ladies were transferred to a town in Umbria, near Perugia, named Collazzone. Eventually the Italian government attempted to reunite families.

Italian-born Jews were not arrested during this first wave of anti-Jewish laws and restrictions. They were able to live in their own homes and villages, albeit with fewer rights and privileges than before. Eventually, in 1941, Ursula's father and uncle rejoined their families. They were transferred to Città di Castello, about fifty miles from Perugia, where they lived with an Italian family in a furnished room paid for by the Italian government, and received a stipend of a few lire a day, and the *same* food rations as the local Italians. Ursula was told by the priest of Collazzone to look up his friend, another young priest, Don Beniamino Schivo, who became a lifeline for Ursula and her family. She did, and an incredible friendship formed that has lasted sixty-seven years.

"When I arrived in Città di Castello, I went to the seminary to see Don Schivo. I didn't know why the priest from Collazzone had suggested it," she said. "When Don Schivo entered the room I saw a tall, blond, handsome man who seemed very kind."

Due to the racial laws, the school-aged Ursula was only permitted to attend school with other Jewish children, but there were not enough Jewish children in Città di Castello to form a class. So Ursula, who loved school, was not able to attend, until Don Schivo arranged it.

"He asked if I wanted to go to school and I said yes," she said with a smile. "He arranged for me to attend a boarding school, run by Benedictine nuns in a convent. So here I was, a nice Jewish girl, going to school in Italy, and a Catholic school at that! In addition, I had many Italian friends, even though

Ursula Korn Selig with boyfriend
Giovannino Bianchino, Città di
Castello (Perugia).

we were not supposed to fraternize with the Italians. Not all racial laws were fully enforced."

"Although Italy was allied with Hitler," she continued, "the Italians did not deport Jews during this time. In the rest of Europe, Jews were being deported by the thousands every day, worked to death in camps, and murdered."

For the years 1941 to 1943, life was relatively good for Ursula and her family.

"We lived a life similar to the Italians, except we had to report to the local *carabinieri* daily, could not work, had curfew, and were supposed to stay in Città di Castello. I continued going to school. I even had an Italian boyfriend, Giovannino. My parents spent their time going to the local piazza, having coffee with the people of the town, waiting for the mail, and signing in with the police. That was our daily existence. My relatives did the same thing, except my cousin chose not to go to school. At some point, my relatives were transferred to Bevagna, near Perugia, where they spent the rest of the war."

Ursula Korn Selig (left) with Italian friends in Città di Castello (Perugia).

This comparatively peaceful existence came to an end for Ursula and the rest of the Jews in Italy on September 8, 1943, when Italy signed an armistice with the Allies. Italy had now officially "switched sides" and its former ally, Germany, was now its enemy. Central and northern Italy, now under German occupation, began rounding up the Jews. In Rome, for example, on October 16, 1943, a total of 1,259 Jews were deported.

The situation was similar in Città di Castello and other towns where the Germans knew or suspected there were Jews. Germany commanded the Italian police to assist in the roundups. On the surface it appeared that the Italian police cooperated with the Nazis, but many took the information and notified the Jews about what was going to happen.

Plaque in Jewish quarter in Rome noting the 16th of October, 1943, when Jews were deported for the death camps.

Parallel to a situation we heard about from Walter Wolff, a police officer came to Ursula's home and said he was going to arrest the family the next morning. So they, like Walter, were warned. But in this case, Ursula and her family remained in the apartment under curfew. Leaving the home was too risky, so they stayed and, as promised, were arrested the next day and taken to Perugia.

But then a piece of good luck. The prison was full, and they were taken back to Città di Castello, spared being sent to German camps for the moment. Ursula turned to Don Schivo.

He had helped Ursula before by enrolling her in school, but this kind of help would be on a completely different level.

Up to that point, Ursula's family had not been in danger in Città di Castello, but now Don Schivo believed the family had a better chance of not being found by the Nazis if they lived in the countryside. He decided they should hide in a convent run by Salesian nuns in the mountains in a place called Pozio, about a seven-hour walk from town. The nuns used this convent as a retreat during the summer months. Because it was the middle of October, the convent was closed until the following summer.

The family went to the convent, as did Ursula's Italian boyfriend, Giovannino. He had been in the Italian army when the armistice was signed and now was considered a deserter. Besides going along for safety, he wanted to be with the spirited Ursula. The caretaker was a man named Lazzaro and, unknown to Lazzaro's wife, Don Schivo had arranged for Lazzaro to bring food to the group. On Christmas Eve 1943, Don Schivo surprised them all by visiting with another young priest from Città di Castello, bringing gifts of food. Two Catholic priests breaking curfew, spending Christmas Eve with Jews hiding from Hitler. Had they been found, it would have meant immediate death for all.

When the Germans wanted to use the convent for their own purposes a few months later, Ursula's family and Giovannino hid in a small nearby building that housed the brick oven the nuns used to bake bread. In Italy, Ursula hid in an oven for safety! What a contrast with what was happening in Germany.

After a while, the group headed back to the protective arms of Don Schivo, who arranged for Ursula and her mother to hide in a convent disguised as nuns. Ursula's father was sent to live with a farmer in the hills of Perugia, and Giovannino went to his family home. Through bombings, raids, war going on all around, this is how they lived. Eventually Don Schivo moved Ursula and her mother to the seminary for further protection.

Città di Castello was liberated by the British in July 1944, and the family was free, alive, and finally safe. They had survived the war because of the generosity of many people in Italy: police officers, officials, Don Schivo, and the nuns. And it helped that they were arrested "Italian style," sent to Italian camps and freely interned. Had they remained in Germany and been sent to the German camps, they would have perished along with her paternal grandmother, who was in Theresienstadt, and her uncle and two aunts, who were in Auschwitz. Another uncle perished in Auschwitz after trying to escape to France from Italy, and many cousins and friends died in Breslau.

Ursula Korn Selig with her parents in Città di Castello (Perugia) after the war.

January 2008. Monsignor Schivo with Ursula Korn Selig.

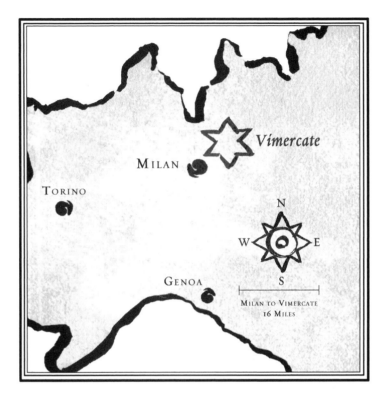

22

HERTA'S VISIT

Herta Mingelgrün Pollak is eighty-nine years old, adores dancing, and loves Italy. She was born in Frankfurt and moved to Milano in 1935 with her parents. When she lived in Germany, her family lived a comfortable life; her father was in the fur business and her mother was a homemaker. As her parents didn't like what was happening in Germany in the early and mid-thirties, they decided to leave for Italy, which appeared to be the safest haven.

The family had a pleasant life in Milano, and Herta and her parents became friends with other Jewish families. It is amazing to know that this group included Horst Stein, Max Kempin, Walter Wolff, and little Marina Lowi, whose story will be told in a bit—all people we have met and interviewed. Each of these people survived the war because his or her family decided to go to Italy. Most left Germany before the Italian racial laws were enacted in 1938.

Everything changed for Herta's family in 1940 when the war broke out. Herta's father was sent to Ferramonti with many other foreign Jews. Herta and her mother stayed in Milano during the first part of the war and continued her father's fur business. In the beginning, they did not believe they were at risk.

"I even went to visit my father in Ferramonti," said Herta.

"They *allowed* you to do that?" I asked. It did not seem possible. Who was allowed to visit relatives in a concentration camp in Germany? I had not heard of family visits for those interned in Italy before. Neither had Vince. Most of the information we read on Ferramonti focused on the camp itself, the number of people who were there, and the lives they led. Nothing discussed family members being permitted to visit.

After additional research, Vince and I learned that in Italy, it was accepted for family members of those interned to visit. Horst's mother could visit his father in Civitella del Tronto, an *internato libero* camp, where people were freer than in most other places. Ferramonti was a traditional camp with thousands of internees, quite a different story, yet clearly family members visited there too. Later, through my travels in Italy, I met Signora Lopes-Pegna in Florence, who said she could visit her father, Sigismondo Smulevich, in his internment camp, which was in Campagna. She showed me a photo to prove it. The photo appears to be of a typical family outing on a Sunday afternoon. These family visits are one more example of the stark contrast in the early 1940s between being Jewish in Italy and in other parts of occupied Europe.

"Herta, when you visited, how did you get to Ferramonti?" asked Vince.

"I took a train from Milano. I made a *domanda*, a request,

to visit my father, and the police officer granted me the *permesso,* the permission," she said matter-of-factly, as if this were normal procedure. "We even wrote to each other."

Herta's father's letter written from the concentration camp at Ferramonti to her in Milan.

We were learning that it was considered normal procedure to ask an Italian official for permission to visit, or to
travel, and the request was often granted. The Jews did not
fear the officials at that time.

"It was a long trip," Herta said. "It took at least twenty
hours to get there, maybe more with all the stops and changes.
Then I had to take a bus to Ferramonti. My father was fine. He
said life in the camp was as good as could be expected. He
was able to go to synagogue; they had built a small synagogue
there. They even had rabbis in the camp. This camp was not
like a German camp at all. Then I returned to Milano."

Herta's father, Isaac Mingelgrun.

"Why didn't your mother get taken away?" I asked.

"Well, we did get a notice for her to go to the police station, but I went in her place. I figured I was younger than she was, and they could take me in exchange for her. When I went there, the police officer told me to go home and not to worry; he wasn't taking me anywhere and wasn't taking my mother anywhere. I could go home. He then opened his drawer and showed me stacks of *domande* in the drawer and just shrugged."

Interesting—*another* Italian police officer who did not obey orders and took matters into his own hands.

"My mother and I continued to live in Milano until 1943. Life was okay. In fact, sometimes I didn't even know there was a war going on. I worked, went to the piscine (the local swimming pool), and went dancing—even though we weren't supposed to," she said with a wink. "Here are some pictures."

Herta with friends in Milan at the local piscine *(pool), 1942.*

Herta Mingelgrun Pollak in Milan, 1942.

We looked at the pictures and were amazed. Herta's clothes were beautiful and stylish, and of course, some were fur trimmed. In fact, by looking at the photos, you would *never* know there was a war going on. But the photos that most captured my attention were those in *piscina*. Here, in 1942, young people were swimming in Milano, Italy, the country of Hitler's ally Mussolini, with seemingly not a care in the world.

"In September 1943, everything changed. We were now at risk, and we left Milano for a nearby town called Vimercate. The Cantú family helped us and sheltered us through that time, and no one turned us in. Everyone we met took a chance by helping us; they risked all for us. If it weren't for them, we would not have survived."

Two women strolling in Milan in 1942. Herta is on the right.

We mentioned we would be visiting Max the next week.

"I'd love to come with you," Herta said. "I haven't seen him in a long time."

"We'll pick you up and take you with us," said Vince.

Herta and I decided to meet at Penn Station. From there we'd take the train to meet Vince in New Jersey and then continue to Max Kempin's home. We all coordinated our visit with cell phones, including Herta. How quickly cell phones became part of our lives. I wondered, then and now, how we ever lived without them.

All of the survivors we know have cell phones and computers and know how to use them well. Walter loved to e-mail me. This shows how well the Jewish internees adapted throughout their lives. In my opinion, being adaptable is one of the reasons they survived during the war.

The next week, Herta and I met at our designated spot, both a bit wet from a summer thundershower. On the surface, we looked like a grandmother and granddaughter meeting for a day of sightseeing in the city. Do you think people going through the station that day could possibly imagine Herta's stories? People walk by us every day, and each person has a story. Who knows what we might learn, if we only ask?

We joined Vince and continued to Max's home. Herta and Max were friends before the war, during the war, and stayed friends after the war. Reunions among old friends are always wonderful, and with a smile and a hug, these two old friends conveyed decades of shared experiences and warmth. You could also see the sadness in their eyes when they mentioned their friend Walter Wolff.

23

MAX

"My father read *Mein Kampf* in 1933 and decided to leave Frankfurt," said Max matter-of-factly. "That decision was crucial. Everyone thought my father was an alarmist, exaggerating the situation. I'm glad he was strong enough to listen to his own conscience and not follow the advice of others."

Max Kempin and his family's survival have a common thread with the others we'd met. The family consisted of Max's twin brother Felix and his sister Erma. (The family name was Kempinski and was changed to Kempin in the United States.) They left Germany in the 1930s at the beginning of Hitler's rise to power. How their families had the foresight remains a mystery—even to them today. They did believe that terrible things could happen and decided to take action rather than take the "wait and see" approach that so many others did. Waiting ultimately cost many Jews their lives.

"My father initially moved us to France, where we had a visa for one year," Max said. "After one year the French would not renew our visas, so we went to Italy, where the doors were open. We had a good life in Italy, my mother and father, me, my twin brother, and my older sister. Even with the racial laws, we managed, quietly, under the table, Italian style.

Felix and Max Kempin in Milano, early 1940s.

"When the war broke out, my father was sent to Ferramonti, and my mother was told to go to another village, Spezzano della Silla, in the province of Cosenza. Jewish friends from Milan had already been sent there for internment and wrote to my mother saying it was a pretty mountain town, almost like a resort. Do you know what my mother did? She had dresses made for the trip. Can you imagine that? My mother was that kind of lady. She wanted to dress for her trip.

"I officially escaped internment due to the kindness of a town official. When I reported to his office, he said that he would not send me to a camp. He opened his desk drawer; 'See those,' he said, placing my paper in the drawer. 'They aren't going anywhere either. Don't worry about it.'" It was just like Herta.

"Why do you think that happened?" I asked.

"What can I tell you," Max said with an Italian shrug. "That was Italy."

Max's family decided he should accompany his mother to Spezzano and stay with her, even though he did not have to be interned. After about one year, he returned to Milano.

"When we arrived, we were taken by the police officer in the village to choose our apartment. It still amazes me, knowing what I now know, that we were able to *choose* our living quarters. As you could probably tell, my mother was . . . precise . . . and the first few apartments did not meet her standards so she kept looking until she found one she liked. This did not happen anyplace else but Italy."

This scenario was similar to what happened to the Wolff family when they went to Casale Monferrato. They, too, were able to choose where they wanted to live.

"And Ferramonti? What was that like?" I asked.

1941. Internees having a picnic in front of the barracks in the concentration camp at Ferramonti.

"As Herta told you, the camp was not a bad camp, and my mother and I were able to visit my father there. Ferramonti was its own small town, with people doing everything you do in a town. There were doctors, dentists, bakers, teachers, rabbis. They even had their own form of government in the camp. Here, let me show you the pictures," he said as he opened an old photo album.

We saw pictures of people at a picnic. Pictures of people playing the guitar. Pictures of men in "Parliament," formed by the internees to "govern" the camp internally. Unbelievable. Then came the pictures of children in school.

Parliament in the Concentration Camp of Ferramonti. © *Fondazione Museo Internazionale della Memoria Ferramonti di Tarsia. See copyright page.*

"They had a school for the children in Ferramonti?" I asked.

"Yes," said Max.

"Children in a camp are unbelievable. And educating children in a camp, that would be sheer fantasy in a German-run camp," said Vince.

Jewish children in school, Campo di Concentramento di Ferramonti.
© Fondazione Museo Internazionale della Memoria Ferramonti di Tarsia.
See copyright page.

"And here, look at this one," I exclaimed. It was a photo of a wedding in Ferramonti. People were allowed to get married? Apparently so.

Wedding in Ferramonti. © Fondazione Museo Internazionale della Memoria Ferramonti di Tarsia. See copyright page.

Concentration camp at Ferramonti, wedding photo in front of barracks. Max Kempin's mother is on the far right; his father is directly over the bride's right shoulder. Note all internees are wearing their own clothes and were not wearing Jewish stars.

"There were a few weddings in Ferramonti," Max said, "at least three or four that I was aware of. My mother and father are in one of the pictures. Do you know that there were even children born in the camp? I believe there were about twenty-one. They even had a Bris."

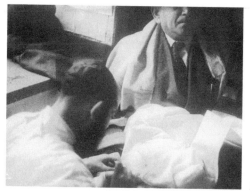

Bris at Ferramonti.

Again and again we saw and heard firsthand accounts of what happened in Italy. If it were not for the pictures and the many different people telling us similar stories, even *I* would not believe it.

October 11, 1942. Marriage certificate between two internees in the Campo di Concentramento di Ferramonti between Karl Hermann Schwarz and Elvira Huppert. Signed by Rabbi Riccardo Pacifici of Genoa. © Foundation Ferramonti.

MILAN

TORINO

Piea

N
W   E
S

TORINO TO PIEA
23 MILES

GENOA

24

HIDING OUT IN THE OPEN

Not too long after Walter passed away, Vince and I met with Giorgina de Leon Vitale. Vince and Walter had participated in a Jewish Community Center program in New Haven, Connecticut, with Giorgina a few months earlier and recognized that her story should be included in the documentary. It is significant because it depicts life in Italy for Italian Jews both before and after the dividing line of September 8, 1943.

July 1940. The de Leon family at their villa outside of Torino.

Giorgina is an Italian Jew who is originally from Torino. Her father was a successful businessman who owned an electrical supply factory and a chain of stores, and, as a result, the family led a comfortable life. When the racial laws of 1938 were enacted, which, among other things, prohibited Jewish people from owning businesses, Giorgina's family's business continued as a corporation. At the end of the war, the business was still intact, and the de Leon family returned to run it.

Summer 1942 . The de Leon family at their Torino villa.

Signor de Leon continued to work secretly for his own company until it became too dangerous for him to do so. Because they already lived in Italy, Giorgina's family was not deported to the Italian camps the way foreign Jews were when the war began, so they continued to live in their family home.

The family had prospered, and due to the growing business,

moved to Milano in 1936. Giorgina attended a Jewish school in Milano until it closed in January 1943 because of the increasing frequency of air raids. To continue her studies, she went to Rome and stayed with her aunt and uncle. She enrolled in a parochial school run by nuns, even though she was Jewish.

After September 8, 1943, when the Germans began marching through Italy, living in Milano was too dangerous. The family became one of the many *sfollati*, Catholic and Jewish people who fled the cities all over Italy, and went to small towns in the countryside for safety. Since Italy was now Germany's enemy, all Italians were suspect to the Germans.

Giorgina's father chose Piea, a small town between Milano and Torino, where he could hide his family in the open. The family included Giorgina's ninety-year-old grandfather, her mother, and her two sisters, Michelina (who was older) and Emilia. The family assumed false identities and became known as the De Giorgis family.

A friend of Giorgina's father who worked in *Comune* in Torino, and whose name Giorgina cannot remember, provided them with false documents that hid the family's true identity. This man was one of the other "Giovanni Palatuccis" in Italy. With new identification cards, Giorgina and her sisters could move freely around the area.

Giorgina's family lived the simple life of the country people of Piea, and she was elected the family representative to attend church. Her family was afraid that if someone didn't go to church, people would begin to suspect they were Jewish.

In fact, for a while, her grandfather even lived with the local village priest.

Piea, 1943. A walk after church with Italian friends. Giogina is on the left.

German soldiers were constantly in the area looking for partisans and army deserters, and Giorgina believes they didn't look too hard for Jews in this little town because they did not expect to find them there. But if Giorgina's family had been found, they would have been taken prisoner immediately, and the people who helped them would also have been at great risk. At one point, while the Germans were searching the towns, the family was advised to split up for a few months. The de Leon girls, who had lived with the name of De Giorgis, assumed a third identity. They were now the Alpozzo girls from Montanaro.

"Emilia was only five years old and naturally quite confused as to why she had so many last names," said Giorgina. "One day she turned to me and said, 'When we were in Milano my last name was de Leon, when we were in Piea my last name was De Giorgis, now in Montanaro my last name is Alpozzo. What will my last name be if we move to Venice?' I didn't know what to say to her. How could she understand at five years old that the world had gone crazy and this is what we needed to do to survive?"

One slight slip, a wrong last name mentioned by an innocent five-year-old girl, and the family would have been instantly deported. After a few months, the family decided to reunite and returned to Piea. Emotionally it was too difficult to stay apart.

"We lived amongst the Italians, and we thought they didn't know we were Jewish," said Giorgina. "At the end of the war, my father felt he should tell the people of Piea the truth, that we were Jews. The mayor answered, 'Yes, we know.' My father asked why they didn't turn us in, because the people of the town were at great risk, and the mayor answered, 'Because you are people, human beings like us. *Cristiani come noi.*'" *They were Christians like us.* In Italy, many times you will hear people use the word "Christian," but it has a different meaning than one we might attribute to it. In Italy it means "human being" or "person." As Horst Stein said, "For the Italians there was no difference; we were human beings."

Giorgina's father also spoke to the townspeople in the *piazza*, and this is what he said:

Dearest Friends,

The day has arrived in which I am again free to return to my own home and especially, to my work amongst my old employees, my own workmen.

In this time of happiness, I want to thank all of you dear Pieesi, citizens of Piea, for having welcomed us to this village. We found in you that warmth, that hospitality, for which today I can do nothing else but thank you and express to you our eternal gratitude.

And so, we leave this town where we have spent two years with you, in the midst of you, doing all sorts of jobs. We leave here proud of your friendship, promising you that I will come to visit every now and then together with my family. I want to express before all of you gathered here my special gratitude to the family Giuseppe and Laurina De Giorgis of Porta di Sotto and to Signor Venturello who have protected us, putting themselves at great risk and danger. To Signor Corio, the tobacconist, who gave us shelter knowing who we were and knowing what could befall all of us. And to all of you who, without exception, guarded our secret with care.

Remember us as we will remember you, with affection, as we are now, here all together. I salute you and I wish you every blessing.

Sincerely,
Giorgio

Spring 1945. Giorgina's parents.

"We survived because of the good people who helped us, and we moved back to our home in Torino after the liberation in May 1945, where we found our apartment was in perfect condition," said Giorgina. "My father had let an Italian-Catholic family live in it while we were in Piea, because their apartment was destroyed during one of the air raids. All of our belongings were there, and both families lived together in our apartment until the Catholic family could find another one.

"Our factory had been destroyed during an air raid, but the stores remained, and when we returned, the stores were returned to us—as promised. The bombed factory was rebuilt, and we resumed our lives, but we never forgot Piea."

In May 2007, Piea was recognized by Italy as *Uno dei Giusti*, a Righteous City, and Giorgina's sister attended the ceremony. The community of Piea d'Asti was recognized, in particular the De Giorgis and Pescarmona families along with Don Ambrogio Isidor, the local priest, for having sheltered and saved Jews during the Holocaust.

Spring 1946. The de Leon family with workers from their factory. The family's factory was returned to the family after the war.

May 2007. Giorgina's sister Michelina de Leon Treves (holding the paper in the middle) honoring the town of Piea.

"It is thanks to the people of Piea that I have lived," Michelina said. "In those years, I learned that even on the darkest night, there is always a bright star in the sky. Mine was called Piea."

Translation of Text:
"The Jewish Community of Torino shows gratitude and recognition to the Comune of Piea for the help they gave the Jews, putting the [entire] community at risk for their lives during the period of racial persecution (1943–1945)."

It is interesting to note that the Jewish community of Torino recognizes the racial persecution of the Jews as beginning in 1943. It is in September 1943 that the Germans began to deport Jews from Italy and when the Jews in Italy felt their lives were at risk. Prior to that time, there were many restrictions on the Jews—but as they stated and the pictures demonstrate, they did not feel that their lives were at risk.

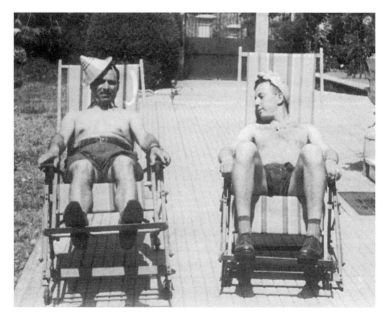

Summer 1942. Giorgina's father (left) with cousin relaxing at the family's villa.

Milano 1941. Felix.

Summer 1942. Giorgina and friends.

Summer 1941. Max and friends.

Summer 1942. Herta and friends.

Summer 1942. Giorgina and friend.

Milano 1942. Herta and friend.

25

THE LITTLE GIRL AT THE POOL

Marina Lowi Zinn, as a little girl, spent time with Horst, Max, and Herta at a swimming pool in Milano. They thought of her as their little sister or mascot. She now lives in New Jersey, but she lived in Italy until 1950. She was part of the group of Jews who were saved by the goodness of the Italians during World War II. Her parents had moved to Italy in 1934 to escape the growing anti-Semitism in Germany, and she was born in Milano.

Life was comfortable for the Lowi family in Italy. Her father was in the textile business, but after the racial laws were implemented in Italy, he decided to move to Belgium because he thought it would be safer. He left in 1939 to see if the situation in Belgium was truly better. If that was the case, his family would join him. It never happened. Italy entered the war in June 1940.

Marina, her mother, and older brother, Gilberto, remained in Milano, and her mother supported them by working in the fur business.

"We tried to join my father in Belgium," said Marina. "My mother arranged for us to be smuggled to Belgium, but my brother and I got the measles and couldn't travel at the last minute. Who would have thought that getting the measles saved our lives?"

The family was devastated. They could not be reunited, and travel became more and more dangerous with the passing of each day.

"Initially, we never feared for our safety because we were Jewish," Marina said. "We feared for our safety because Milano had air raids. When life became more dangerous, we moved out of Milano and to Gandino, located in the province of Bergamo. A man who worked in Comune, Giovanni Servalli, arranged for us to have false papers. We were now the Carnazzi children and, of course, we were 'Catholic.'"

After September 1943, the family stayed with various families in Gandino who helped shelter the "Carnazzi" family. Because of the cold weather, the children were sent to a Catholic boarding school in a convent. The mother superior knew they were Jewish but kept their true identities from everyone else. Only the priest knew the truth.

"One day we were in church, and because my brother was a few years older, his class went to receive communion. Naturally he had to go, otherwise he would arouse suspicion. As he came back, he looked at me, smiled, and slightly shrugged his shoulders as if to say, 'what can you do?'" recalled Marina.

"My mother was not with us. She stayed with various families in the province of Bergamo. She was here, there, everywhere, is what she told me. We never knew the truth because she was afraid we might accidentally reveal her hiding place."

Marina Lowi and her brother   *Mariem Lowi.*
Gilberto Lowi.

In 2006 Yad Vashem honored six residents of Gandino who helped hide Marina and her family: Vincenzo Rudelli, Giovanni Servalli, Francesco and Maria Nodari, and Bortolo and Battistina Ongaro. To this day Marina keeps in close contact with the Ongaro family and calls them at least once a month.

"It is truly amazing. The people of Gandino knew we were Jewish and hiding in their town, but no one ever betrayed us. That is why I am here today. It would be lovely to have the entire town honored by the Yad Vashem. They truly deserve it. Those people risked everything to save us." Her words and story were similar to those of Giorgina.

"My father was not so lucky," she continued. "Unfortunately he went to Belgium, what he thought was a good idea at the time, but it turned out to be a death sentence. He ultimately perished in the hands of the Nazis at Auschwitz. Everyone I know who was in Italy survived. That is the difference."

The wedding photo of Marina Lowi Zinn's parents,
Mariem and Leo Lowi, January 31, 1934.

26

AN UNEXPECTED DETOUR

I don't like what I see," said Dr. Poyman. "The cyst is a bit over five centimeters," he continued, his voice drifting off as I began a noisy conversation with myself.

I knew what this meant. Surgery. Again! And this was *not* the time to have surgery. I had important work to do because the people involved in this story were all of a certain age. There was little time to spare. My mind was racing. I was to leave for Italy in a few weeks for additional research, and I had appointments scheduled for the middle of September. I just *had* to put off any surgery until after I came back. I had postponed surgery before. I could have this one after the trip.

Why was this happening *again*? I asked God. What possibly could be the purpose of a fourth surgery? What was I supposed to learn about *this* time? Didn't I get a pass? Didn't God know I was working on a good story and did not have time to be sick for six to eight weeks? If, for some reason, I needed surgery, couldn't God make it happen after I had finished all the research so that this story could be documented?

" . . . and this time I am concerned," Dr. Poyman was saying.

"What does that mean? 'Concerned'?" I questioned, coming back to the voice on the phone, briefly leaving the one in my head.

"Well, it isn't quite clear what it is this time. It is not presenting clearly as a dermoid cyst," he said with a different tone in his voice than in past conversations. Three prior surgeries made me almost a pro, and I could tell this was different.

My heart began to race, and my hands got sweaty. What exactly was I hearing?

"I need you to go for further testing as soon as possible. You need an MRI."

"What are you telling me? If you are not sure this is a dermoid, and dermoids are almost always benign, are you telling me this cyst might be malignant?" I asked.

"Well, I'm not sure from the report. What I am sure is that it isn't clearly a dermoid, so we can't rule out the possibility of it being malignant," he said. He was talking about ovarian cancer. Cancer. Two of my cousins had died of cancer, as had some uncles and a good friend from college. I held her hand as she passed from this life to another a few years ago.

"How much of a possibility?" I whispered. Was I hearing this correctly? It was a nice summer day. This couldn't be happening to *me*.

I had gone for the sonogram as a precaution before an extended trip to Italy to do further research on this story. I had not expected a problem. After I stopped cursing, I played "Let's Make a Deal" with God. *Please let this be a simple surgery. I can handle six to eight weeks being down and out. You can get rid of the other stuff. I can't have cancer.*

"I can't tell what the possibilities are from the report I have. An MRI will be more precise, and we can go from there. But, I do suggest that we move on this right away," he said with a calm, but assertive, voice. I knew what that meant: the sooner the better.

In seconds I went from "I don't want to have surgery" to accepting a simple surgery—with no complications. Five minutes earlier I was working on my calendar, making plans. Ha. So much for that.

"I'll schedule you for the MRI, and we'll meet as soon as I have the results," he said. "I am sorry, Elizabeth. I know this isn't what you wanted to hear."

I hung up the phone and sat there, not moving as I looked out the window. The summer sun was still shining—but it was shining for other people. A thunderstorm was over my head. It was the end of the day, and people were on their way home. And I was going . . . I wasn't sure where.

Then it came, a flood of tears. Thank goodness the door was closed so no one could hear me. I picked up the phone and called Michele, one of my best friends from childhood. She has been with me through every surgery. I told her what happened.

"Mishy, I don't want to die," I whispered. "*This* time, I am scared." At this point, she could barely hear me through my sobbing voice. She responded with silence. Finally she spoke.

"I will be there for you; you know that," she said in her re-assuring voice. "You will get through this. We will all help you."

I called friends who were doctors, to get their opinions. I could tell they were not pleased with what I was saying and didn't want to let on. But with friendships of twenty and thirty-plus years, well, it is hard not to hear the tones in their voices. They all said the same thing: wait until you get the MRI. Until then we can't tell you much more than you already know. I called Vince. His wife, Dorothy, the OR nurse, said the same thing: let's see what the MRI has to say.

So the "waiting game" began. We all know about that. The MRI was taken, but showed nothing more conclusive. Basically, I had a fifty-fifty chance of having a malignancy. I was terrified.

Surgery was scheduled. No trip to Italy for me in September. I was afraid but tried not to let it show; I needed to keep my wits about me as I waited. There was nothing more to do until surgery, and I did not want a pity party. I adopted a "need to know" policy and told very few people what was happening. On the list were work friends and a few others, and naturally my family, but not Nanny. What was the point of having her worry?

Also included on the "need to know" list was Cardinal Ruini's secretary, Monsignor Filippi. He needed to know I would not be traveling to Italy in September.

"*Ciao Elisabetta. Come stai?*" he asked.

I wasn't exactly sure how to respond.

"*Eh, potrebbe andare meglio,*" I said. Things could be better. My voice quivered as the words were spoken. "I won't be seeing you in a few weeks. I need to have surgery."

"Ah," said Monsignor Filippi, with a note of concern.

"It has the possibility of being cancer," I said in a whisper. Maybe if I didn't say it too loudly, the cancer possibility would disappear.

All the way from Rome, I heard the tone of Monsignor Filippi's voice change.

"*Elisabetta, mi dispiace.*" I am sorry.

"Well, they don't know. We'll only know after surgery. It's a fifty-fifty chance. May I ask you a question? Why now? Doesn't God know I'm working on a good project, and the people are all of a certain age, and I need to finish this? I don't have time to be sick. Make me sick when I've finished the project, if I have to be sick at all," I said. It was a bit daring to question God's will with a Vatican priest, but it was how I felt. Maybe there was an answer he could give me.

"*Non lo so, Elisabetta.*" I don't know, responded Monsignor Filippi. "God has His ways."

Well, to be honest, I was quite upset with those ways, and frightened too.

"We will pray for you," Monsignor Filippi continued. "Cardinal Ruini and I are going to Lourdes in a few days, and we will pray."

"Thank you for your prayers. I am not sure how much *my* prayers are being answered these days, but you and the cardinal,

I am certain yours get heard a bit quicker. You must have a more direct line than I do!" I said with the first laugh in days.

Monsignor Filippi chuckled. "I don't know why this is happening, but there is a reason."

Honestly, I had my doubts but was willing to consider his point. There are reasons for everything, as my friend Ann Marchesano constantly tells me. It just takes time for the answers to unfold.

I ended the conversation knowing that prayers would be said for me by a man that most people in Italy consider to be next to the pope. And his wonderful Monsignor was going to pray for me too. I truly hoped their prayers would be heard. They surely had a better "in" than I did!

The day of the surgery, I asked my mother and my childhood friend, Ellen Auwarter, to promise they would tell me the truth, no matter what the outcome after surgery. So, on a bright, sunny September day, I entered the hospital not sure what would happen or if I would ever see the world as sunny again. One thing I would see was the operating room. I asked to keep my glasses on until they needed to give me anesthesia. Without my glasses, I can't see a thing and I wanted to see the operating team before they knocked me out. It was one last act of independence for a while.

The surgery was complicated. I was in the operating room for more than five hours. Finally, I began waking up in the recovery room and tried to talk. Ellen and my mom were at my side. My throat was sore, and I could barely ask, "Do I have cancer?" I wanted to know. I *needed* to know. The prayers were answered. No cancer. A small smile appeared on my face, and I asked for my glasses before I fell back asleep. Ellen laughed and got them for me. She and my mom knew I would be okay.

The road to recovery took awhile—a full week in the hospital and many more at home. But each day I improved, and I knew I would be able to continue my work. The irony in this was receiving many lovely calls from the survivors. Vince and I had to tell them what was happening because we had to postpone additional filming. They knew about the surgery, but I spared them the possible cancer details. I had many offers of chicken soup, and their love certainly helped the recovery process.

27

URSULA'S GASP

While recovering at home, I kept working on the story, reviewing some of the tapes we had made and learning as much as possible about that time in history. I was determined to go to Italy (with the doctor's approval) and tried to will that my recovery be "fast-tracked." I wanted to be in Italy for All Saints' Day and All Souls' Day, which were November 1 and 2. My Aunt Ida would be in Campagna, and my friend Agnes Bundy Scanlan was traveling to Rome the first week of November and would visit Campagna if I was there.

A few weeks after surgery, I slowly returned to work, and Vince and I continued interviewing and videotaping Holocaust survivors. Each interview proved more eye-opening than the last. We spent hours with the interviewees, looking at their pictures, listening to their stories, hearing the gratitude in their voices. They were determined to let the world know why they survived. Without fail, there was always a surprise that made us gasp.

Vince usually began with basic questions: Where were you born? Where were your parents born? How did you get to

Italy? What happened when you got to Italy? Where were you taken? And so on.

In addition to the individual interviews, we scheduled a roundtable discussion so that all the survivors could hear each other's stories and freely converse. We couldn't wait to see what the results would be, both the similarities and the differences.

So, on a brisk October day, our group of survivors—Horst Stein, Herta Pollak, Max Kempin, Gerda Mammon, Edith Birns (Alfred Birns's widow), Giorgina de Leon Vitale, and Ursula Korn Selig—met in the Engel studios in Manhattan. Eva Deutsch Costabel and Marina Lowi Zinn could not attend.

The spirit in that room was palpable, and the "Walter Wolff" group was thrilled to have a mini-reunion. They were excited to finally meet the others who had been participating in this ever-growing project.

When the filming began, each survivor was intent on hearing about the journeys the others had taken. They listened to each other, nodding in agreement because they, too, had experienced something similar, or shaking their heads when they knew something bad had happened.

What we found most surprising was that most of them had only begun discussing their experiences about fifteen years earlier. Why then? Because the Holocaust was far enough behind them that they could face what had happened so long ago. And because no one was telling the story of Italy and its people. It had not hit mainstream media. These survivors believed they owed a debt of gratitude to Italy and, as Max Kempin said, "must set the record straight while we still have a chance."

"I began speaking because of you and Walter," Horst said to Vince. "You made me realize how important this was, and I knew I had to tell my story." After that statement, you could hear a pin drop. Vince's lip quivered, as he had not known he was the catalyst behind Horst's publicly telling his story.

Giovanni Favilli, the deputy consul of Italy, came to the taping with his staff, as did some of our family members. The survivors were deeply honored that the vice consul wanted to hear their stories. In addition, they loved being able to speak Italian with him. (They all speak Italian fluently.) They did not know then that this wouldn't be the only time they would meet. A few months later they would be invited to tell their stories at the Italian Consulate.

Perhaps Giorgina de Leon Vitale, whose family "hid openly" during the war, said it best: "After us there is no one to speak and let the world know what the Italians did for us, for our families, for the Jews. They saved our lives, and we are grateful for this opportunity to record what happened so that future generations will know another part of that time in history."

Vince continued with the questions. Although we had interviewed Ursula before, we found a new development in her story. Sometimes a question needs to be asked again in a different setting, in a slightly different manner, and it jogs a slightly

different response that could go unnoticed if we were not paying attention and already thought we knew all the facts.

✦

"Ursula, where was your family during the war?" Vince asked.

"I was taken to small towns in Perugia with my mother, as
I told you before. My father wasn't with us in the beginning."
This was the first time we'd heard that.

"Where was your father?" I asked.

"Salerno," she said.

Vince and I looked at each other with wide, questioning
eyes, and my heart started pounding. Where was this coming
from? She had never mentioned that her father was anywhere
else but in the Perugia area.

"Ursula, there were no camps in Salerno," I interrupted,
"but there was one in Campagna, in the province of Salerno.
Does that name sound familiar?"

Ursula said no, but I just *knew* that her father was in
Campagna. I felt it, and Vince did too.

"Ursula," he asked, "what is your father's name?"

"Paul. Paolo Korn."

I had not brought my books with me to the taping. I was
still recovering from surgery, and carrying heavy things was a
no-no. I could have kicked myself. In "the book" there is the
list of 272 Jews who were in Campagna during the war. What
if Paolo Korn was one of them? If we were super lucky, maybe
he was in one of the pictures. My mother was coming to the

taping and probably hadn't left the house yet. She had a copy of "the book" and could bring it with her. Maybe the question would be answered here, during the taping.

The taping continued with Edith Birns. As Edith was speaking, my mother arrived, and I went out to meet her. My hands trembled as I turned to the list of names, Campagna's version of "Schindler's List." I looked under "K." There he was: Paolo Korn!

79.	Korn	Paolo	Davide	1895	commerc.	germ.
80.	Körner	Szloma	Feibisch	1880	maestro	germ.
81.	Krausz	Arturo	Guglielmo	1898	vetraio	germ.
82.	Krausz	Massimiliano	Ermanno	1890	commerc.	germ.

Ursula's father and Walter Wolff were in Campagna at the same time, their whereabouts captured in a simple, typed list. I left the room with the book in my hand. Vince was still interviewing Edith, so I nodded my head. He knew that I had found Ursula's father's name.

We decided to catch that moment on tape, so we waited until it was time to conduct the roundtable interviews and surprise Ursula with the news. As we sat down, Ursula was to my left and Edith was seated next to her.

"Ursula, earlier today you mentioned that your father was in a camp in Salerno. The camp was actually in the *province* of Salerno in the town of Campagna—the same town that Walter Wolff and Alfred Birns were in."

My finger was on the page pointing to his name.

Everyone in the room gasped, including the film crew.

Ursula stared at it and finally said, "I can't believe it—my father in Campagna."

Now it was time to search the pictures. Only Ursula would know her father. She looked at picture after picture and then finally, there he was. He was greeting Vescovo Palatucci on the steps of the *Chiesa di San Bartolomeo,* the church.

"I have that picture at home," she said. "I just thought it was Salerno."

Edith was sitting next to Ursula and pulled the book toward her, staring at the picture, "What I wouldn't give to have a picture of my father after over sixty years," she said. "I have nothing left. Nothing. Barely my memories."

1940. Ursula Korn Selig's father in Campagna at the former convent of San Bartolomeo greeting Bishop Palatucci. Rabbi Wachsberger is on the right.

Reunion after the war. Milano 1946. (Back Row) Horst Stein, Clara Stein, Herta Mingelgrün Pollak, Max Kempin, (Front Row) A young Marina Lowi (Zinn) between two of Herta's friends.

Everyone in the room realized the significance of this moment. In Manhattan, on a bright fall day in 2007, three Jewish women—Ursula, Edith, and Gerda—had a direct connection to a former convent in the hidden little village of Campagna. Ursula found a piece of her past that she did not know existed, and Edith made us realize the significance of a simple photograph. So simple, yet so powerful. While we all were stunned, my mother truly couldn't believe it. Her parents' small village had a history that was not well known, and new pieces were being discovered right before her eyes.

October 2007. Elizabeth Bettina, Horst Stein, Giorgina de Leon Vitale, Max Kempin, Vince Marmorale, Clara Stein, Herta Mingelgrun Pollak.

28

MORE DISCOVERY

I opened the window of my hotel room, and there it was before my eyes again—the symbol of Rome, the Cupola. What an incredible view. I felt a tear roll down my cheek. Just a few weeks earlier, I had not been sure I would ever see Italy again. Monsignor Filippi and Cardinal Ruini's prayers in Lourdes must have worked. Amidst the beeps in the recovery room, the voices of my mother and childhood friend, and the noisy din of doctors being paged, the only words I'd been praying to hear were, "You don't have cancer." And I heard them.

Time is a precious commodity and something we too often take for granted. We think we will have tomorrow to do things, knowing all too well it's not necessarily true. We act as if we have infinite tomorrows, when the only thing we have for certain is *now*.

Many ask why I've spent so much time on this project, time spent away from other things. The answer: if it was going to be done at all, it had to be done *now*. No more "woulda, coulda, shouldas" in my life. So as soon as I was given the okay from my doctor, I went to Italy to do more research. Like I'd hoped, I was able to be there for the Catholic holidays of All

Saints' Day and All Souls' Day, a time when Italians and Catholics around the world remember their dead.

They are still important holidays in Italy—especially in the smaller villages, where it seems the entire population goes to the cemetery to visit relatives who have passed. I'd never been in Campagna during that time, and it was like watching a scene from a movie. Almost everyone I knew in the village brought flowers to the graves of their loved ones. I couldn't help wondering if maybe their respect for the dead was somehow connected with why they helped the Jews so long ago.

Italian graves are different from those here in the United States. Each grave has a picture of the person buried there, which as a young girl, I thought was downright spooky. I imagined the people who were buried looking back at me from their tombstones. But now I find the idea comforting. I feel as if I am really visiting *them*, not a slab of marble with just their names carved on it. Born on this date, died on that date. I can "look them in the eye" and remember *who* they were and the times we shared. When I was there, I visited the graves of my great-grandparents, aunts, uncles, and even some cousins, members of the younger generation taken before their time. Then came the grave of Zia Maria. We so miss her. I thought about how she never elaborated on the Jews who lived just up the cobblestone street from her home. Oh, the questions.

I spent the night in my great-grandparents' home with my Aunt Ida amongst faded pictures of family members at various stages in their lives. It is something special to be in a home that has been in your family for generations, where your great-grandparents lived—and where they died. I realize how lucky I am to have this. The Jewish people I have spent so much time with do not have this luxury. There is no ancestral home to return to; there are no faded pictures of extended family on the wall. They can't stroll through the village with the older people who say they remember your great-grandfather as a no-nonsense man and your grandmother as a beautiful young woman who married the handsome son of the *farmacista*, the pharmacist, and went to America.

✦

Vince met me in Campagna a few days after I arrived. We weren't exactly sure what we would discover while in Italy, but we knew we needed to go to learn more about what happened in Campagna and Ferramonti during World War II. He asked me who specifically we would be meeting with, and when. For the most part, Italy just doesn't work that way. "Show up and things happen" has been my experience. I couldn't say what would happen, but I knew something unexpected would!

✦

Being in Campagna for a few days was wonderful. We were able to speak to Michele Aiello in depth about his work as president of the *Comitato Giovanni Palatucci*. If Vince is a search engine of all that is the Holocaust, Michele is a search engine of all that is Giovanni Palatucci. We also had a chance to speak with Gianluca Petroni, whose thesis had become "the book" that I carried with me everywhere, my bible of sorts. Had he not written in depth about the Jews in Campagna, I probably never would have known any more than what I knew as a child. His hard work was having an impact on the other side of the world.

My uncle told Vince and me a story about how my great-grandfather and his older sons helped hide a few Jews on the land he had in the mountains when the Germans arrived after September 8, 1943, to round up the Jews and take them to extermination camps.

"You could see that the Jews were upper class. They dressed nicely and were well educated; in fact, Dottore Tanzer saved my life when I was sick. We would not let the Germans take them. We knew the Germans were on the way, and the convent was emptied, and the Jews dispersed into the mountains in small groups. We took a few and hid them in the cellar on our land where we kept the cheese and sausage. We saw the Germans coming, and we knew they weren't coming to bring us presents—we knew what they wanted. They wanted the Jews, and we were ready for them. We were ready to shoot."

The things one discovers so many years later. I could picture my great-grandfather with his shotgun, protecting these innocent people.

The extra days in Campagna allowed for a visit with my friend Agnes Bundy Scanlan, who was traveling in Italy. She knew about my passion for this story and decided to break away from her group when they visited Pompeii, and spend the day with us in Campagna instead. It was wonderful to show her around "my" little village and take her to the Camp of San Bartolomeo.

29

THE CAMP THAT IS NOT A CAMP

We went to Ferramonti, the camp I call "the anti-Auschwitz" for many reasons. It is located about two and a half hours southeast of Campagna. Driving in Italy is always an interesting experience, and the only way to get to Ferramonti is by car, but we could not go directly. Vince and I had to travel first to the town of Tarsia, about ten minutes away, to have an "official" take us to the former camp. Up we went on the narrow, winding road that hugged the curves of the mountain. Tarsia was the opposite of Campagna. Instead of being embedded in the folds of the mountain, this town was perched on top of the hill, its buildings looking down on relatively nondescript countryside and swampland.

Vince and I followed the signs for *Comune*, where we were to meet town officials who would escort us to what is now the small museum of Ferramonti. The Italian Consulate in New York had sent the mayor of the town an e-mail, explaining we were two Italian-Americans doing research on Jews in Italy during World War II and requesting they have someone available to escort us to the former camp. Due to limited budgets, many small museums in Italy are not open to the public on a daily basis, and special appointments must be made in advance.

Although the mayor of Tarsia received the e-mail, he looked upon us as a bit of an intrusion to his otherwise seemingly uneventful day. He introduced us to the police officer who was to be our guide, but first he had to find the keys to the museum. He grabbed a bunch but was not certain that they were the right ones. "*Proviamo*," we will try, he said with a shrug. I looked at Vince, he looked at me, and I, too, shrugged— Italian style. The mayor gave the keys to the police officer, and we hoped for the best.

In our little Italian car, we followed our police officer— now our tour guide—back down the winding road. That was an interesting experience. Vince is a great driver, but the police officer was going so fast that we had trouble keeping up. One thing about Italians: they do know how to drive those curvy roads. Our police officer must have looked in his rearview mirror and seen us far behind, because his brake lights went on and he slowed down. Finally we could follow him without being concerned about going off the road.

All of a sudden he stopped under the overpass of the main highway in a desolate area with nothing around it.

"Vince, is this it?"

"Well, it must be. He's getting out of the car."

We got out and followed. What we saw ahead were a few long, barrack-type buildings, two that had been restored and a few that were quite run down. There was also an old watchtower that gave me a creepy feeling. It reminded me of the footage I have seen about German camps—how the Nazis were on guard at all times in the event any Jew tried to escape to save his life. What usually happened was the direct opposite. Death was accelerated by being shot on the spot. That did not happen in Ferramonti. Many things did not happen in Ferramonti.

Vince and I looked around. All the other barracks and buildings had been torn down long ago, as something else was to be built on the land, but that never happened. What was left now was a fraction of what was. Curious, we walked toward the building that was the "museum." Now it was time to see if the keys worked. Wouldn't that be something, coming all this way, having a police escort, and not have the keys work. I kept my fingers crossed. The first key did not work, nor did the second.

"*Non si preoccupi, signora.*" Don't worry, madame, said our police officer. "I can call a professor who also has a set of keys, and he can come and open the gate after he finishes his work." That would mean waiting for at least two hours, until one PM. Lunchtime is sacred in Italy, especially in the south, and under no circumstances would the professor be at work at one PM. Good, now we had a backup plan.

Again, as had happened so many times on our trips, Vince looked at me and we both thought the same thing. As the police officer inserted the last key in the door, I was thinking, *Please let this key work. We travelled so far, and it just has to work.* The key turned in the lock, and the door was open.

We entered a barrack that had been restored into a museum of sorts. Documents and photographs told us what happened more than sixty-five years ago. Although we had seen copies at Max's home, we were amazed at the other photos, especially seeing them in the camp where they were taken.

We saw pictures of happy couples on their wedding day, dressed in typical wedding attire: a suit for the groom and a beautiful, traditional white dress for the bride. I wondered where in the world they got the wedding dresses. Internment camp or not, there was a war going on, and such luxuries were limited. I had visions of an Italian woman in the town taking down her white embroidered curtains to make a wedding dress. Like that famous scene in *Gone with the Wind*—when Scarlett O'Hara needed a new dress, she just tore down the green velvet curtains and made one.

Other pictures showed people well dressed in their own clean and pressed clothing, not official uniforms, doing what people do on a daily basis. As Max said, Ferramonti was more like a small town than an internment camp. Depending on the exact time, anywhere from two to three thousand internees, mostly foreign Jews along with some Italian political prisoners, lived there as they would in a town. Families were able to live together. A school for the children was organized. Jewish internees who were doctors created a small clinic, and the rabbis in the camp could be rabbis. No one did forced labor, and no one was executed. Max and Herta were able to visit their fathers in Ferramonti. I still find that amazing. Imagine "visitation day" at

Auschwitz. You can't, because it didn't exist, and if it did, what would the visitors have said when they left?

"Elizabeth, do you realize what's here—or more importantly what's *not*?" asked Vince.

At first glance, the faded pictures of the ninety-two barracks that made up the *Campo di Concentramento* in Ferramonti look eerily similar to German concentration camps. But that's where the similarity ends. When you look at them again, there are no smokestacks, and there never were.

"It wasn't right for these people to be interned and lose their status and property," said Vince. "But Italy, at that time, didn't turn the Jews over to Germany to be sent to death camps."

"These pictures are amazing," I replied, "especially compared to images I have in my head of Jews in the camps, wearing threadbare, striped uniforms, literally skin and bones, with the men and women separated from each other."

In contrast, the Jews who were in Italy continually told us stories that circumstances were nearly normal—almost as if they were not in camps. But nothing about that time was normal, was it? Was it "normal" to decide to annihilate an entire group of people? Was it "normal" to decide to give people "gas showers" and put them into ovens to become ashes? Was it "normal" to think about this—let alone *do* it? When was it "normal" to create factories that manufactured death?

What amazes me is that this happened during a time when there was decent communication—not like today's instantaneous everything—but communication nonetheless in the form of telephones, film, radio, and newspapers. This was not the Middle Ages, yet what was supposed to be a civilized, well-educated group of people created mass murders on an assembly-line basis—not unlike any modern-day factory. Imagine knowing that you could be promoted for figuring out how to speed up the "murder assembly line." Working at the "Factory of Death"—that was your job. Good day at the office today, wasn't it?

At Ferramonti there was no "murder assembly line." Murder did not occur in here. Instead there were weddings, children, and prayer—Jewish prayer. Ferramonti also had a synagogue, as did the camp in Campagna. The difference was mind-boggling.

Synagogue at Ferramonti. © Fondazione Museo Internazionale della Memoria Ferramonti di Tarsia. See copyright page.

30

SATURDAY NIGHT LIVE IN CAMPAGNA

As the car made its way up the dark, winding road to the *Ristorante Avigliano*, I remembered something. It was *Saturday night* in Campagna.

"Vince, the restaurant will be filled with people from the town this evening. Think of a catering hall in New York, Italian style," I told him, laughing.

"Okay," replied Vince, who wasn't exactly sure what to expect.

As we approached the hotel, the road became packed with cars overflowing from the parking lot. And when we opened the door to the restaurant, we found it filled with several hundred people of all ages, from their eighties to little babies and everyone in between. Italians tend to not have baby-sitters, so children go everywhere with their parents, especially in the small towns. This place was hopping. In addition to serving delicious food, the restaurant also had a live band, and people were dancing the night away. We ordered the incredible brick-oven pizza. There's nothing like brick-oven pizza in Italy, especially in the mountains.

We sat down, happy to eat, and watched the activities of the evening. We were exhausted. The day had been tiring, and the next day was going to be packed. We were returning to Salerno to pick up Tagliaferri and bring him back to Campagna, as he requested. Then we were heading to Rome to meet Consuelo and Antonio Bandini. They were now back in Rome. His tenure in New York had concluded. The people in *Ristorante Avigliano* took note of the two *stranieri*, foreigners. We apparently added a bit of spice to their Saturday night activities. It was quite welcoming, and if I hadn't been so tired, I could have danced myself.

Sandro Scannapieco, a magnificent trumpet player.

Sandro Scannapieco was playing his trumpet beautifully, and I recalled how he played "Taps" for Walter last year. A knot was in my throat. Suddenly I heard the melody of the song

"New York, New York." Vince and I smiled because we knew Sandro was playing the song in honor of us. He is an excellent trumpet player and can play with the best in New York. The problem is that in this area, there were not a lot of options to play professionally, so Sandro worked at the *Autogrill* in Campagna. The *Autogrill* is a chain of rest stops on the *autostrada* that has delicious food and snacks. You can always get a great *espresso, panino,* or even a full meal. Even at the rest stops in Italy, the food is exceptionally good.

After playing his set, Sandro came over and sat down. He was also one of the members of the *Comitato Giovanni Palatucci* and was so happy that we were researching this story.

"I hear you are going to Rome tomorrow," he said as he joined us at our table.

"Yes, after we bring Tagliaferri here in the morning," I said.

"*Ah, bene, bene. Sai,* I have a very good friend. Dottoressa Savoia is in Rome, and you should meet. She works for Monsignor Clemens—he was Cardinal Ratzinger's secretary for twenty years. I will call her."

Vince looked up at me. Cardinal Ratzinger is now Pope Benedict XVI.

"Sandro, how did you meet Monsignor Clemens?" he asked.

"Well, about ten years ago, I was at work at the *Autogrill* and Monsignor Clemens and Cardinal Ratzinger came in for an *espresso,* and we began talking," he said. "Over the years we became friendly, especially concerning the Giovanni Palatucci story. When Cardinal Ratzinger became the pope, Monsignor Clemens was put in charge of the laity division." Laity are non-clergy who assist in church matters.

Vince still had an "I don't believe this" look on his face.

"We would be delighted to talk to your friend about what we are doing," I said.

This was one of many unexpected encounters that happened when we were in Italy. We never knew what we would find—or where.

31

CUT IRON—TAGLIAFERRI

When we asked Remo Tagliaferri if we could meet with him during this trip, he invited us to visit him in his home in Salerno, about thirty-five minutes from Campagna. After we got comfortable, we asked him to tell us about his time as a guard in the Camp of San Bartolomeo.

"I dressed in civilian clothes, because I wanted to respect these people," he said. "They didn't do anything bad. You could tell that the Jews were *professionisti*, professionals, educated people. The world was crazy, but we were not. We treated them with dignity, and I took them many times to play soccer on the outskirts of town."

Tagliaferri showed us his old uniform, and then he took out the whistle he used for roll call. He had used it last year with Walter Wolff. "Here, you take it. I want you to have it," he said, handing the whistle to Vince. "You care about this story."

"No, you should keep it," said Vince. "It is part of your past."

"And when I die, no one will know what it was. You know, I have something else to show you." Tagliaferri left the room and returned with his revolver. "This never left my side all those years, and it was always *caricata*, loaded."

The gun was in good shape and came with bullets housed in a separate case.

"I would like to do something. I would like to go with you to Campagna tomorrow, to show you Campagna through *my* eyes," he said.

This was quite an opportunity, and I knew I could delay our plans to go to Rome in the morning. We would be delighted to visit Campagna with Tagliaferri. Besides, he was holding a gun.

"*Ecco*, here, I would like you to have . . . this gun," he said as he handed it to Vince.

Vince explained that while he was extremely honored, he could not accept the gift. "I'll get arrested at the airport if I try to bring this on the plane, plus I don't have a permit for a gun," he said.

"I would like for you to have it, but I understand you can't take it with you," Tagliaferri said reluctantly.

Vince said he would accept the whistle instead, and we made plans to return in the morning to take the former police officer back to Campagna. Vincenzo, Zio Peppe's son, graciously accompanied us to Salerno in the morning.

Early the next day, the car sped along the *autostrada* from Campagna to Salerno. Speed limits for Italians, well they tend to be a mere suggestion. Salerno is located on the coast, about an hour south of Naples. It is the beginning of the Amalfi Drive, the famous and extraordinarily beautiful coastline seen in so many postcards. It is also where you can catch a ferry to the chic Isle of Capri, where the world's glitterati vacation. There is a famous picture of Jackie O walking in Capri holding her sandals in her hand. All this, less than an hour from Campagna.

It was difficult to imagine that more than sixty years earlier, there was a bloody battle in Salerno—the Allies versus the Axis. Thousands of men died fighting Hitler's soldiers on these shores, and for one long stretch, you can see the white crosses at the Salerno War Cemetery where so many young American soldiers are buried.

When we arrived at his home, Tagliaferri was waiting for us in his doorway and looked quite handsome in his suit jacket. I wondered if he had the revolver with him.

Remo Tagliaferri at the train station in Eboli

On the drive to Campagna, we stopped at a small station, Eboli, where trains filled with Jews from all parts of Italy had once arrived. From the train station they were taken in buses or army-like trucks to the camps in Campagna. Again, it was here that comparisons to German-run concentration camps end.

As we drove into Campagna, local townspeople slowed down and stared into the car. We got out to get a coffee, and a gentleman in his early eighties who had been staring at our group from afar turned to me, exclaiming, "*È lui, è Tagliaferri.*" It is Tagliaferri.

"*Era terribile—ma buono,*" said the man. He was terrible, but good.

Now I understood why Aunt Ida always looked terrified, as a child does when she is afraid, whenever Tagliaferri's name was mentioned. Tagliaferri still had a commanding presence, and the older people took notice; the sheriff was back in town! Before I knew it, he was holding court in the *piazza*, reminding everyone how he had enforced the blackouts.

"Instead of walking up to a house that had a light on, I would just shoot it out," he said, lifting his arms and using his hands to simulate a gun in his hand. "Bang! Then the next morning I'd go and give them a fine. Why waste my time at night? Soon, everyone obeyed curfew—and blackout, no more problems."

Vince and I laughed. "He is one heck of a guy, but I wouldn't mess with him," Vince said. I was still hoping the gun was back in Salerno.

We walked through the town and arrived at the bottom of Via San Bartolomeo.

"That is the street that the Jews came down every day, and I would take them to what I called the *confine di Campagna*, the confines of Campagna," said Tagliaferri. "I will show you later. Now for the camp."

We entered the *Campo di San Bartolomeo*, and Tagliaferri gave us his personal tour.

"Here, this is where they would pray. We let them pray," he said. He then showed us how they prayed. Religious Jews tend to rock back and forth during parts of their prayers, and after years of watching the Jews pray, he knew exactly how they moved.

We climbed up the stairs of the old convent, and he showed us where the Jews had their rooms, and also where they ate. Finally he showed us the "window" that the Jews escaped from. With the signing of the armistice, Italy withdrew from the war on the side of the Germans and become allied with the United States. One country, two sides. Germany felt betrayed by its former ally. Italy was now the enemy. German soldiers in Italy tried to gather the Jewish internees who were confined under the Fascist government, and others who were now in hiding, and deport them to Germany. The Jews were now in danger. It was September 8, 1943.

The Germans planned to move the internees from the *Campo di San Bartolomeo* in Campagna to extermination camps in Poland and Germany. But, thanks to many people like Tagliaferri, the Germans were not able to execute this evil plan.

"Two German soldiers came up the street of San Bartolomeo. I didn't know what to do, shoot them or talk to them. My gun was ready," he said. Vince and I had no doubt about that. "I decided to hear what they had to say. They told me they were going to return the next day to gather the internees, so we decided to have the Jews escape as soon as it was dark.

"During the night, with the help of a crowbar, we opened this window on the second floor, and the Jews escaped into the mountains right out the window of the camp. I fled into the mountains with them. I knew my mountains and the caves where they could hide; plus, when the Germans got back and didn't find the Jews, they would not be very happy with me."

Fortunately, when the Germans arrived in Campagna, a German tank got stuck in the narrow streets. Meanwhile, at the camp, a sign was placed on the door that said: "The internees were transferred by official order—Destination Unknown."

The people of Campagna were afraid that the Germans might retaliate, given that the Jews they were looking for were no longer there. For a few days the town was virtually empty, as many local residents had also fled into the mountains for safety from the Germans and from bombs dropped by Allied forces.

On September 17, 1943, many people, even some from Eboli, the *sfollati,* were in a small *piazza* next to town hall celebrating the fact that the Germans had been forced out.

These people were also eagerly anticipating the arrival of the Allied forces and their daily ration of bread. They could hear an airplane approaching, but they weren't afraid. After all, it was the Allies. What they didn't realize was the pilot had seen a tank, and, thinking the enemy was nearby, began to bomb the area—killing hundreds of innocent people. I know of many Campagnesi who were killed there that day.

The Jewish doctors who were in hiding came down out of the mountains to help the wounded. Those who were not wounded helped gather the dead and brought them to the cemetery, which was about two kilometers away around the curve of the mountain. Many of the dead could not be identified, and the doctors, hoping to avoid an epidemic, decided to cremate the bodies. At that moment it was the ex-internees who organized the town and helped the citizens of Campagna deal with the tragedy.

The Camp of San Bartolomeo remained in operation until the fall of 1944. After the war ended, some Jews returned to Campagna to revisit the place where they were interned and to thank yet again the people of the town. Some Jews sent money to Campagna to restore the convent of San Bartolomeo that kept them safe from the atrocities of the Nazi regime, a regime that killed many of their family members. A plaque from former internees is located in the former convent, thanking the people of Campagna for their kindness during World War II.

Translation of plaque: The Jews of Long Island City, particularly the family of Ignatz Wohl, in appreciation for the kindness received by their countrymen in Campagna during the Second World War and for the personal intervention of Judge Alessandro Del Giorno, contributed to the reconstruction of the ex-convent for the purpose of welcoming the youth of Campagna.

Tagliaferri, Vince, and I left the old convent and made our way down the winding cobblestone road to the edge of town, where Tagliaferri stood in the middle of the main road leading to the town, paying no mind whatsoever to the fact that cars were coming in both directions. The drivers of the cars took one look at him and just stopped. He still had "it." Tagliaferri stuck out his foot and dragged his heel across the road.

"This was the line. I put a big white line in chalk and wrote in five languages that it was the *confine*. No one went beyond it—ever."

"I wouldn't have either," said Vince with a wink. You just didn't mess with Tagliaferri. Not even now!

We continued on to a soccer field. "This is where I took the internees to play soccer. Many of them were very good. Wolff was a good player."

It was time for lunch, and we went to the *Ristorante/Hotel Avigliano* for a delicious meal. Tagliaferri held court once again with the people of Campagna before we had to leave to drive him home to Salerno. For Vince and me, another piece of history had clicked into place.

32

CONNECTING THE DOTS

When we arrived in Rome, I called Sandro's friend, Dottoressa Savoia. She had been expecting my call and, yes, she would be delighted to meet with us. An appointment was made for noon that day. We took a cab to her office and realized that it was not far from the Jewish quarter. Quite fitting.

We entered the office and met Dottoressa Savoia, a woman who was about fifty years old. She ushered us into a conference room where we explained the journey thus far: how Vince met Walter Wolff, how I saw the picture of the rabbi with Bishop Palatucci, and all the rest. We also showed her how Walter's story and the Giovanni Palatucci stories intertwine.

"This is one of the most important stories of the Holocaust because it demonstrates the goodness of the Italian people amongst the evil in the rest of Europe at the time," said Vince.

We spent about half an hour with her, reviewing the journey. Toward the end of our visit, she smiled. You could tell she got it.

"We're continuing our research and filming Jews who survived the Holocaust because they were in Italy," I told her.

"Their stories will be told in their voices, and they will teach people of future generations what the people of Italy did during the war." We closed by giving her a brief history on the survivors we knew.

"I think you should meet Monsignor Caccia, a colleague who works with international matters in the office of the *segretario di stato,* the secretary of state's office," she said. "This is a wonderful story, and I think he should hear about it from you."

"We would love to meet with him," we said, "but we're leaving tomorrow at eleven for a two thirty PM flight, so we don't have much time."

"I'll call him right now," she said, and went to her office to get his number.

Dottoressa Savoia called Monsignor Caccia and explained who we were and what we were doing. It was decided that we would meet with him the next morning, at eight forty-five in his office in Vatican City. She explained that we were to enter at Porta Sant' Anna, located under the Colonnade of Saint Peter's Square. It is to the right as you look at the Basilica. The Swiss Guards would then give us further instructions.

Dottoressa Savoia could not have been nicer. She had known about some of our work from Sandro, and also from Michele Aiello. We were *raccomandata.* Recommended. Basically, being *raccomandata* is how Italy works. If you know someone who can vouch for you, things happen. Being *raccomandata* was how many Jews survived. We were now going to meet someone else in the Vatican, all because one *racco-mandata* led to another.

✦

The next morning Vince and I had breakfast in the rooftop restaurant at our hotel, the Atlante Star. "What a way to wake up. I love breakfast here. It's truly something when you can wake up to cappuccino and drink it while looking at Saint Peter's Basilica," I said to Vince. "No matter how many times I see it, I'm speechless."

"I know what you mean," said Vince. "Imagine, that is where we are going now."

We walked to Porta Sant' Anna. As described, at the entrance we found the famous Swiss Guards and other police officers.

"*Buon Giorno*. We have an appointment with Monsignor Caccia." I gave the guard our names and he gave me a piece of paper. A "hall pass" to the Vatican!

"*Signora, avanti alla prossima entrata*." Ma'am, go ahead to the next entrance.

We walked up the cobblestone street where cars were parked along the way. On the right was a Vatican post office. The Italian mail system can leave something to be desired, but the Vatican postal system is quite reliable. There's another Vatican post office in Saint Peter's Square that's available to tourists, and it's the place to go to send your postcards.

We continued walking toward the next gate and were

met by another police officer. He checked our "hall pass" and told us to go left and enter a large doorway. I saw Vatican fire trucks barely bigger than overgrown Tonka Toys. Given the size of the trucks, I'm glad most of the Vatican is made of solid, thick stone that can't burn too easily! My father, a retired New York City firefighter, would find these tiny fire trucks amusing, so we took a few pictures for him.

Vince and I continued following directions, entered the door on the left, and got on an elevator. I have never been in an elevator this large in Italy. Most of them barely hold one or two people. This one came with an elevator attendant as do many of the apartment houses on Fifth Avenue in New York City.

Swiss Guards on duty at the Vatican.

We went to our floor and were met by another Swiss Guard. I do wonder how these guards feel when they put on their colorful "uniforms" every day. The uniforms remind me of court jester or clown outfits, more decorative than practical. We then walked down several splendid corridors covered with frescoes. One even featured a map of the world as it was in the late 1400s. Australia was missing—it had not yet been discovered!

We were greeted by Monsignor Caccia's assistant, Bruno, and were shown to a meeting room where Monsignor Caccia joined us a few minutes later. He is a handsome, soft-spoken man in his early fifties with graying hair and was wearing the typical "priest clothes." Vince and I explained our journey and research. We discussed in-depth aspects of the Holocaust, and I have to say that Vince never ceases to amaze me. He knew every treaty, speech, and policy that was mentioned. Even Monsignor Caccia was impressed. I don't think he knew exactly what he was getting into that morning, and to be truthful, I was not certain either. What I expected to last half an hour became nearly an hour and a half. Monsignor Caccia was very interested in our research and travels. As we were ready to leave, he asked if we had a few more minutes. Of course we said yes. I was glad our bags were already packed!

We followed Monsignor Caccia down another corridor; this one was covered with frescoes from the school of Raphael. It is hard to imagine that the frescoes are approximately five hundred years old and are still in such good condition. Until recent times the Loggia was not enclosed, and the frescoes were exposed to the elements of nature—yet they lasted.

We then went through doors that led onto a Vatican terrace that overlooked Saint Peter's Square and the Basilica. The Cupola was looming over us, and I felt as if we could touch the statues. From the terrace, Vince and I saw all of Rome. Monsignor Caccia then gave us a bit of Vatican history. I wanted to pinch myself to make sure I was truly awake.

"And those windows are the windows of the pope's apartment," he said, as he pointed to a building not one hundred feet away.

"Wow." It was about all I could manage to say. Vince was speechless.

It was time to leave, and Monsignor Caccia accompanied us to the elevator. As we walked, I explained that I didn't know Vatican politics very well and that when we were here with Walter Wolff, I didn't know who Cardinal Ruini was until my cousin explained his role to me. Monsignor Caccia laughed.

"All I knew was that Cardinal Ruini should meet Mr. Wolff, because of the Giovanni Palatucci connection," I said. "But I had no idea of his specific position. I knew he was a cardinal, that was all."

"*Elisabetta*, that is exactly why you are here. Because you *don't* know the politics," he said with a twinkle in his eye. We all laughed.

Monsignor Caccia was truly interested in our project, and we promised to keep in touch as we continued our research.

Before we said good-bye, he pointed to a door down the corridor and told us it was the entrance to the pope's offices. I nodded, again not truly believing where we were.

Vince and I went back the way we came, but in a bit of a daze. How did that happen? A private, unexpected visit in the Vatican?

"Well, you were right," Vince said.

"About what?" I asked.

"You said in Italy you 'show up and things happen,' and you were 100 percent right."

As we drove to the airport, we passed Saint Peter's Basilica and I thought to myself that a simple pizza in the mountains of Campagna had twice led to surprises in my life: discovery of the Jewish story and unexpected meetings in the Vatican. The journey kept getting more intriguing.

33

MORE DOTS CONNECTING

Until the moment I was invited to hear her speak, I had never heard of Ruth Gruber or the fascinating story of her voyage on the army transport, the *Henry Gibbons*. Vince, of course, knew who she was.

During her speech, I learned that in 1944, Ruth Gruber was asked to secretly accompany one thousand Jewish refugees on a transport ship, the *Henry Gibbons*, from Naples, Italy, to New York. This was arranged by an executive order from President Franklin Delano Roosevelt. The plan was that the refugees would "visit" the United States, and then return to their home countries at the end of the war. In the end the Jewish refugees were allowed to remain in the United States.

When the Jewish visitors arrived in the United States, they continued to Oswego in upstate New York, where they were housed at an old army base. It had taken several years, from the beginning of the war until 1944, for the United States to make provisions to help one thousand persecuted people stay in a country that was safe.

Ruth Gruber was still feisty at the age of ninety-six. I could only imagine what she was like in her thirties during the war.

As she spoke, I shook my head and found it hard to believe that here was yet another Italian story that began near Campagna.

"Ultimately the *Henry Gibbons* carried 982 Jewish refugees," Ruth Gruber explained. "Some remained in Naples for medical reasons. As you can imagine, the trip was not easy, and the ship was under constant threat of attack."

Ruth accompanied the refugees to Oswego to acclimate them to their new surroundings. She also helped document their stories as witnesses to the unimaginable horrors that were taking place in Europe.

I wondered whether people who had been in Campagna were on the *Henry Gibbons*. It was entirely possible. I would later discover that there was a Campagna–Henry Gibbons connection.

After the presentation, Vince and I spoke with Ruth Gruber, and we also met a lovely woman, Doris Blumenkranz Schechter. Doris was a little girl, just six years old, when she was on the *Henry Gibbons* with her parents and sister. They, too, had been in Italy, in a small town called Guardiagrele in the province of Chieti, in Abruzzi on the Adriatic Coast of Italy. According to Doris, Guardiagrele had seventy Jews interned during the war. Her experiences echo those of the other survivors. If she had not been in Italy, she would not have survived. One of her favorite stories is how her father wrote to the Vatican requesting matzo for Passover, and the Vatican sent the matzo. Doris loves Italy and has been back to Guardiagrele several times in the last few years.

Just back from a recent trip, she showed me extraordinary documents that list the rules the interned Jews were to abide by and funds provided by the Italian government. I had always heard about these rules from the many survivors we had interviewed, but never seen them written. Neither had Vince. (A copy and translation are located in Appendix C.)

I compared the list of 982 people on the *Henry Gibbons* to the list of 272 in Campagna. There were twenty-five people from Campagna who traveled with Ruth Gruber to New York. I went from never having heard of the *Henry Gibbons* to learning that quite a few internees from Campagna traveled on it. Amazing.

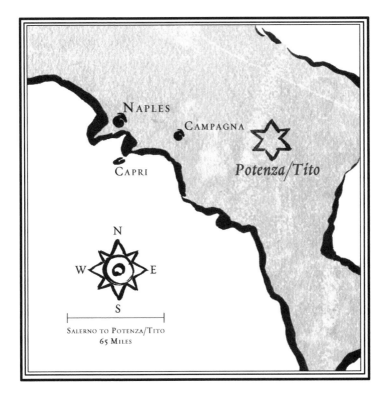

34

NASHVILLE: BRINGING ME TO CAMPAGNA

A s my friend Ann Marchesano says, there is a reason for everything, and sometimes it takes years to know exactly what it is. Ann offers perspective on things, much as an older sister would. Her words have proven true over the years.

A few years ago, I traveled to Nashville on business and befriended on the plane two wonderful families, the Martin/ Orlands and the Jamisons, who found the story of Jews being saved in Italy during the Holocaust fascinating. Unbeknownst to any of us at the time, they each would play a role in this story, and many more trips to Nashville would follow.

An invitation to Eli Orland's bar mitzvah led to another discovery. I met a guest, Felicia Anchor, who said I must speak with her friends Eva and Eric Rosenfeld, Holocaust survivors originally from Germany. They said I would find Eva's story of particular interest because she survived the war in Italy. Now imagine the look on my face when I heard that a woman who lived in Nashville, Tennessee, the home of country music, had survived World War II in Italy. The next day I was able to meet Eric and Eva. They invited me to their home so I could view their photographs and documents. I was so excited about meeting them that I called Vince in New York.

"You must be kidding me. In Nashville!" Vince said. "Call me as soon as you're finished. I can't wait to hear what she has to say." I could picture Vince shaking his head in disbelief.

Eric and Eva are a very sweet couple. She is soft spoken, and Eric is filled with energy. From the moment I met them, it felt as if I were being reacquainted with old friends. This has occurred with almost all of the survivors. The "Italy bond" is an incredible ice-breaker through time and generations. Eva gave me a hug, and we began to talk.

As a young girl, she was first interned in Potenza, a town about one hour (or about fifty miles) southeast of Campagna, and then in Tito, a smaller town about ten miles from Potenza. Vince and I had traveled through Potenza by train on our way to Ferramonti just a few weeks earlier. During our trip to Italy and at the various conferences we attended, not once did any-one mention Jews in Potenza. This just proved what Vince and I already knew—that this untold story of the Holocaust was bigger than we ever imagined.

Eva and Eric showed me several documents that were dis-played on boards they use for their educational speeches. There was a picture of a seventeen-year-old Eva in a newspaper, one of the people brought to America on the *Henry Gibbons*.

Eva explained how she got to Italy. Her parents, Kurt Lepehne and Margarite Neuberg, decided to move from Germany to Genoa in 1937 to escape the persecution of Nazi Germany.

Kurt Lepehne was a pharmacist, but he was prohibited from working in Germany under the Nazi regime. In Genoa, the couple worked endlessly trying to run a bakery. Eva's parents became friendly with a newly married doctor and his wife, Dr. and Mrs. Max Kleinmann. This was a friendship that would become vitally important to young Eva. Eva's brother remained in Germany with other family members to finish the school year and planned to join the family a few months later. During this difficult time, Eva's mother became sick, and she died of heart failure in January 1939. Twelve-year-old Eva was now alone with her father in Genoa. Her brother never did join the family—it was too dangerous. Fortunately, he was able to escape Germany and get to England, but it would be twenty-eight years before Eva and her brother were finally reunited.

Then, for Eva, the unimaginable occurred. Her father was arrested, and she was left alone. The Kleinmanns took care of Eva during this time, and her father later was released from prison, but with a warning: he had to leave Italy in just a few days and was advised to go to France. Because it was too dangerous to travel with his young daughter, Eva stayed behind. This decision would prove fateful for both Eva and her father. Kurt Lepehne arranged for the Kleinmann family to care for his daughter in his absence. She and the Kleinmanns already had boat tickets to sail to America a few weeks later, and Eva's father would attempt to join them when he could.

What I have learned in life—especially from this story—is that timing is everything. The timing of these tickets definitely worked against Eva and the Kleinmanns. Tragically, the war broke out just four days before they were to leave Genoa. The few weeks that Eva was supposed to live with the Kleinmann family turned into four years. Eva's father never was able to escape from Europe. Years later, Eva finally discovered that he was captured in France and died in Auschwitz. To this day, Eva wonders what would have happened if her father had stayed in Italy with her. "If my father had not gone to France and had stayed in Italy, he would have probably survived," Eva said wistfully. This reminded me of Marina Lowi's father going to Belgium after Italy, because he thought that things might be better in Belgium than in Italy. Neither man was ever seen again by his family—their fates sealed in Auschwitz.

In October 1940, Eva was sent to Potenza with Mrs. Kleinmann—pregnant with her first child—as part of the internment program in Italy.

"For some reason her husband was first sent to a different camp in a town not too far from Potenza and joined us several months later," said Eva. "I think the town is the one you mentioned before—Campagna."

I rummaged through my black bag and pulled out "the book" with the list of people's names. My fingers trembled as I went to "K." Yes, Kleinmann, Massimiliano!

61.	Klein	Isacco	Salomone	1912	medico	germ.
62.	Klein	Maurizio	Isidoro	1893	autista mec.	germ.
63.	Kleinmann	Massimiliano	Wolf	1909	medico	apol.ex germ.
64.	Klüger	Gustavo	Gerson	1892	impiegato	germ.
65.	Kniebel	Leopoldo	Simone	1882	chimico	germ.

"Right here!" I said, pointing. Eva and Eric couldn't believe what we were learning on this quiet Sunday afternoon.

I began doing the math in my head. Dr. Kleinmann was born in 1909, which made him ninety-eight years old. I didn't think he would still be alive, but before I had a chance to ask, Eva told me he lived in New York. Flushing, to be exact. Flushing? Dr. Kleinmann was alive and lived approximately *one mile* from my grandmother, who was born and raised in Campagna! Eva added that Mrs. Kleinmann had passed away earlier in the year and that the couple had three sons.

My hands went again into the big black bag, this time to get out my cell phone to call Vince. Less than five minutes had passed since I last called him.

"Are you sitting down? Because you're not going to believe what I have to tell you this time!"

✦

Max Kleinmann's son, Walter, was having a nice, quiet Sunday afternoon in New York and was surprised to hear Eva's voice on the phone and learn why she was calling. Yes, he said, he would be delighted to meet as soon as possible. So we set it up for Thursday afternoon at his father's house.

Eva made us a soothing cup of tea, and I spent the rest of the afternoon learning about Eva and Eric and their experiences. Over and over again, Eva said what so many others had. I could almost finish her sentences: "The Italians were wonderful, and I thank God I was in Italy. If I was not in Italy, I would not be here today."

Eric then told me his story. He had attended the same high school in Frankfurt, "Philantropins", that Walter Wolff and Horst Stein had. What are the chances? You can imagine Eric's surprise when he realized I knew the name of his school. At sixteen years old, he was on one of the last transports out of Europe in 1941. That trip saved his life.

Eric wound up in the United States in 1941 and joined the United States Army in 1944. Because of his ability to speak German, the army sent him to Germany, where he was stationed in his hometown village of Seeheim, assigned to the 103rd Infantry Division. This was totally by chance; it wasn't planned for him to be sent to his hometown.

Imagine when the mayor of the town saw Eric return as a uniformed United States soldier. One day Eric took the mayor out to a field. It was just the two of them, no witnesses.

"What happened to my mother?" Eric asked.

"I was only following orders," the mayor said sheepishly. "I was ordered to send her to Darmstadt [a small town nearby]. I didn't know that she would end up in Auschwitz."

Eric told me that he wanted to choke the mayor to death that day, but decided against it, not wanting to carry that burden for the rest of his life.

Eric and Eva, both orphans of the war, met in Rochester, New York, and were married in 1951. They created a life together and have four children and six grandchildren.

Before leaving, I hinted that it would be quite something if Eva and Eric considered visiting Italy with Vince and me, with Walter Kleinmann and others from our group. Eva and

Eric smiled and said that would be nice, but it probably was not going to happen. After all, they were in their eighties, and a trip to Italy was a big undertaking. I told them I had done it before and was capable of doing it again.

"Trust me," I promised. "One day you will get to Italy."

Eva Lepehne (Rosenfeld), ID card from Potenza, Italy.

The Rosenfeld family.

35

THE NASHVILLE-CAMPAGNA-NEW YORK CONNECTION

Fresh from my time with Eric and Eva Rosenfeld in Nashville, I met with Vince, Dr. Max Kleinmann, and his son Walter in Flushing on Thursday afternoon. At ninety-eight Dr. Kleinmann was a bit frail in body, but full of spirit and an active mind. He greeted us with an animated remark.

"*Now* you come to visit! It took you almost seventy years, and now you come to talk to me about the war?"

Vince laughed. "Some of us had to be born and grow up before we could learn about this story."

We settled in and listened to what Dr. Kleinmann had to say, still amazed that a chance meeting in Nashville led us to someone in our own backyard.

In 1933 Dr. Kleinmann was a young medical student at Friedrich Wilhelm University in Berlin. The Nazis had begun beating Jewish students there, and the young Max Kleinmann decided to leave Germany and continue his medical studies in Pisa, Italy. Something else helped influence his decision.

"I read *Mein Kampf* and decided to leave Germany by page three," he said. He made us laugh and sounded a bit like

Max Kempin describing his life in 1935. Kempin's father had done the same thing—read *Mein Kampf* and decided to leave the country. Dr. Kleinmann's family and friends, including his hometown sweetheart, stayed behind. None of them believed things would get worse. Life, they thought, would get better with time.

"I told them I would come back when it got better, but it never did." Dr. Kleinmann finished his medical studies in Italy, the only country that allowed him to enter without a visa.

He received his medical degree at the University of Pisa in 1936 and spent eight months in the Italian army near the French border before World War II. He had convinced his sweetheart, Felicitas (Lizi), to join him in Genoa, and in 1938 they married.

Dr. Kleinmann was not allowed to practice medicine because of the Italian racial laws, and in 1940, he was arrested and taken to Campagna. He was there at the same time as Walter Wolff and Ursula's father, Paolo Korn, and Fred Birns. I now had a direct connection to four people in Campagna.

Lizi Kleinmann, newly pregnant, was sent with young Eva Lepehne (Rosenfeld) to Potenza, an hour or so away. While in Campagna, Dr. Kleinmann contracted typhus, and the Italian authorities sent him to the hospital in Salerno, where he recuperated. After he recovered, he was sent back to Campagna. While he was fighting his own health battle, Lizi was having a difficult time with her pregnancy.

"The camp in Campagna was a nice camp. High in the

mountains. I wasn't there long, a few months," Dr. Kleinnman told us. "During my time in Campagna, we were treated well, we were able to mix with the people of the town, walk around, play soccer, and I helped the people with medical questions, as did the other doctors in the camp. After I became sick, I contacted my former commanding officer, and they let me join my wife and Eva in Potenza. It was a different experience from Campagna. We were confined to the town, but otherwise we were, for the most part, free. This kind of freedom would not have happened in Germany."

It was the same story we'd heard so many times—people requesting to be reunited with their families and the request being honored.

"In Potenza," Dr. Kleinmann continued, "we lived in town, among the Italians, in a small apartment, *internamento libero*. The only rules the town had for the Jews were curfew, and each day we had to report to the police. After I said, '*Buon giorno*' each morning, I usually had coffee with the chief of police at the local café," he recalled with a smile. "The people treated us well, and we went about our lives like other people in the town. We were also allowed to get together with other Jewish families, pray, observe the holidays. In fact, we even were able to bake matzos for Passover. None of this would have been imaginable in any German-run camp in Europe.

"I was not officially allowed to practice medicine, but . . . " Dr. Kleinmann's voice trailed off, and he gave us one of those

Italian shrugs, raising his shoulders and tilting his head. He had learned well! Everyone knew he was a doctor, and they all needed his help. It was wartime. No one had money.

"The people brought me whatever they had—some eggs, some milk, some bread, those types of things—to say thank you. I am ever grateful to one special woman whose actions demonstrate the compassion of the Italians during that time. How can I ever thank the woman who nursed my son Walter in 1941 when my wife was unable to feed him?"

Such stories of goodness never cease to amaze me. An Italian woman breast-fed a Jewish baby in the middle of what Hitler had hoped would be a complete extermination of Jews.

We began looking at Dr. Kleinmann's documents—his university papers, his military papers, his marriage certificate, his citizenship papers. Yes! Dr. Kleinmann even became an Italian citizen. He had an attaché case filled with papers that reminded me of Walter Wolff and his documents.

Dr. Kleinmann continued his story about Potenza and how the family was eventually transferred to Tito, a village about ten miles away.

"Whenever Germans were in the area, the Italians would take the Jews to Tito and to other small towns in the area that didn't appear on most maps at the time," he said. "After September 8, 1943, we remained in Tito, and a family named Goldman was also with us."

"You must meet Ruth Goldman Tobias," said Walter Kleinmann. "She lives in New Jersey—her sister, Cilla, was born in Tito, and her brother, Jeffrey, was born in Potenza. My brother Erwin was also born in Potenza."

Birth certificate for Walter Kleinmann.

Dr. Kleinmann was leading us to other people who were connected to Italy and World War II. The best part was that this "new" survivor was right here in the New York area.

"When the war ended, we stayed in Italy," said Dr. Kleinmann. "We were waiting to go to the United States, and in 1948 we moved to New York."

It was getting late, and we could see that Dr. Kleinmann was tiring, so Vince and I decided to return at a later date to continue our conversation. He was an amazing man with a story that was inextricably linked to the stories of the other survivors we had met.

Dr. Max Kleinmann's ID card from Genoa.

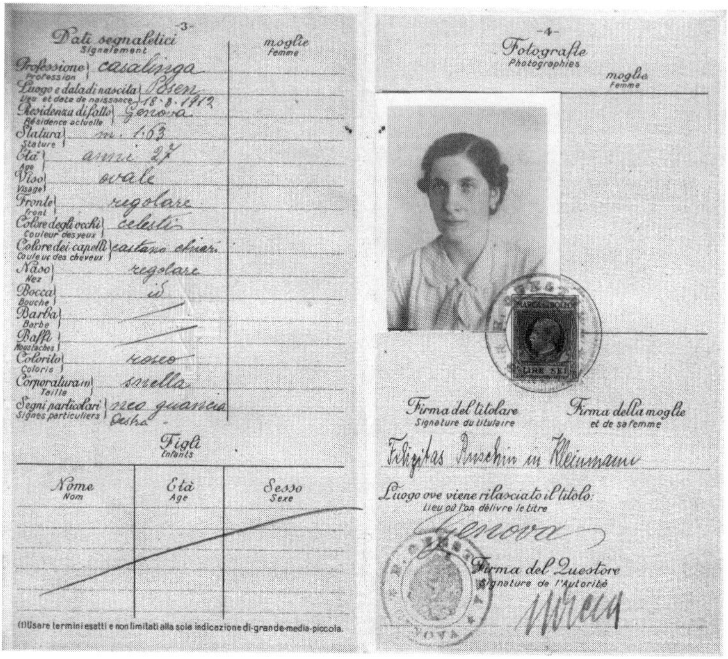

-3-

Dati segnaletici
Signalement

	moglie Femme
Professione / Profession: casalinga	
Luogo e data di nascita / Lieu et date de naissance: Posen 18.8.1912	
Residenza di fatto / Résidence actuelle: Genova	
Statura / Stature: m. 1.63	
Età / Age: anni 27	
Viso / Visage: ovale	
Fronte / Front: regolare	
Colore degli occhi / Couleur des yeux: celesti	
Colore dei capelli / Couleur des cheveux: castano chiari	
Naso / Nez: regolare	
Bocca / Bouche: id.	
Barba / Barbe: —	
Baffi / Moustaches: —	
Colorito / Coloris: roseo	
Corporatura (1) / Taille: snella	
Segni particolari / Signes particuliers: neo guancia destra	

Figli
Enfants

Nome / Nom	Età / Age	Sesso / Sexe

(1) Usare termini esatti e non limitati alle sole indicazione di-grande-media-piccola.

-4-

Fotografie
Photographies

moglie
Femme

MARCA DA BOLLO
LIRE SEI

Firma del titolare
Signature du titulaire

Felizitas Ruschin in Kleinmann

Firma della moglie
et de sa femme

Luogo ove viene rilasciato il titolo:
Lieu où l'on délivre le titre

Genova

Firma del Questore
Signature de l'Autorité

Lizi Kleinmann's ID card from Genoa.

36

THE SOUNDS OF MUSIC

Whenever I tell people about Campagna, I explain that the town is embedded in a valley with only one road leading into it, and that mountains surround the town. If that road were to disappear—be blown up during a war for example—the town would be completely inaccessible. The only way to get in or out would be to climb the mountains like Julie Andrews did in *The Sound of Music*. When I explain it that way, people immediately understand. What I didn't know was exactly how many similarities I would find between *The Sound of Music* and Campagna.

I attended the famous Macy's Thanksgiving Day Parade on a nasty, rainy day, the kind that chills you to the bone and certainly not ideal for a parade. Next to me was a family, and in our camaraderie of trying to keep dry under our umbrellas, we began to chat. I asked what brought them out to the parade in the "lovely" weather, and the woman told me her mother was participating in the parade. How interesting. I envisioned her mother being one of the famous balloon handlers. It was then that she told me her mother was not a balloon handler—but Julie Andrews! I laughed out loud and told the woman how often I used her mother's movie, *The Sound of Music*, to explain a little village in Italy—not only the geography, but the importance of what so many nuns did during World War II to help people. I also mentioned that I had seen her mother's last performance in *Victor Victoria* years before.

As a child, I saw *The Sound of Music* many times. But only now do I fully understand the historical context and underlying meaning of the movie. Even children understand that Captain von Trapp and his family wanted to escape the soldiers who wanted him to join the Navy of the Third Reich. The family sought refuge in the convent—with the nuns' full cooperation and blessing. In one fondly remembered scene, the nuns thwart the efforts of the Germans by pulling the spark plugs from their cars. As amusing the thought is of nuns misbehaving, we do not necessarily see the *true consequences* of that action in the family-friendly movie. The "bad guys" in this movie are Nazis, and in real life, the nuns could have been sent to concentration camps or shot immediately for their well-meaning gesture.

Recently, I watched *The Sound of Music* with a more informed eye. I now understood the tension Captain von Trapp must have felt in 1938 when he was required to accept the German annexation of Austria—known as the Aunchluss. Upon returning from his honeymoon with his new wife, Maria (Julie Andrews), he was given a telegram with orders to report for naval duty in the new regime the next morning. By not obeying orders, he would put his entire family at risk, but obeying orders was unthinkable. It was apparent that he would have to leave that night.

The nuns played an extremely important role in this story and in so many stories of people I interviewed. If you recall, the nuns in *The Sound of Music* were cloistered and did not pass the Abbey gate and enter the church when Maria walked down the aisle to marry Captain von Trapp. I had never thought twice about that, believing it was just what cloistered nuns did—but now I understand how significant that scene is.

Cloistered nuns did not leave the convent, and visitors to the convent required specific permission from bishops, or others in the Vatican. Yet all during the war—and throughout Europe—Jews were being hidden in convents by nuns who knew the risks they were taking. They took those risks because it was the right thing to do.

Vince called at the very moment Rolf, the young Austrian who was smitten with Liesel, appeared on the screen. He was singing with her—wonderful, youthful flirting.

"Rolf is the most important person in the movie," Vince said, "because he started out as a normal boy who was doing his job delivering telegrams, and turned into someone willing to turn in the entire von Trapp family to the Nazis. It showed how the Nazis were able to transform him from a nice young man to a disciple of the Nazi regime. The Nazis were able to get the support they needed from the youth of the countries they occupied."

He was right. The character of Rolf is an example of those who followed Hitler's orders. At one point, Captain von Trapp almost convinces Rolf to join him and his family. The audience is rooting for Rolf to leave, because we know what the future holds—the horrors of World War II. We want Rolf to see the light, do the right thing, and escape with the von Trapps. We see Rolf's uncertainty. Should he pretend he didn't see the family and let them go? Should he join them in flight? That flicker of doubt quickly disappears when Rolf does what he has been trained to do—turn them in. He doesn't shoot Captain von Trapp, but instead blows his whistle to alert the other soldiers. Vince was right. Rolf is the perfect example of why the Nazis were successful for so long with their brutal "Final Solution."

For me, *The Sound of Music*, a charming family film broadcast each year during the holiday season and regularly on cable, has serious new meaning. Subtle facts are now glaringly apparent to me, confirming everything the people I interviewed said.

The movie ended at eleven. I was tired, but I had a gnawing curiosity to know more about the von Trapp family. I knew they eventually made it to America and opened a hotel in Vermont, but didn't know much more than that. So, to the Internet I went—and I couldn't believe what I read. Captain von Trapp and his first wife, Agathe Whitehead, met and married in Fiume. Giovanni Palatucci was the *Questore di Fiume*! Of all the cities in Europe, the von Trapps had ties to Fiume!

"Unbelievable," I said out loud. That meant that Captain von Trapp and his wife were most likely registered in the *Questore's* office in Fiume, the same office that years later would be Giovanni Palatucci's! It was another uncanny discovery that connected the pieces of this ever-growing puzzle.

37

URSULA'S PHONE CALL

My cell phone rang as I sat by my grandmother's bed in the hospital. It was Ursula exploding with good news regarding Monsignor Schivo. He had called to tell her he was being honored January 24th by the president of Italy for being one of the "Giusti," or one of the Righteous. This was January 11th. It always amazed me that such events, usually planned months in advance in the United States, are only finalized at the last minute in Italy.

Monsignor Schivo was ninety-eight and still as handsome as ever. He had been blessed with good health and a sharp mind. Ursula was so excited that this priest who saved her life was being recognized by his country.

I was happy for her and grateful for the cell phone. For a few minutes, I could smile and share her happiness, even though I was at the hospital with my grandmother. In teaching me to love Campagna and Italy, my grandmother unknowingly set the stage for this extraordinary journey.

Ursula asked about Nanny, and I said she was doing as well as could be expected. What I did not add was, "for a woman who was almost ninety-five years old." I am always sensitive when discussing illness—mine or anyone else's—with the survivors because they are in their eighties and nineties and constantly remind us that they won't be around forever.

Time passed that weekend as if in a black hole. Somehow when you enter a hospital, the clock stops. You bring a book but rarely reach the second page because you read the first page again and again. I found myself eating Oreo cookies and Rice Krispies Treats, two snacks I rarely touch, but in moments of stress, they comfort me.

On Sunday night, I returned to my apartment. Nanny was in good hands with my mother and Aunt Ida. By Monday morning, I started to catch up with my work and planned a quiet day. Then the phone rang, and once again it was Ursula. She had just received a phone call from the office of the president of Italy inviting *her* to the ceremony for Monsignor Schivo. She was so delighted, because having him recognized had been part of her life's work for the past twenty years at the Hidden Child Foundation. She asked me to go with her to Italy, because she did not feel up to traveling alone. She knew my situation with my grandmother was uncertain and even apologized for asking. I was honored to be asked, but even though my grandmother was stable for the moment, I did not wish to risk leaving her. Instead, I suggested Vince go in my place.

I woke up the next morning at five thirty and called Rome. That had become one of my habits, calling Rome early New York time. My first call was to Dottoressa Savoia. I told her about the Nashville coincidence, Dr. Kleinmann, and

Ursula's good news. She believed these were things that God had arranged. What else could explain it?

I, on the other hand, wanted to ask God why all this was happening at the same time. Nanny was sick, and I couldn't leave. I wanted to stay with her, yet a small piece of me also wanted to go to Rome with Ursula, meet Monsignor Schivo, and be part of another historic moment. Why now? What lesson was to be learned here? If God controlled everything, couldn't He have spread things out a bit? I recognize that such thoughts appear selfish, but most of us can relate to the need and desire to be in two places at once.

Ursula Korn Selig, Monsignor Schivo, and Mordecai Paldiel (former director of the Department of the "Righteous among the Nations" at the Yad Vashem) planting a tree in honor of Monsignor Schivo for saving Ursula and her parents during the Holocaust.

I became bold and asked Dottoressa Savoia to help me make a dream come true. I explained the significance of Monsignor Schivo's and Ursula's potentially meeting the pope. Monsignor Schivo had been honored in Israel many years earlier by the Yad Vashem, and now was being honored in Rome by the president of Italy. To add the honor of recognition by the pope, *with Ursula at his side*, would truly make things complete.

I could tell Dottoressa Savoia liked the idea. I sent her information about Monsignor Schivo. I also spoke with Amy, my wonderful Embassy angel. She, too, was excited about this possibility. If you "wish upon a star" long and hard enough, your dreams may just come true.

38

GOOD-BYE AND HELLO

My grandmother died in the hospice unit, and timing wasn't on my side. I had spent the weekend at the hospice taking turns with my mother and sister—Friday through Monday. Aunt Ida had arrived on Sunday evening and intended to go back to her home in Brooklyn Wednesday evening. My plan was to return Wednesday afternoon and cross paths with her. We didn't want my mom to be there alone, so I intended to stay at the hospice unit for the rest of the week.

Vince arrived at the hospice late Monday afternoon to visit us and discuss the details for his trip with Ursula. I thanked him for going to Italy in my place. Vince knows so much about all aspects of the Holocaust and—as he would be meeting the president of Italy—it really was better for him to accompany Ursula on this particular trip. My mother and Aunt Ida were happy to see Vince again. They just wished it was under better circumstances. Vince was now considered part of the family, especially after having been to Campagna twice, the last trip only two months earlier. After all, how many people did we see in New York that we also saw in Campagna? Not many! Before he left, Vince said, "Because of

Nanny, there was a *you*, and because of you, this story has grown. I am grateful to your grandmother for taking you to her town."

Vince knew that this was a difficult time for us and promised he would have prayers said for Nanny in the Vatican. To think that Nanny would have Vatican priests praying for her at her time of need . . .

Mom called on Tuesday morning to say that Nanny had an "okay" night. I accepted that, under the circumstances, "okay" would have to be good enough. I gathered my thoughts and approached my "to do" list. Lists are always helpful, especially in a time of crisis; they add a sense of order. I called Ursula to say I would stop by at four o'clock to see her off before she left for the airport at five. I reviewed final details for the trip with Vince. Then came "the call."

Mom said that things had changed, and Nanny wasn't doing so well. What did that mean, not doing well? Translation: it meant "come back now."

I called my sister Victoria at her office and asked her to leave the office *now* and meet me at the train station. My father and brother Louis were already on their way. Twenty minutes later we boarded the next train. I called Ursula from the train and apologized for not being able to see her off, but I needed to get home.

The train ride seemed like an eternity, and I had a feeling we would not get there in time to say good-bye. Our parents' friend John Wimer picked us up at the station when the train arrived at 2:59. The hospice was about fifteen minutes away—the longest fifteen minutes ever.

When we arrived at the hospice, I knew by the look of the nurses at the main desk that we were too late. Victoria and I ran into the room and saw my mom crying with my aunt Ida and Rika Wimer, John's wife. Nanny was in her bed, her eyes closed forever. She had died at 2:56.

The rest of the afternoon was a blur, filled with tears and soft whispers of "I love you." The woman whose life touched so many, and had changed mine so much, was gone.

We went back to my parents' home. How ironic that Nanny had died the day I would have left for Italy with Ursula.

On Wednesday we tended to all the details for a funeral. It is almost as if a funeral is an impromptu party to which no one RSVPs, yet so many show up. The wake would last just one day, Friday, as per Nanny's wishes. The funeral was scheduled for Saturday.

I returned to the city Wednesday night, exhausted and relieved to sleep in my own bed. On Thursday I awoke a bit confused, and then remembered what had happened. I called Gerda, who wanted to attend the wake or funeral but couldn't, due to Shabbat. I was careful to avoid the others in the survivor group because I was afraid to tell them that Nanny had died. She was only a few years older than they were, and they had already told me very frankly about their own mortality.

By now it was lunchtime in New York, and I called Rome to see how the day had gone. Nanny would have wanted me to continue to be part of Ursula's visit, even from afar. I had many questions: How did the presidential ceremony go? What was Monsignor Schivo like? Was he as handsome in person as he was in Ursula's photographs? I was curious to learn about the meetings with Monsignor Caccia and Monsignor Filippi. Vince and Ursula were with Amy at the hotel. They asked how I was, and I said okay, under the circumstances. Vince recounted the day's events and told me they had all prayed for Nanny.

Entering the funeral home for the wake was difficult, but it was worse watching my mom and Aunt Ida look at Nanny, so peaceful in the "Italian" coffin. I knew we had done the right thing in selecting the Italian one. It was decorated with pictures of the Last Supper and my favorite statue, Michelangelo's *Pietà*—very Catholic and very Italian. As crazy as it seems, it was just perfect for Nanny.

So what was Nanny's nearly ninety-five-year journey all about, I wondered? As an adult, Nanny lived far away from where she was born; as young newlyweds, she and my grandfather created a new life for themselves from nothing. Just then, I recalled Nanny cooking and making *struffoli* (fried dough balls rolled in honey), plates and plates of spaghetti, the sauce simmering on the stove. Her hard-working hands were now forever still, folded with rosary beads.

How did Nanny spend her entire adult life in the United States? It was only to be for a few years, but World War II and Hitler changed all that. So seventy-seven years later, here we were at her funeral in New York, rather than in Campagna.

Throughout the evening, people came and went as they do at these things. As my childhood friend Ellen Auwarter and I were talking, out of the corner of my eye I saw Vince and Dorothy enter the room. How could that be? Apparently Vince had landed two hours earlier, gone home, picked up Dorothy, and come straight to the funeral home. So much had happened since he left on Tuesday. Vince and Ursula had met with Monsignor Schivo, the president of Italy, Monsignor Caccia, Monsignor Filippi, Dottoressa Savoia, and Amy Roth and then come back to New York. The day he left, Nanny was alive. Now she was no longer with us. All in just four days.

Rome, January 2008. (left to right) Monsignor Schivo, Ursula Korn Selig, and Mayor Fernanda Cecchini of Città di Castello (note the "Miss America" sash), and Vince Marmorale.

Ursula Korn Selig watches Monsignor Schivo receive the Righteous Award from the president of Italy, Giorgio Napolitano.

Ursula Korn Selig with Monsignor Filippi.

39

THE POSTCARD

After Nanny's death, my family and I began the inevitable—packing up a lifetime of her possessions. During a break over tea, my mom and I watched part of the documentary. The tragedy of World War II changed so many lives, including those of my grandparents. While going through Nanny's dresser drawers, I found our own connection to World War II in a simple postcard, another piece of the puzzle of life—in this case, my life.

My grandmother, like many others, saved letters and cards she received over the years, and I am so glad she did. She kept them in her drawers, neatly tied with ribbons making pretty bows. These papers often shed light on why our ancestors chose various paths and how their choices may have affected us. At the time, no one knew what they would signify years later.

The postcard was a black-and-white image of Saint Peter's Basilica, signed by my grandfather and sent to my grandmother in Campagna, Salerno—only her name, town, and province—no street address, again proving that people in little villages know everyone and everything about everybody. Despite such little information, the mailman knew exactly where to deliver it. The postmark is 1935 from Livorno-Torino. My grandfather was headed back to New York—alone.

This postcard symbolized more than loving wishes before a trip to New York. It is a symbol of the unexpected detour that life took for Nanny and my grandfather. After their marriage in 1930, they moved to New York. They planned that children would be born in the United States to give them United States citizenship; that they would work and build their nest egg; and that, ultimately, they would return to Italy to raise their children and live their lives. That process began—my uncle and mother were born in New York, and in 1935, the family of four headed back to Italy. The children were United States citizens; my grandparents had their nest egg. But Adolf Hitler altered this plan and those of many others. My grandfather decided that Hitler was growing too powerful and sensed that war was on the horizon. He decided to return to New York to avoid being drafted into the Italian army. (Note: He had fought in World War I.)

Had it not been for Hitler, my grandfather would not have returned to the United States, and my grandparents would have lived out their lives in Campagna, not New York. My mother would have been raised in Campagna; she would not have met and married my father; and, well, I wouldn't exist—at least as I am today. Until that moment, I never thought of Hitler as having a direct impact on *my* life. He had a direct impact on the six million Jews and five million other "undesirables" murdered, and on the millions of lives interrupted—

changed forever. But I never considered my immediate family and Hitler as being connected.

In fact, my grandparents' lives and choices were similar to those of the foreign Jews who survived in Italy. They all decided to leave their countries to escape the unrest and bad sentiment surrounding them and to avoid potential military action. The postcard we found that day is more than just a message from husband to wife—it symbolizes why I was born in the United States, and not in Campagna.

40

INDIANA JONES

Vince had asked me to contact Gloria Virey, a woman Max Kempin had met on vacation in St. Maarten. All he had was an e-mail address. At times I felt like Indiana Jones, finding clues in the craziest of places. I wasn't exactly sure how Max and Gloria had met, or how they started talking about concentration camps in Italy, so this was a shot in the dark at best. I e-mailed Gloria and prayed my note wouldn't bounce back.

The e-mail went through (yippee!), and Gloria replied a few hours later. We made a phone appointment for five PM that Sunday afternoon. Gloria was delighted to meet me on the phone and share her story with me.

"I was born April 1, 1944, in Arezzo, about an hour south of Florence," she said. "But before my parents were in Arezzo, they were in southern Italy. My mother was with my father."

"Do you know what the camp was called?" I asked.

"Campagna. It was called Campagna."

"My family is from Campagna, and I was just there a few months ago!" I practically shouted into the phone as I dove for "the book."

"What is your father's last name?" I asked as my finger trailed down the list.

"Jeithner," she said.

"He's in my book; he's on my list in Campagna."

47. Igel	Adolfo	Giacobbe	1885	commerc.	germ.
48. Iwanicki	Antonio	Stefano	1918	agronomo	pol.
49. Jacob	Alfredo	Luigi	1905	commerc.	germ.
50. Jacob	arberto	Luigi	1904	agricoltore	germ.
51. Jeithner	Rodolfo	Riccardo	1901	commerc.	germ.
52. Jellinek	Oscar	Bernardo	1904	commerc.	germ.
53. Jellinek	Teodoro	Leopoldo	1885	commerc.	germ.
54. Jockl	Giorgio	Edmondo	1903	impiegato	germ.

Here was another connection to Campagna—this one in the Caribbean. Gloria on the island of St. Maarten, me in New York City, and the little hidden village in Italy. Campagna was part of this triangle.

"Gloria, can you hold on for a second? I want to call my colleague." I picked up my cell phone and called Vince. *How many times*, I thought as Vince's phone rang, *has this happened*?

"Hi. I'm on the other phone with Gloria Virey in St. Maarten, and she says her father and mother were in Campagna."

Once more I got a "You are kidding me. Not again!" from Vince. I explained to Gloria what Vince had said.

"You know, I have many pictures of Campagna in my apartment in Milano," said Gloria.

We then discussed how her mother and father wound up in Italy. They were on their honeymoon during the *Aunchluss* in 1938, when Germany took over Austria, so the two newly-weds stayed in Italy.

"That was *the* decision that saved their lives," she said. "The rest of my family on both sides perished in Auschwitz."

"What do you know about their life in Campagna?"

"They said their lives in Campagna were pleasant. The people were kind and helpful, and my parents were quite free and passed their time playing bridge with other people. I have pictures of them playing cards," she said. At some point Gloria's parents left Campagna. She isn't sure exactly when, but she knows they were in Arezzo when she was born in April 1944. The family stayed in Italy after the war, with her father working in the fur business.

One day we will meet Gloria, hopefully in Milano, to review her pictures and documents.

"Imagine what will happen when the book is published and the documentary is out," Vince said to me later. "Who knows how many more stories there will be!"

✦

A few months later, while looking through the book, I stopped on the photo with my great-grandfather in it. For some reason I reread the names of the people surrounding him. There was a woman standing next to him, and the caption read: "Mrs. Jeithner, wife of an internee." My great-grandfather was standing next to Gloria's mother.

41

MAMMA MIA!

At first glance we looked like a group of friends having a quick meal before seeing a Broadway show. The billboard facing the Così sandwich shop window advertised the play *Mamma Mia!* I couldn't think of a better phrase to be on a billboard for this particular meeting.

Walter Kleinmann was able to join us at the last minute—a surprise for Ruth Goldman Tobias and her husband Teddy. Walter had put us in touch with Ruth, whose family was also in Potenza and Tito with the Kleinmanns. A few years had passed since they had last seen each other, even though Ruth and Teddy lived just over the river in New Jersey. (A sad note: Walter's father had passed away a month earlier; Vince and I were grateful to have met Max Kleinmann and recorded his story.)

Ruth is a very attractive woman who looks at least ten years younger than she is. Today, she wore jeans and a sweater. Looking at her, you would *never* imagine that she was a Holocaust survivor. Ruth's parents were from Poland and had moved to Italy in 1935. Ruth was born in Milano, and after the war began, her family was sent south to Potenza, where they met the Kleinmanns. Dr. Kleinmann was her mother's doctor in the village.

Ruth and Walter reminisced the way childhood friends do, except they talked about their experiences in a little Italian village during World War II, which was quite different from where they raised their families just outside of New York City. Imagine a Goldman and a Kleinmann in Potenza in the 1940s!

In fluent Italian, they described gathering water from the *fontana*, the fountain, in the central town square. There was a glow on Ruth's face that I have seen in other survivors, and her expressive blue eyes sparkled when she spoke of Italy and the Italians. Her gratitude showed, and her husband Teddy jumped in to add stories that he had heard her parents tell over the years. Teddy passionately told us how his beautiful wife, her family, and so many other Jews were saved in Italy.

He reached into his briefcase and took out documents and numerous letters that he had written to the mayor of the little village, Tito. Tito is approximately eleven miles from Potenza, which is about fifty miles from Campagna. The Kleinmann and Goldman families were moved from Potenza to Tito in the middle of the war, where their internment was always *libero*, free. This was another family that could live in the town, but not leave it without permission.

Ruth and Teddy described a trip they took to Tito in 2002. Upon arriving in the village, they asked a *carabiniere* if he knew anything about Jews that lived in the town during World War II. The *carabiniere* emphatically stated to Ruth and Teddy that *no* Jews were in Tito during the war. Ruth knew she had to show him something written to prove that this did occur in

---

COMUNE DI TITO
Provincia di Potenza

DIVISIONE SERVIZI DEMOGRAFICI
- Ufficio di Stato Civile -

Estratto per riassunto dai registri degli atti di nascita

Dal registro degli atti di nascita dell'anno 1944 n. 16

Parte I Serie A risulta che:

il giorno venticinque del mese di febbraio

dell'anno millenovecentoquarantaquattro

alle ore dodici e minuti ===

in Tito è nato un bambino di sesso femminile avente il cognome

di GOLDMANN ed il nome (*) di Cilla

di Abraham e di SCHCINDEL Rachel

ANNOTAZIONI

NESSUNA

ha contratto matrimonio con

il in

Il presente estratto è conforme all'originale e si rilascia per uso

amm.vo.

Tito, lì 15/05/2001

L'Ufficiale di Stato Civile

(*) leggere avvertenze a teroo.

Cilla Goldman's birth certificate from the city of Tito (Potenza).

his town, so she asked to go to *Comune* and look up her sister Cilla's birth certificate.

It was lunchtime, sacred time, especially in a small village. Stores close, schools finish for the day, and offices, particularly government offices, come to a complete stop. Everyone is home with their families having a big Italian lunch—then a siesta. Around four thirty or five o'clock, the towns slowly awaken.

Naturally, no one was in the *Comune*, and it was locked.

"Let me guess," I said to Ruth. "Your *carabiniere* knocked on someone's door, and like magic he had the key to the closed office."

She laughed. "That is exactly what happened." And sure enough, Ruth found Cilla's birth certificate!

Imagine the look on the *carabiniere's* face when he saw a birth certificate saying Cilla *Goldman*. That certainly was not a last name of anyone in Tito. He was surprised to learn from these Americans that they were right—there *were* Jews in Tito in the 1940s.

Vince and I listened and at times finished Ruth's and Teddy's sentences. They were surprised we could do that, but we had heard so many similar ones. No matter where the event occurred in Italy, they all had comparable elements. The courage to care and the willingness of people to risk their lives to help others was spread across the entire boot of Italy. All the survivors we interviewed said the same thing: it was in the Italian character to help.

Thousands of foreign Jews survived in Italy, and to this

*Summer 1942, Tito (Potenza). The Goldman/Tobias family
(lower left to right) Walter Kleinmann's mother, Felicitas Kleinmann;
Mr. and Mrs. (Gerta) Barnass, Ruth Goldman, and Sabine Goldman.*

*(second row left to right) unidentified man (probably Franz Hayek),
Mr. Abraham Goldman, Eva Lepehne (Rosenfeld), Walter Kleinmann,
and Dr. Max Kleinmann.*

day, there is no total number. People like Ruth, Walter, and their families are most likely not listed in the official census of the time.

Our discussion then turned to why the Italian story is not known. "Perhaps some historians feel that the number of Jews saved in Italy, approximately thirty-thousand or more, was too small when compared to the tragic loss of six million Jews who were brutally and systematically murdered by the Third Reich," said Walter Kleinmann. "The Italians treated us well."

"I would love to have you return to Potenza and Tito with Eric and Eva Rosenfeld," I said, trying to figure out how I was going to get them there. If I could take Walter Wolff to Italy, imagine what could happen with the others! Ruth, Teddy, and Walter loved the idea.

Being in front of the billboard for *Mamma Mia!* made us chuckle. "Mamma Mia" is an expression Italians use when things are unbelievable, and it perfectly captured our feelings. This was not the last time we would hear it.

I couldn't wait to call Eva and Eric in Nashville to let them know that our chance meeting had led to more connections. Teddy added another piece of a puzzle and gave me a book called *Dottore,* written by Doctor Salim Diamand, another person who survived in Italy. In *Dottore* were pictures of Campagna and Ferramonti—additional evidence that many people who were in Campagna were transferred to Ferramonti and survived the war. Some of the photos featured the same people in "the book." Unfortunately, we could not interview

Dr. Diamand, as he had passed away, but the following passage from his book is significant:

> The townspeople were indifferent to our status as Jews, or enemy aliens, or prisoners. We made friends among the local populace and the police. We met them in cafés, spent afternoon hours in conversation with them and we met them in football matches. Like tourists, we took pictures of the town and our newfound friends. Of course, we missed the variety and bustle of the big city, but it was a relaxing and healthy existence. If one must be a prisoner, then [Campagna] *Eboli* in the summer of 1940 was as good an incarceration as one might have hoped for.

After Dr. Diamand had been in Campagna for a time, he was transferred to Ferramonti. It is definitely a small world.

THEODORE K. TOBIAS, MD

11 February, 2002

Sindaco
Municipio P Del Seggio
Provincia Potenza
Tito, Italy 85050

Dear Sir,

In May of this year my wife Ruth and I visited the city of Tito to reminisce the time she lived there with her family We were gratefully received at the Municipio where we reviewed the birth record of my wife's sister, Cilla Goldman born on 25 Feb 1944 Afterwards the Polizia gave us a personal tour of the area where the Goldman family lived in 1943 and 1944 Ruth recalled many of the landmarks that she remembered as a small child living in Tito

Everyone who met us was surprised to learn that Jews once lived in Tito My wife Ruth was born in Milano and was the daughter of Abraham and Sabina Goldman In 1941 Ruth and her mother were sent to the Internment camp in Potenza and her father was sent to the Farramonte concentration camp located in the Province of Cosenza near the village of Tarsia Later he joined them in Potenza In 1943 the Jews in Potenza were dispersed to smaller villages such as Tito.

Ruth also remembers going to the basement of the house they lived in during the Allied bombing raids Abraham Goldman recalled one event when a German convoy with a disabled truck remained in Tito The German soldiers were unable to communicate with the Italians and therefore my father in-law who also spoke german was introduced as an Austrian citizen He was able to assist in the repair of the truck so that the convoy could move on and Tito saved from any bombing After the German retreat and liberation by the Canadian Army, the Goldman family moved back to Potenza where they lived until 1946

Ruth's mother Sabina (97 yrs) is well and remembers the friendly neighbors who helped her during her pregnancy and afterwards in caring for Cilla who was born prematurely

Ruth and I want to wish Tito and its citizens a Merry Christmas and Happy New Year Heartfelt thanks for the hospitality they showed us recently and the Goldman family during the War years

With warm regards,

Letter written by Teddy Tobias to mayor of Tito, 2002.

42

THE POPE CALL

For many, Saturday is a day to catch up and run errands—and in my case, there was lots to do, as I had just moved. My new apartment was across the street from the Park Avenue East Synagogue, where the pope would visit during his spring trip to America. Of the hundreds of synagogues in New York, the pope chose the one across the street from my home. Was it coincidence, or was it something else?

This particular Saturday in March was gray with a bit of a winter chill in the air, the kind of day you want to curl up with a good book or watch a movie—not be outside running errands. To procrastinate, I began reviewing e-mails, and there it was: an e-mail from Gary Krupp. Krupp is founder and president of Pave the Way Foundation, an organization that promotes peace by removing obstacles between the religions and by initiating gestures of goodwill. Vince and I had met with Gary regarding the documentary, and he offered to help us arrange a meeting with the pope.

I *knew* even before opening the e-mail what it would say, and I was right.

"I am pleased to inform you that the Secretary of State has

honored my request for a private audience with the Holy Father for your group in June."

I could not help staring at the words. I was stunned that we had an appointment to see the pope in a private audience! What I had envisioned for Walter almost two years earlier would now take place with some of the other survivors.

I reached for the phone to call Vince, somewhat reluctantly. Dorothy was attending her nursing school reunion, and the husbands were spending the afternoon together. But it isn't every day I have the chance to tell someone he is going to meet the pope!

"I'm sorry to disturb your afternoon with the guys, but I just opened an e-mail from Gary, and you must hear this." I could tell in the background that Vince was being teased. The "work wife" was calling. If they only knew *why* I was calling. I read the e-mail aloud, and Vince, who always has a lot to say, kept repeating one sentence: "Oh my God . . . Oh my God . . . Oh my God!"

Well, that would be correct now, wouldn't it!?

What was it going to be like? What happens when you meet the pope? Does your life change drastically?

On to more practical things. What is the protocol? Will we be given a list of things to do and not do? And for the women, the ultimate question: what does one wear to meet the pope? What an excuse to go shopping! How many women ever need to find a dress specifically to see the pope? *Men,* I thought, *have it easy.* The dark suit, white shirt, and tie work for them every time, almost anywhere.

43

THE POPE VISITS NEW YORK

What a weekend! Pope Benedict's visit to Park Avenue East Synagogue marked only the third time in history that a pope had visited a synagogue. The first was by Pope John Paul II to the Great Synagogue of Rome (*Tempio Maggiore di Roma*) in 1986, and the second occurred when Pope Benedict went to the Synagogue of Cologne in Germany, August 2005.

Because the pope would be right across the street, I could not resist a chance to see him in my neighborhood; my childhood friend Gail Greenwald joined me. Security was like something out of a James Bond movie—police everywhere and helicopters in the sky. The police would not allow us to stand on the street near the synagogue, so we had to find another spot. The Pope would be driven in an armored limousine, which somehow needed to travel five blocks down from the corner of 72nd Street and Madison Avenue, where he was staying, to the synagogue on 67th Street and Lexington Avenue.

So we walked to Park Avenue, the most logical route to the synagogue. Surprisingly, Park Avenue itself was lined with very few people. I guess most people were waiting to see the pope on Fifth Avenue on Sunday, when he was scheduled to greet the people of New York. The motorcade was unbelievable—at least forty police motorcycles with their lights flashing, followed by many large black vehicles that looked as if they housed Darth Vader. I am certain that a team of "super officers" was inside with machine guns ready to jump out if needed. Next came emergency vehicles, ambulances, more black vans, and SUVs with the windows down, men with machine guns pointing outward. Finally, two limousines drove by, both with Vatican flags.

Which one was the pope in? There. He was in the second one, and sure enough, he looked out the window and waved!

Now, standing on the street corner in my neighborhood, I couldn't believe I was going to see him again—in the Vatican!

The next day the pope drove up Fifth Avenue in the "Popemobile" greeting enormous crowds. Even my Jewish friends were excited about his visit, and on the news, one reporter referred to Mayor Bloomberg as "giddy." Mayor Bloomberg is not known for being "giddy," and at first I didn't believe the reporter, but he was right. Interviewed on the news, the mayor said he never thought a guy named Bloomberg would meet the pope once, let alone five times.

That weekend, I went to Ursula's home, only a few blocks from mine in New York City, for Passover. It was not lost on me that sixty-eight years earlier, Ursula's father had celebrated Passover in Campagna down the block from my great-grandparents' home. It is a small world, isn't it?

44

VISITING THE VATICAN
RUDOLFO'S WAY

Victoria Duggan, Horst and Clara Stein's daughter, called. "My parents are so excited that they're going to meet the pope! In fact, my father didn't sleep at all last night. I want you to know that I never really knew much about this from my parents. They never talked about it in depth. It's amazing what you got out of them."

Her words reminded me of that powerful moment when Vince asked Horst and Clara, at what point did they begin telling the story? And they answered: "When we met you, Vince."

The next day, there was a message from Vicky on my home phone that made me smile. Vicky asked if she and her two brothers, Rob and Ron, could join the trip to Rome. *How exciting it would be for Horst and Clara to share this trip with their children*, I thought. And yes, of course they could all go to Rome.

✦

A few days before the trip, an event was held, presented by Vincent Marmorale, at the consulate regarding Italy's role during World War II. Horst Stein, Ursula Korn Selig, Herta Mingelgrün Pollak, Max Kempin, and Walter Kleinmann spoke about their experiences and expressed their gratitude to Italy to Consul General Francesco Maria Taló. In addition to the people of Italy, many diplomats also helped get the Jews out of harm's way during World War II. Kristen Parrish, my wonderful editor, and Joel Miller, the publisher of this book, were able to attend and hear the stories of survival in Italy directly.

At long last, all the work and hours of planning were coming together, and we would be on our way to Rome in a few hours. The "Pope Group" totaled nine: the Stein family of five, Vince, Giorgina, Ursula, and me. I gave the group two simple instructions; First, call me when leaving for the airport. Second, put your "pope clothes" in a carry-on bag, just in case the luggage is lost.

We had a lengthy weather delay leaving New York, but a very sunny Rome greeted us. We quickly checked into the hotel and had dinner. Consuelo Bandini and her daughter Elisa met us at the *ristorante*, and we were delighted to see them again. Consuelo had been there at the very beginning, and Vince and I could not wait to introduce her to this group of survivors.

On Monday morning we had a visit to Saint Peter's Basilica arranged by a man named Rudolfo, a special envoy to the Vatican. And what a visit it was. Only afterward did I fully comprehend that *how* we visited the Vatican was a perfect example of how the Jews were saved in Italy.

To this day, when Italians want certain things to happen, they just happen with little or no documentation. This is a contradiction of sorts, because generally Italians love creating paperwork, and they have a special knack of stamping papers with a fanfare that only Italians can provide. I am convinced that Italian children are given toy stamps to play with, and it becomes a game for them to see who can stamp with more pomp. How else can you explain how they manage to stamp papers so elegantly, with the stamp in the right place, not upside down? I even have problems with those "paid" stamps on invoices.

Rudolfo met our group of nine at the hotel, and off we went. Rudolfo was our very own private Vatican tour guide. We walked two long blocks toward a wall located on the right side of Saint Peter's Basilica. By going in the private back way, we could walk the group there. Otherwise, we'd have had to take taxis to the main entrance a few blocks away.

Rudolfo led us to a gate, and the guards stationed there were obviously expecting us. As you know, Italians tend to speak with their hands. In this case it was a certain flick of the wrist with the hand making about two and a half circles and then stopping. This movement occurred as Rudolfo looked at them directly in the eyes and said, "*Sapete tutto.*" You know all.

The two policemen nodded, and our group continued. I am not sure how often groups of people get to enter Vatican City through the back door, but it is a real treat! Besides skipping the regular tourist route—the front of Saint Peter's

Basilica—and waiting in a long line to go through security, you get to see things you would *never* see otherwise.

Passing the walls of Vatican City, the first thing I saw was not what I expected. I expected a statue, a fountain, a small garden, a cross . . . something religious. No. The first thing we saw was a small gas station. Imagine that! A gas station on the Vatican grounds. I guess even the Vatican uses earthly fuels.

We proceeded to walk past a small garden and several Swiss Guards. They all looked at us and nodded at Rudolfo. Obviously they knew we were not some tourist group that had lost its way. We continued toward the building in front of us and entered a door that had modern bronze sculptures for door handles. Rudolfo continued and once again did the circular flick-of-the-wrist thing. The guard jumped to open the door, and as we were going through, Rudolfo pulled the guard and me aside and said our group would be leaving the church the same way. I was to go to *this* guard as we were leaving. I understood that we were getting special treatment, and I was to follow all instructions *exactly*.

Through a relatively small, non-descript door we went, into Saint Peter's Basilica. Everyone was oohing and ahhing and looking up as tourists do in New York City. I was trying to figure out exactly where we were in Saint Peter's. It turned out we were in an area closed off to tourists behind Bernini's bronze spiraling columns on the main altar. Bernini is famous for being one of the architects of Saint Peter's Basilica as well as a master sculptor. As we continued to follow Rudolfo, we emerged behind red velvet ropes. Guards parted the ropes for us, and Rudolfo explained, again, that we would be going out the way we came in—our "group of nine."

He also explained, in that insider way, that many times when notable people visit Saint Peter's, they have members of their group enter through separate doorways so they don't attract attention.

We were now in the main part of the Basilica, and it was packed with tourists. Rudolfo took us on an extraordinary tour, told us about some of his experiences inside the Vatican, and explained to us what it was like to be alone with the art in this amazing building when it is empty. I tried to imagine this massive building empty, quiet, without thousands of tourists milling about. I felt so insignificant here, surrounded by such a sea of humanity. What would it be like to be the only person here, walking down the massive aisles, hearing only the click of your heals on the beautiful marble? What would praying in complete silence be like?

My favorite statue in the world is Michelangelo's *Pietà*, and once again I was looking at it. The first time I saw the *Pietà* was when I was a little girl at the New York World's Fair. I will never forget the slow-moving escalator that brought us down to the lifelike statue of Mary holding Jesus. I would see the *Pietà* again years later with Nanny when we visited Italy. The statue also reminded me of Nanny's funeral, I thought with sadness. She would have been delighted to know that, so many years after our trips to Italy where she showed me these wonders, I had returned on a very special mission: I was going to meet the pope.

Rudolfo explained that he was present when the *Pietà* was being shipped to New York, and he oversaw the process. While he was telling us the story, I imagined the statue being wrapped in silk cloth, then bubble wrap, then being put in a huge crate surrounded by Styrofoam popcorn. Rudolfo told us, "It is the smoothest piece of marble I have ever touched," he said. "You can feel the muscles and veins—it is almost real."

Rudolfo eventually left us to explore this amazing building on our own. We were able to reach the second level of St. Peter's via a relatively new addition—an elevator! Thank goodness for modern amenities. The view of Rome from there was extraordinary. Those who wish to go higher can climb the Cupola, the dome that looks like the top of the Capitol in Washington, D.C. Climbing the Cupola with this group was out of the question as it was something akin to the "original Stairmaster." You needed to be in decent shape for that.

For those who do climb the Cupola, the journey begins on well-worn stone steps located between the thick outer stone wall of the Cupola, which can be seen from any spot in Rome, and the inner dome that people see when looking up from inside the church. As you go higher, your body bends to the curves of the building. There is no turning back, but once you get to the top, you realize that the climb was well worth it. The statues located on the second level—which are large when you are standing next to them—appear small from this height. It is then that you truly wonder how this building was built so long ago without electricity and modern construction equipment.

It was time to leave the amazing Basilica of Saint Peter. We had a busy week with more visits to the Vatican ahead of us. We followed Rudolfo's instructions and went back the way we came. Back behind the velvet rope, back behind the Bernini columns (where we snuck in a few photos), back through the small door that was hidden in a massive wooden structure, and out to the Vatican gardens. Suddenly we were stopped by a Swiss Guard. He had just come on duty and didn't know who we were—nine people just wandering through his post. At that moment, one of the guards at the gate signaled that we were okay, and we continued on.

Horst's three children wanted to explore Saint Peter's a bit more, and I explained to the guards that they had only accompanied us to the side gate and would like to go back in to Saint Peter's Basilica. The two guards looked at each other and had a conversation. No, that would not be possible—they could not go back in with another person.

Apparently there was a misunderstanding; another person would not be joining them; it was just the three of them going back in, I explained. *Ah, va bene così.* I realized that Rudolfo had told them that we were all "okay." We had been vetted, but we could not have someone join our group if Rudolfo had not given his approval of the new person with his famous hand movement. That movement was worth more than hundreds of official stamps.

This is when I *realized* I had just witnessed how many Jews survived in Italy during World War II. People were often moved with a nod, a look, and a wave of the hand—no documentation, no written orders—just trust, and a very specific understanding between two people of what needed to be done. It reminded me of how Walter Wolff received his fake papers in *Comune*.

45

A VISIT WITH MONSIGNOR CACCIA

O ur appointment was at four o'clock in the Vatican. We walked up the cobblestone street. Ursula had been to this part of the Vatican in January with Vince, so she knew her way. Giorgina and the Stein family were looking around in awe. For the second time in two days, we were in Vatican City.

We slowly walked toward the next gate and took the elevator to Monsignor Caccia's offices. His assistant, Bruno, met us and directed us to a sitting area in the Loggia. And again I admired the frescoes.

The looks on everyone's faces were priceless. They couldn't believe they were overlooking Saint Peter's Square and the Basilica. We sat down and began a game of musical chairs. What was the appropriate seating arrangement? We decided that the survivors and Clara should sit together in one part of the circle, and the rest of us would be on the other side. Monsignor Caccia entered the room and quickly put everyone at ease as he began to ask the survivors to tell their stories, one by one. He intently listened as Giorgina and Horst told their stories. He knew Ursula's story from her January visit.

Ursula, Giorgina, and Horst turned to Monsignor Caccia

and told him how grateful they were that we were working on a documentary and that their stories would live forever through our work. Then Horst turned to Monsignor Caccia and said, "To the Italians, we were *'cristiani come noi'*—Christians or human beings like us.

"In addition, I want you to know that Vince and Elizabeth know more about my story than my three children do." We all looked at each other and knew this was true. It was something we had heard time and again from survivors' families. Somehow, they were able to open up to us. Horst's children nodded in agreement.

We then received Monsignor Caccia's tour of the "house" and private terrace. Horst's family was busy taking pictures that no tourist ever gets to take. Being in these special areas of the Vatican is like being allowed backstage on Broadway before the performance. Tomorrow would be the "performance," but today we again were backstage. And let me tell you, backstage is fantastic!

Before we left, Monsignor Caccia presented all of us with special medals of Pope Benedict and accompanied us to the elevator. Everyone was thrilled that he spent so much time with our group.

June 17, 2008, on a private terrace at the Vatican. Horst Stein, Monsignor Caccia, Elizabeth Bettina, Giorgina de Leon Vitale, Ursula Korn Selig, Vince Marmorale.

46

MEETING THE POPE

When I woke up that morning, I had that feeling you get when you are a child, and it is either your birthday or Christmas. You open your eyes, and before you are truly awake, you know that for some reason, today is a different day. A few bleary moments later, I remembered why today was different. It wasn't my birthday, and I wasn't miraculously ten years old again, nor was it Christmas. Well, almost! Today was the day I was going to do what very few people ever get to do. I was going to meet the pope. What had begun as an idea while walking to work in Manhattan was, in a few hours, going to be real.

I called everyone in our group to make sure no one had overslept. No one had. We all met after breakfast in the lobby of the hotel, dressed as per the instructions we received from Gary Krupp: women in dark dresses and men in dark suits with white shirts. We did not look like the other tourists in the lobby who were getting ready to board their tour buses. Instead, we looked like a group dressed as if we were going to an evening cocktail reception—except it was nine o'clock in the morning.

For this special occasion, I was also carrying my grandmother's veil, the one she wore to church.

The sky was a clear blue, with not a cloud to be found. Beautiful for pictures, but offering no shade, which is why we carried umbrellas. We could keep the umbrellas up until the pope's arrival. Of course, it was the hottest day of the week.

Black book bags are a great thing to bring on trips. You never know when they might be needed for other items—like water. I fit nine water bottles in mine that day, one for each of us!

We headed out a bit after nine thirty, led by our trusted friend Rudolfo. We walked slowly and entered Saint Peter's Square. Once again, Rudolfo had alerted the guards to our group's arrival, and with that famous circular movement of his wrist, we were guided to a special security line just for us. We then proceeded to what I call center stage. We walked past a group of about two hundred seats in a special section and were led to seats just for our group—with *nothing* between us and the pope's chair.

Out on Saint Peter's Square, thousands and thousands of people gathered to hear the pope's blessing. Because we had about forty-five minutes until the pope arrived, we took a few pictures and chatted with the bishops seated behind us. Everyone was glad we had umbrellas, and the water did come in handy. I wondered what the protocol was for drinking water during a long blessing, but given the heat and the ages of the survivors, I didn't think God would see this as a problem.

Horst was beaming and looking back at his family—a

family that wouldn't exist had it not been for the goodness of the Italian people. Ursula said that meeting the pope was something she could have never imagined as a young girl dressed as a "nun" in the convent. Giorgina, the only Italian Jew of the group, wanted to acknowledge the people of Piea who helped her and her family so many years ago.

It was approaching eleven o'clock, and the crowd was getting excited. Then came the roar. The pope had arrived in an uncovered "Popemobile" and was touring Saint Peter's Square. Naturally, the "Popemobile" was surrounded by security guards. Suddenly the vehicle just "climbed" the steps in front of us. How it did that, I don't know, but it was headed right for us. Then there he was, the pope, just an arm's length away.

Vince and I looked at each other and exchanged smiles. It was another "can you believe this?" moment.

Vince leaned over and said, "I have a confession."

Great, a confession in front of the pope. This will be interesting.

"When I met you," he said, "I thought you were a nice person, but certifiably crazy when you said that one day we were going to meet the pope. Who gets to meet the pope? This lady is dreaming." Vince paused, looked me in the eye, and said, "I will never doubt what you say again."

I nodded and laughed. I never doubted that this would eventually happen. I just didn't know exactly how it would happen. It was meant to be. We looked at Ursula, Horst, and Giorgina, who all had looks of awe on their faces. The roads they had traveled all these years had ultimately led to this special meeting.

The pope began his blessings, and twice he spoke about having Holocaust survivors present on this day. He spoke of Judaism and Christianity and how the religions were related. The time passed quickly, and now it was time for each survivor to meet and speak with the pope. It was also time for me to put on Nanny's black veil. It was a way to have Nanny with me and show old-fashioned respect for the pope. It did both, but it also made me look like a Sicilian widow right out of central casting.

The pope descended the outdoor altar and made his way to us. Somewhere along the way, he had put on an unusual red hat, a sort of papal cowboy hat. It was explained to me later that there are many hats the pope wears, and this one was to offer some shade. After greeting Gary and Meredith Krupp, the pope spoke with Horst. So here were two German men—one Jewish, one Catholic—meeting on the steps of Saint Peter's Basilica. One had avoided Germans to stay alive, and one had become the leader of the more than one billion Catholics across the globe—something unimaginable many years earlier.

Giorgina greeted the pope in Italian, and Ursula spoke in German. They briefly told him their stories of survival and how grateful they were to have been in Italy during the Holocaust. Ursula told the pope that she would not be alive today if it was not for Monsignor Schivo.

Then it was my turn. The pope! I blinked. *The pope* was in front of me with his shocking white hair and sparkling eyes, his hands stretched out to take mine. I told him I had seen him in front of my home in New York, near the synagogue. He smiled and nodded. It had only been a few weeks since his historic visit. I was probably one of the first people to tell him that I saw him on his way to the synagogue and in Rome!

Vince was the last of our group, and he expressed gratitude to the pope for acknowledging the survivors' pasts on this special day. By doing this, Vince said, the pope also honored those who helped them survive and recognized that good can triumph over evil, even at the worst of times.

We all slowly and quietly left the platform, passing many people in Saint Peter's Square who looked at us with quizzical glances. Many realized that *these* were the Holocaust survivors the pope had mentioned. Rudolfo was waiting for us and guided us out of the square the way we came. All of a sudden, everyone was talking at the same time, thanking Vince and me for making this happen. But *we* did not make this happen. *They* made it happen by having the courage to speak of their experiences and revere those who risked their lives to save them. (Note: Monsignor Schivo was invited to meet the pope as well but was unable to attend.)

47

A JOURNEY BACK IN TIME

The next morning we met in the lobby of the hotel, ready for our next adventure. This journey would take us across southern Italy and back in time more than sixty years. Today, Horst was going back to the town where he was interned. We had arranged for an air-conditioned minivan and driver, and off we went—Horst, Clara, Victoria, Ron, Rob, Ursula, Vince, and yours truly. Giorgina remained in Rome to spend the day with her sister Michelina who lives in Siena.

Within half an hour, we were deep in the countryside. You would not know that Rome, a city of over six million people, was nearby.

Small town after small town appeared, almost all perched on the hills. No matter how many I saw, I always wondered how they got there, who built them, and what life was like in these secluded places. Although many of the towns are only a few linear miles apart, they are hours away by foot, donkey, or horse. From a distance, you usually see a bell tower attached to a church and ancient stone walls surrounding them. Building towns high up in the hills enabled townspeople to keep watch for those possibly intent on attacking them.

We continued on the *autostrada*, following winding roads carved into the edges of the mountains, and tunnels that went right through them, sometimes for miles. As we drove further away from Rome, Vince and I realized yet another reason the Jews were able to survive in Italy during the Holocaust. They were sent to remote, hard-to-reach places—and if we found them hard to reach in 2008 on modern roads, imagine what it was like during the 1940s with a war in progress.

After several hours, we arrived at the village of Teramo, and I realized that the driver was lost. Basically, traveling in Italy is not complicated as long as you know which major city or town is near your final destination. Just follow the signs for that town, and when you get there, look for local signs with an arrow that points in the direction you need to go.

Of course that was all before GPS systems. Today people rely on GPS and, generally, travel is easier, but that requires the GPS to be in working order. Our minivan did not have a working GPS, so our driver depended on the good-old arrow system. But for some reason, once we got to Teramo, there were no signs pointing to our destination of Civitella del Tronto. We were, however, equipped with a cell phone, so I asked the driver to call the mayor, who was waiting for us in Civitella. Hopefully *he* would know the way to his own town.

Our driver was a typical Italian male who didn't want to admit he was lost—merely because his trusty arrow sign was missing—so he avoided the "I need directions" phone call. Men and directions are men and directions, even in Italy!

Picture an Italian male with an American woman telling him what to do because she figured out he was lost. Our driver finally pulled over to ask some local people, but after a few useless turns, we still weren't on the right path.

At this point I convinced him it was time to make "the call."

"The man who is waiting for us knows exactly how to get us from Teramo to Civitella, as he lives here and you don't," I said.

The driver grudgingly made the call, and thirty minutes later, we could see Civitella in the distance, perched on a hill like the other towns we passed along the way. We started up a long, narrow, winding road and finally arrived. Horst still did not know exactly what was in store for him.

We found Mayor Ronchi exactly where he said we would find him, in the only *piazza* in town. Several other officials, including the chief of police, accompanied him, and together they formed a local welcoming committee.

Horst was overwhelmed with emotion. He was not expecting people to greet him. He and his family couldn't believe they were actually in Civitella. His family had heard so much about this town that had played a big role in Horst's survival.

We entered Civitella through an old stone doorway—the type seen in movies set in the Middle Ages. One can imagine that the town is about to be attacked, the warning is given, the enemy's horses are charging up the mountain, and just as they are about to enter the city, the massive door at the main gate is slammed shut and the town is saved—at least for that day. I half expected to see a knight on a horse in front of me.

Once we entered Civitella, a small, almost Disney-like town appeared before us. On the right was the Hotel Zunica, which belonged to one of the families that helped Horst and his father during those dark days. On our left was a view of the rolling hills we had just driven through, and in front was a street that was so narrow in spots that you could practically touch the walls of the homes on either side with outstretched arms—typical of so many ancient Italian towns. We followed the mayor down this beautiful picturesque street and continued our walk to the town hall, where Horst and his family were officially greeted by the town historian, Tonino Pantanelli, who also reviewed with us a number of documents about internment in Civitella.

When we walked through the narrow streets, it became apparent that Civitella was not a town invented by the magical people of Disney. The mayor pointed to scrape marks on the stone walls, demonstrating that the narrow streets were made for an ox and cart—not cars—and certainly not German jeeps or tanks. In fact, during World War II, a German tank tried to navigate this very street, scraped the walls, and got stuck. That delay allowed a little village boy to run down the back hill and warn the Jews, interned in various homes, that the German soldiers had arrived. After all those years, the scrape marks were still there. Oddly enough, at the very same time we were looking at the scrape marks, several German tourists walked by. How times had changed.

Today, Civitella has been named one of the top one hundred picturesque towns in Italy. It is a wonderful place to spend a few days eating delicious Italian food, reading a good book, taking a stroll in the countryside, or perhaps a drive to the beach—less than an hour away. There was no hustle and bustle in Civitella as there was in nearby Teramo, where there were traffic and people rushing about. In Civitella it felt like a Sunday, even though the calendar told us it was Thursday.

We arrived in *Comune*, and Tonino couldn't wait to show Horst his notebook filled with details of each of the Civitella internees. He had notes on each internee and had attempted to document their paths and their fate after leaving the security of the town. Some were transferred to Ferramonti, some to other towns; others unfortunately ended up in Auschwitz. In Horst's case, Tonino was not certain what had happened and assumed Horst and his father had been killed in Auschwitz.

"Until September 8, 1943, I didn't fear for my life at all. Everything was okay in Civitella," said Horst. "While Italy was Germany's ally, we were left alone. It was only when Italy became Germany's enemy that we had to hide in order not to be deported. We were lucky. Many people helped us survive those horrible days. One day, we all had to run into the woods to escape the Germans, who had come to take us away. By some good chance, I was wearing dark green pants that helped camouflage me while hiding in the brush. I can still remember seeing the Germans looking through the woods for us, machine guns ready. They would have shot me if they had found me. From my hiding place, I could see their boots— only inches away. We survived because the Italians had warned us, as opposed to turning us in."

As Horst looked over the documents, a short, stout woman about eighty years of age entered the room and headed toward him. Signora Violanda Zunica was a young girl during the war and vividly remembered Horst. I gathered that she had a bit of a crush on him at the time, and why not? He was a tall, handsome young man, a bit different from the local boys. The two embraced. She, too, thought he had perished.

(left to right) Tonino Pantanelli, Mayor Gaetano Luca Ronchi, Horst Stein, Violanda Zunica, police officer Michele Biondi, Clara Stein.

We then went to the first place of Horst's "internment," an old palazzo that was showing its age. The stone stairs leading up to it were worn with time and lit by a dim bulb. The apartment that had once been his home was now empty, and Horst looked around, remembering. He later told us it had been slightly modified over the years, but generally looked the same. He couldn't believe where he was—back in this town, back in this home.

It was about two o'clock—way past the traditional Italian lunch hour—and the mayor invited us to lunch at Hotel Zunica, a fitting place honoring Horst's ties to the family. During the meal a parade of citizens came to greet Horst. It was remarkable.

Some who stopped by were children of people he knew, and all had their own stories to share.

The Stein family visiting Horst's former internment apartment.

There is no reason to Google anyone in small Italian towns. Just ask someone who lives there. Out came cell phones, and this made me laugh at how advanced Italy has become. Just fifteen years earlier, it took months to get a land line hooked up in an apartment, and that was if you knew someone and were *raccomandata.*

At this point, people who lived outside of Civitella, who might remember Horst, were called. Horst even spoke with the man who gave him a saxophone many years ago.

We walked to the old hospital, which was the second place Horst was interned in Civitella. It was now a nursing home. When we arrived, many of the people who lived there were out front waiting to greet Horst—especially one former student who was given English lessons by Horst and eventually wound up living in England, where those lessons came in handy. The two men laughed like old classmates at a reunion, and an impromptu party developed. We were offered wine, *pizzette, dolce,* and *gelato* (small pizzas, cake, and ice cream). The nurses and doctors were happy to see that someone who lived in their building so many years ago had survived and lived to be almost eighty-eight years old. In fact, Horst was older than most of the current residents of the building. What would have happened to Horst if not for the Italians?

Soon it was time for us to return to Rome. For a brief moment, Horst had gone back in time to a place he referred to as "*paradiso*," and now I know why.

Horst and residents of Civitella del Tronto.

48

THE CONTINUING SAGA
BECOMES HISTORY

Friday morning. Did this trip really happen? So much thought, so much planning, and then it is over. Like a wedding or any special event, when it ends, you almost cannot believe that it took place.

The group left for New York on Friday, June 20. Vince and I stayed in Italy to do more research, but we accompanied our friends to the airport and waited until they went to the gate. Then we headed back to Rome.

"We did it," Vince said with a big smile on his face. "I would have never believed it—but we did it."

"I know," I said, tired but happy. "Sometimes dreams do come true."

"Yes, they do. You truly dreamed—dreamed big—and never stopped dreaming. That and an extraordinary amount of hard work made this happen."

It's true. This trip started with a dream. I reached for the stars with my feet on the ground, found people who could help make it happen, and added the never-ending belief that *somehow* it would happen, with a little extra help from above.

Back in Rome, Vince and I went to Consuelo Bandini's home for iced cappuccino.

"The two of you look so tired," she said.

We told Consuelo everything that had happened since she joined us for dinner the past Sunday evening.

"I remember when we talked about this the first time we met in New York," Consuelo said to me. "Did you ever think this story would lead you down this path?"

"Absolutely not! I simply wanted to know more about the Jews in Italy. Then my curiosity got the best of me and one thing led to another. Now here we are, but we're not done. There are many more people we want to bring back to Italy so they and their families can visit the camps and see where they were during the war."

"There she goes again. This group has barely even taken off, and she wants to bring another group back," laughed Vince. "She is unstoppable."

We soon left for the train station to head to Forte di Marmi, a beach town near Pisa. My friends Mario and Elena had invited us to stay at their vacation home for the weekend. Then we would go to Casale Monferrato to visit Giorgio and Adriana Ottolenghi, Walter Wolff's friends whom we had met two years earlier. Vince and I were delighted to have a day to gather our thoughts, to stop and recharge our tired batteries on a beautiful Italian beach.

Then it happened.

"*Elisabetta, sai che il papà di Mario era in parte ebreo?*"

said Elena. Elizabeth, do you know that Mario's father was half Jewish?

I pulled off my sunglasses and stared blankly at Elena. I have known Mario and Elena for more than twenty years and did not know *this* little tidbit.

"This story gets crazier by the minute," Vince remarked.

"*Cosa?*" I said. "What do you mean his father was half Jewish? *Now* you tell me!"

"*Sai*, it is like this. Mario's father had a Jewish mother, but he was baptized when he was fourteen; thus he was Catholic for the rest of his life," said Elena.

"Yes, but we all know during that time it was best not to be Jewish and have documents proving otherwise," Vince said cautiously.

"My grandmother was Jewish and my grandfather was Catholic. Like many Jewish people in Florence, my grandmother was quite assimilated," said Mario. "Because she was Jewish, my grandparents raised their children Jewish, but when the racial laws were enacted, they thought it best for the children to take the religion of their father."

"Why didn't you tell me before?" I asked.

"Well, it was such a long time ago, and no one in my family gave it a second thought. That's the way things were then, and once the war was over, we went on with our lives," said Mario. "But I realized with the work you are doing, it is important that you know."

DIOCESI DI *Firenze*

Parrocchia di *S. Jacopino*

Provincia di *Firenze*   Comune di *Firenze*

CERTIFICATO DI BATTESIMO

A dì *13 Marzo 1942*

Certificasi per Me infrascritto, *Curato Strolli* della Parrocchia

suddetta, come dai Registri di BATTESIMO che si conservano in questo Archivio Parrocchiale,

Reg. *I* a carte *113* Atto N. *108* resulta la seguente partita:

L'anno *1938* a dì *16* del mese di *Novembre*

(Cognome e Nome) di

e della di

Nat o a *Firenze* il dì *26 aprile 1924*

fu battezzato a questo Sacro Fonte (ovvero: fu supplito alle S. Cerimonie dal

Sac. *Mons. Santoni* essendo Padrini *Don Marino Squarci*

Annotazioni (¹) *Benedetto fino dal Marzo 1938 ebbe il*
suo frequentando la scuola e ricevendo l'istruzione Cattolica e
soltanto per motivi indipendenti dalla sua volontà. L'amministra-
zione del Battesimo è stata rimandata a questa data.

Rilasciato in carta libera per esclusivo Uso Ecclesiastico.

IL PARROCO

Il Curato Strolli

(¹) Annotare se ha ricevuto la Cresima, il Matrimonio, gli ordini Sacri o ha fatto la Professione religiosa.

Baptismal certificate for Mario's father. Note the two dates given for baptism, 1938 and 1942.

"Do you have documents, like a baptismal certificate?" I asked, not expecting Mario and Elena to have anything.

"Yes," said Elena. "We do."

And with that she produced a yellowed document, Mario's father's baptismal certificate with two dates on it—November 16, 1938, and March 13, 1942. Which date was real?

Why would a boy born to a Jewish mother on April 26, 1924, choose to be baptized into the Catholic faith fourteen years later—approximately at bar mitzvah age? The answer: Hitler.

Generally, if a person were baptized before the racial laws were enacted in Italy, that person would probably not be considered Jewish; he or she would likely be considered Catholic. But any baptism after the racial laws came into effect might not be valid.

In 1938, the thought that people would be physically harmed because they were Jewish had not yet entered anyone's mind. They were not worried about being *killed* because of their religion. Jews in Italy were mostly concerned with their ability to attend school, work, and live amongst the Italian population. They were not worried about being murdered because they were Jewish.

So, on the beach on a hot summer day, we learned another unexpected story.

✦

On Sunday afternoon, Vince and I went to visit Giorgio and Adriana Ottolenghi. Casale Monferrato—where they live—

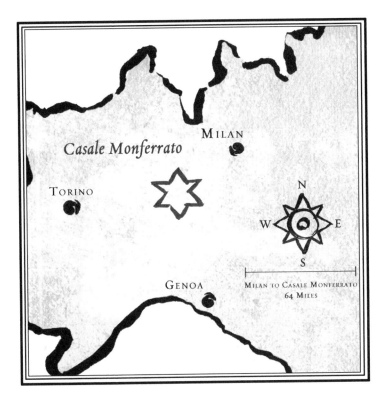

was a beautiful three-hour train ride from Forte di Marmi. Glancing out the window, you can see the glistening blue Mediterranean Sea.

Seeing Giorgio and Adriana again was lovely, although we all missed Walter. They took us to their ornate synagogue, still decorated with flowers from a wedding the night before.

Giorgio and Adriana reminisced about their time with Walter in Casale, and we asked why they thought they had survived the war. Before September 8, 1943, they believed they were not in harm's way. The racial laws affected them, but only in lifestyle, not in life.

"My father continued to work as a lawyer, under the table, like most people," Giorgio explained. "We felt our liberties were limited, but we never felt threatened. Our neighbors and the local people helped us when the Germans came through, rounding up Jews for deportation to their evil camps.

"Under the German occupation of Italy, I found refuge in a convent that also hosted my maternal grandmother and my sister," said Adriana. "My parents stayed with a woman named Anna Bedone Ferrari in a small village near Lago Maggiore called Trarego. Anna Bedone Ferrari and her husband received the honor of the 'Righteous Among the Nations,' as did Mother Giuseppina, head of the Benedictine convent where I stayed. Without their help I would not be here today."

"I also want you to know that *not all* Italians helped," Giorgia said. "Some didn't, and that is why Jews did perish at the hands of the Nazis. My neighbors and others assisted my family and me during those dark days after September 8, 1943, and we were able to hide for a few months in the countryside until we could sneak into Switzerland.

"In addition, after the war we returned to our homes, and all of our possessions were here," he continued. "That's not how it was in other places in Europe. When those people tried to go back, there was nothing for them: not their homes, not their possessions, not their photos. Nothing."

Both of their stories reminded me of Giorgina's; all their

possessions were given back to them after the war. They returned to the town and the lives they had before the war. For them, life continued, not too different than before the war.

✦

I stayed in Italy longer than Vince, taking a few more days to visit friends in Tuscany, Borgo San Lorenzo, about forty-five minutes outside of Florence. *A little time in the country,* I thought, *would be a nice way to end a once-in-a-lifetime trip.* One evening my friend Liana invited friends and family to her home for dinner. And as has been so true throughout this journey, one of her mother's friends, a man named Marcello, had a story. His wife was Jewish, and during the war—for many Italians, "during the war" meant after September 8, 1943—she and her family hid with the *contadini*, the peasants, on the farms in the very hills we were now looking at.

"Mostly, the Jews here lived in their own homes until the Germans came through in 1943," said Marcello. "That is when my wife's family needed to go into hiding. Everyone in the little village where they were hiding knew they were Jewish, but no one told the Germans. And that is how they survived. In addition my uncle, Don Facibene, hid Jewish children in convents in Florence during the war to keep them away from the Nazis."

This was another powerful and unforeseen story that, like many others, was told simply, during a meal. I had heard many such stories, but how many more, I wondered, were still out there?

49

HISTORY THEN AND NOW

The "September Trip" began several years ago on a rainy Columbus Day weekend. In New York City, the week surrounding Columbus Day draws Italians from Italy to celebrate and march up Fifth Avenue in the traditional parade. That weekend, I attended an event and met a woman named Nicla, who was quite interested in this "Jewish story." She, like so many other Italians, knew little of it and invited me to breakfast the next morning so I could further explain.

Naturally, I brought the book with the picture that prompted this unusual journey. When I spoke of Giovanni Palatucci, a man at the next table leaned over and asked how I knew about him. This man was Carmine Nardone, president of the *provincia* of Benevento. (A *provincia* is like a county in the United States.) Benevento is where Giovanni Palatucci went to high school and, for the last few years, the town had been honoring him and remembering the Holocaust.

During the ensuing years, President Nardone and I kept in touch. He met with our survivors in Rome in June, and we discussed having an event honoring Palatucci by inviting the survivors to Benevento and the areas where they were interned.

If this event was to occur, it needed to happen within a narrow window of time: the second half of September. After the customary August vacation, the first fifteen days of September the Italians are getting over what I call "Summer Jet Lag," and it could still be too hot for the survivors.

Also, we needed to consider the Jewish holidays. This year, Rosh Hashanah began on September 30 and the survivors needed to be home a few days before that. That left one choice: a ten-day window in the second half of September, or postponing to the following spring. With most survivors in their eighties, postponing the trip by six months was simply not an option. So, plans were under way for our group to be guests of Benevento for one week in September.

The "September Group" consisted of people who were either in Campagna, Potenza/Tito, and Ferramonti, or had family members in these places: Gerda, Edith, Ursula, Max, his wife Helen, Eva and Eric Rosenfeld, Walter and Elaine Kleinmann, Ruth and Teddy Tobias, and Alec Pollak, Herta Pollak's grandson and a very talented photographer. Kristen Parrish (my very patient editor) joined us on this journey. As Alec Pollack stated, "Whoever you meet becomes part of this story—they wind up in it somehow." He has a point.

The day finally arrived—another "Christmas" or "birthday" for me. Everyone was able to travel, and, miraculously, all the baggage arrived! A big orange bus, the "Pumpkin," and a friendly driver named Ivano greeted us at the airport. We were en route to Rome—the Eternal City.

Years previously, I had led a "teen tour" across the United States on a bus. This felt eerily similar—except none of us were teenagers!

"Remember how I asked you to pack your good clothes in the carry-on bag? Well, you will need to change into *those* clothes after you check into the hotel. At four-thirty PM, we have an appointment in the Vatican with Monsignor Caccia."

Everyone was excited for this visit. I promised that once in Italy, they should be prepared for anything on a moment's notice.

Because Kristen had never been to Rome, I asked her to follow me before she went to her room. I took her to the hotel restaurant, covered her eyes, and led her to the window—then took my hands away.

"Oh my gosh! I can't believe it," she exclaimed, as she stared at the Vatican.

"That is where we are going now!" I happily said.

Even though the Vatican was only down the block, it is a long block for people of a certain age, so we took four taxis. Each group had a map of Rome, showing exactly where to go— the Porta Sant'Anna entrance on the right facing the Vatican— and we would meet at the Swiss Guards.

My cab, which started out leading, suddenly became second in line. Down Via della Conciliazione, we went, but the cab in front of us turned left!

"Where is he going? Follow him!" I said. "Otherwise who knows where they will wind up?"

At that point, we were chasing the cab in front of us and

the other two were following, all going the wrong way. Thank goodness we caught up to the first cab and the situation was corrected—after a little screaming out the window from one cab to the next, Italian style!

When we finally arrived at Porta Sant' Anna, the Swiss Guards were waiting for us. Once again, Vince and I were escorting a group of survivors to a special meeting with Monsignor Caccia.

Monsignor Caccia greeted everyone in the library, a room Vince and I had not yet seen. To Ursula, Monsignor Caccia said, "Ah, la signora Ursula and I know each other. We meet again!" (In nine months, Ursula had visited three times.)

The weather was glorious, and after spending time in the library, Monsignor Caccia invited us to the terrace to continue the conversations. Vince and I smiled, knowing how extraordinary such an invitation is. It was a joy watching everyone step onto the terrace and see Rome beneath them.

As the survivors told him what happened to them in Italy during the war, Monsignor Caccia listened intently. All I could think was, *here they were, out in the open, high above Rome on a Vatican terrace—as opposed to so many years ago, when they were in hiding.*

Monsignor Caccia has a way about him that makes everyone feel comfortable. This occasion was no exception. As he had done before, he gave the group some Vatican history, invited them to take photos, and this time presented them with a memento from the pope's trip to the United States.

It was the dinner hour, and everyone wished Monsignor

Caccia could join us. In a short period of time, he and the group had become friends. When he visits New York, many dinner invitations will be waiting!

Max Kempin and Monsignor Caccia. © Alec Pollack, 2008.

Vatican Terrace. The "September Group": Kristen Parrish, Anita Parker, Eric Rosenfeld, Eva Rosenfeld, Elizabeth Bettina, Edith Birns, Gerda Mammon, Ursula Korn Selig, Walter Kleinmann, Elaine Kleinmann, Vince Marmorale, Ruth Goldman Tobias, Teddy Tobias. © Alec Pollack, 2008.

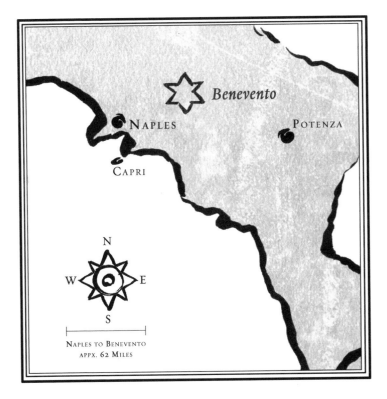

50

BENEVENTO SYMPOSIUM

The next day, the "Pumpkin" was loaded, and off we went, south of Rome to Benevento. The trip took about three hours with a stop at the Autogrill. I reminded the group that the "Autogrill connection" led us to the Vatican. Cardinal Ratzinger (now the pope) and Monsignor Clemens met Sandro, the trumpet player, at the Autogrill years ago. You never know who you will meet having espresso on the *autostrada*!

Upon arrival in Benevento, we were greeted by officials wearing "Miss America" sashes. The next day, we toured the town. Benevento has about fifty thousand people in the city itself and two hundred thousand in the surrounding areas. It is truly the crossroads of Italy, because it linked the Mediterranean and Adriatic coasts during the Roman era. We met with the new president of the region, Presidente Aniello Cimitile, who welcomed the group and acknowledged the reason for their trip—the Palatucci symposium.

In the courtyard of the government building, we discovered a beautiful modern sculpture. We admired its many different colors, and we were astonished to learn that it is called "Memoria" and that each of its hues represents various persecuted groups.

Its base forms a Star of David—something we certainly did not expect to see.

This beautiful piece of art is called "Memoria," and its colors symbolize persecuted groups, including Jews. The foundation is the Star of David.

We spent the early part of the afternoon reviewing the group's symposium speeches. Those who could speak Italian wanted to practice with me, and those who did not, reviewed their stories in English—I would translate for them that evening.

The auditorium was filled, especially with students from the high school that Giovanni Palatucci had attended. It was probably the first time most of these people had met anyone who was Jewish, let alone several Jewish people who could speak Italian.

And then the survivors started, and one by one they spoke—first Gerda, then Edith. I translated their stories and the stories of Walter Wolff and Alfred Birns. Here were two women—who survived the Holocaust in different countries—comparing and contrasting their experiences with those of Walter and Alfred. The room was silent.

Ruth Goldman Tobias's parents' Italian identity cards.

Then Ruth Tobias spoke. Ruth became emotional as she told the crowd, "I am here today because of you and your ancestors. Without them, I would have not survived the war, and neither would any of us. Not only did we survive, but we were treated well by all. Until their deaths, my parents remembered and spoke fondly of their time in Italy." Ruth continued with her story of Potenza and Tito, and how she had returned there in 2002.

The next two speakers, Walter and Eva, told of how fate had brought them together, almost like brother and sister.

Walter added that one woman in particular uniquely contributed to his survival. "My mother had a difficult time and was not able to breast-feed me. She had to resort to a wet nurse. This woman nursed me, and if not for her, I wouldn't be here," Walter told them. "At the time, it was unheard of for a Catholic woman to nurse a Jewish baby."

It was now Eva's turn. Quiet but determined, Eva explained why her family came to Italy, and described how, in 1939, her mother had died, a few months later her father was arrested, and later he tried to escape to France, which proved fatal. "We [she and the Kleinmanns] all survived," she said, "because we were in Italy. He was not. He did not survive, and the Kleinmanns cared for me as a daughter."

Once again, survivors had silenced the room.

Alec Pollak was the last speaker—a symbol of the future generations that Giovanni Palatucci had saved. Alec, too, thanked the people of Italy for his life. Had the Italians not done what they did, neither his grandmother Herta nor his grandfather would have likely survived the war. Alec's grandfather, Branko Pollak, was hidden in Bologna during the war. Hence, without his grandparents, Alec, too, would not be.

Alec Pollak speaks about what the Italians did for his family.
© 2008, Alec Pollak.

Later that night, when we returned to the hotel for dinner, everyone was tired and emotionally drained, but pleased they could convey their messages of gratitude.

To enjoy some free time, the next day we visited *Apice Vecchia*, Old Apice. It is like a modern-day Pompeii, and only an hour away from Benevento. In 1962, a massive earthquake rendered the entire town uninhabitable, so it was abandoned and rebuilt a few miles away. The silent streets of Apice greeted us as if we were the first humans to appear there in decades. We walked cobblestone streets now overgrown with weeds. It was an eerie place that local tradition says is haunted by witches. Apice is an example of natural destruction—an earthquake—that was *out* of the control of man; our orange bus was filled with people who survived destruction that was *in* the control of man.

Recently, there has been talk in Benevento of creating a museum in the abandoned part of Apice focusing on natural disasters around the world. Imagine volcano eruptions, earthquakes, tsunamis, hurricanes—events that kill thousands each time they occur—displayed in a town destroyed by a natural disaster.

We then went to Museo Sannio (MUSA), a museum of agriculture that depicts the farming life of a bygone era. Eva was enthralled with a specific display, a reproduction of a farmhouse in the early 1900s. It featured bed warmers, clothes, a kitchen and utensils, and a high bed (so that animals could crawl underneath to provide warmth for those sleeping above). Eva said it reminded her of Tito.

51

BACK TO CAMPAGNA

The group next traveled to Campagna, where Ursula Korn Selig's and Walter Kleinmann's fathers had been interned. Edith visited one of the places that helped save her husband, Alfred Birns. Gerda returned, this time, sadly, without Walter Wolff.

When we arrived, several people chose to walk the cobblestone road that the internees walked so long ago. Thus, up Via San Bartolomeo we hiked. We passed my cousin's home, where we met their beautiful new grandchild. When we reached my great-grandparents' home, the group could see that it was indeed just yards from the church.

"This is the back of the church," I said, gesturing to the building up the hill, "and sometimes, if you're lucky, you'll see the goats come right down this road."

Then, there it was, the little *piazza* with the fountain, the steps, the church, and the former Convent of San Bartolomeo. A few months earlier, a museum dedicated to the goodness of Giovanni Palatucci had opened, the "Museum of Memory and Peace."

Outside the museum, we saw a photo of the internees

taken on the very steps on which we were standing. Walter Kleinmann stopped in front of it—he saw his father in the doorway. And here was Walter in the very same doorway, sixty-eight years later.

Walter Kleinmann on the steps of the Museum of Memory and Peace. Note the tall poster next to him, which depicts his father (at the far upper left) in the doorway of the former Convent of San Bartolomeo.

We toured the museum, which was remarkable. It even included a re-creation of a bedroom resembling the rooms of the time.

All Edith could do was shake her head. This is not at all what her experience during the war had been like.

"This is *not* what I had in Auschwitz," she said, looking at the beds. "I was lucky to have a slab of wood to share with three other people. And blankets? Ha. I had a thin piece of fabric that did not keep me warm."

Edith Birns explains the differences between the room where the internees lived in Campagna and the one she lived in at Auschwitz. Her husband, Alfred, was interned in Campagna and Ferramonti.

Then we came to the synagogue. We knew there was a synagogue in Campagna during the war, but seeing one was something else. That synagogue goes against *everything* the Holocaust represented. The Jews and their religion were not to exist; yet in Italy, when Italy was Hitler's ally, Jews could be *openly* Jewish and pray in a former convent attached to a church.

A museum re-creation of the synagogue used by the Jewish internees.

In one of the displays, Ursula saw an enlarged photo of her father. It is the same picture she has at home in New York. Ursula said later that she never thought she would visit the place her father had been before he joined her in Città di Castello.

In addition, there was a special section devoted to Walter Wolff; Vince and I felt sad that our friend was no longer here.

We continued to tour the convent and saw "the window" from which the Jews famously escaped with Tagliaferri's help. At that precise moment, we heard bells. Leaning out the window, we discovered they were the bells of local goats who appeared on cue, as if this were a movie. It offered everyone a much-needed laugh in the midst of an emotional morning.

Ursula Korn Selig looking at the poster in Campagna's Museum of Memory and Peace that shows her father as an internee in Campagna.

Vince and I could hardly believe the museum was a reality. Was it just two years earlier that we were in Campagna with Walter Wolff, and it was an empty shell of a building? We were delighted to see it had been done in an appropriate, authentic way. Walter Wolff would have been pleased to see that his visit had helped move the museum plans forward.

As we descended the steps, Vince and I turned around and looked back at the group. When we were here, only a few months earlier, we could not possibly have envisioned this. To think, we didn't even know some of these survivors *existed* at that time!

Former internees, and survivors of the Holocaust, and some of their family members, visiting the former camp in Campagna. Bottom Row: Elizabeth Bettina, Gerda Mammon, Ursula Korn Selig, Edith Birns, Eva Lepehne Rosenfeld, Eric Rosenfeld.

Top Row: Helen Kempin, Max Kempin, Walter Kleinmann, Teddy Tobias, Ruth Goldman Tobias, Elaine Kleinmann, Vince Marmorale, Alec Pollak.

Before we knew it, it was time for lunch. I could think of no better place to go than where this journey began, the *Ristorante Avigliano*, high in the mountains of Campagna, where Zio Peppe gave me "the book" with "the picture."

Lunch was delicious: homemade ravioli, ricotta and mozzarella di buffalo, eggplant parmigiano, luscious figs, and more. We would have loved to stay longer, but it was time for "the pumpkin" to make its way to Potenza, truly a "back to the future" trip for some.

52

POTENZA AND TITO

In Potenza we were met by Dottoressa Piera De Marca, an assistant to the mayor who accompanied us to *Comune*. There we met Sindaco Vito Santarsiero and other members of the town government. Of course, to make it official, the mayor wore his "Miss America" sash. The local RAI television station was there to film Eva Lepehne Rosenfeld, Ruth Goldman Tobias, and Walter Kleinmann, who were all returning to Potenza after more than sixty years. Vince was also taping this for the documentary.

The sindaco welcomed everyone back to Potenza and said, "Until we received this letter from the consulate in New York, we did not know you were coming. In fact we did not know that *Ebrei* [Jews] had been in Potenza during World War II."

We all looked at each other.

"How could that be? There were over one hundred fifty families in Potenza at the time," said Walter Kleinmann. "That makes at least four hundred fifty people."

"*Infatti* [in fact]," said the mayor, "we have a book that was written on the history of Potenza—over two thousand pages—and there is not one word in it about *ebrei* being here in World War II."

"All you have to do is ask the *le vecchiette vestite di nero*," I said, "the little old ladies dressed in black, and they can tell you everything about the town and the people. They can even tell you who is fighting with whom, who is secretly dating whom. They know everything!" Those gathered around the table laughed in agreement.

The sindaco continued, slightly embarrassed. "Forty historians worked on this, but none of them discovered this part of our history."

Pulling the camera away from his face, Vince gave me a look that said, "I must have gotten this wrong. He could not have said *forty*, he must have said *four*." Vince's Italian is pretty good, but every so often I need to translate, especially in official matters. This he got right on the very first try.

Everyone, including the Italians in the room, was flabbergasted by this piece of news. How did forty historians miss this? Where did they do their research? *How* did they do their research? Did they try to talk to people who lived there at the time, witnesses to history? I guess not.

The Sindaco had some *documenti* he wanted us to look at. It was a letter written in 1945 by Dr. Max Kleinmann, Walter's father, requesting space in Potenza's cemetery so a special section could be designated the "*cimitero ebraico*," the Jewish cemetery.

Dr.Max Kleinmann
Comitato Ebraico di Assistenza
Piazza San Luca 5-25
POTENZA.   20 November 1945.

Al Commissario Prefettizio di Potenza

                                        P O T E N Z A .

Mi pregio di informarLa che a Potenza,durante l'internamento,morirono
IO persone di diverse nazionalità,ma tutte di religione ebraica.Esse
furono sepolte sul Cimitero di Potenza.

Ora,d'accordo coll'Unione delle Comunità Israelitiche di Roma,la quale
scrisse già a questo Comune di Potenza,vorremo acquistare sul Cimitero
di Potenza uno spazio di 8 a IO metri quadrati,allo scopo di tumulare
tutte le tombe ad un posto,e precisamente per evitare che i resti
vengano esumati dopo 5 o 6 anni,come si usa a Potenza.

Secondo il rito ebraico,i morti dovrebbero riposare eternamente dove
furono sepolte,e così i parenti dei defunti troverebbero anche dopo
molti anni il posto dove riposano i loro cari.

Sono convinto che Lei,quale Commissario Prefettizio di Potenza,farà
tutto il possibile per venirci incontro in questa pia richiesta.

Attendo pertanto la Sua risposta in merito,con cortese sollecitudine.

                              Con i dovuti rispetti

                                   (Dr.Max Kleinmann)

*Letter from Dr. Kleinmann to the Commissioner of Potenza requesting "eternal" space
in the cemetery of Potenza for Jews.*

"One plus one here is two," I said. "This is not that hard to comprehend. Didn't anyone wonder *perché,* why, if in 1945 a man name Dr. Kleinmann, a very non-Italian name, made a *domanda* for a Jewish section of the cemetery there must have been Jews who died here in Potenza during that time?" (Note: Any Jews who died in Potenza during World War II died of natural causes. They were not persecuted.)

The Sindaco turned to me and said with the "shrug," "What can I tell you? For some reason, we did not put the pieces together. We needed the spark, and that is you."

As Eva, Ruth, and Walter each told their stories of gratitude to the group in *Comune,* the hidden history of Potenza came alive.

"We were not the only ones here," Ruth explained to them. "Many other families were in Potenza, and we took good memories back to the United States with us. We are forever grateful to the people of Potenza and Tito for the way we were treated during the war and for saving our lives. We would not be here today if we were in Germany during that time. When the Germans were coming for us, a police officer said to my parents that they could leave me with him and his family so that I would be safe."

"I am especially grateful," added Walter, his voice quivering with emotion, "because my mother could not breastfeed me and a woman from Potenza was my wet nurse. If she hadn't fed me, I would have died." Unfortunately, over the years, Walter had forgotten the woman's last name. He hoped one day to find her family to express his never-ending gratitude.

These proud mothers holding their babies were interned in Potenza when this photo was taken. Lizi Kleinmann and baby Walter, Mrs. Goldman and baby Ruth, another internee and her baby, name not known.

As on other such occasions, the Sindaco and his staff were moved by the survivors' stories. They were also surprised at how many documents the survivors had proving they actually were in Potenza.

N. ___ Vol. ___ Mod 6.
Visto pel bollo di L. 4.
Il Procuratore del Registro

CITTÀ DI POTENZA
SERVIZI DEMOGRAFICI

ÚFFICIO DI STATO CIVILE
DIVISIONE III

Il Podestà

Esaminati gli atti di ufficio, ed assunte debite informazioni

CERTIFICA

Che **LEPEHNE** Eva di Kurt e fu Neuberg Margherita, nata a Koenigsberg il 22 Aprile 1927, dal giorno 27 Luglio 1940 data in cui risiede in queste Comune, ha serbato buona condotta morale e civile.-

In fede ne rilascia il presente, a richiesta di parte **in carta libera per uso visto Consolare.+**

Potenza, **19 Dicembre 194,0** (Anno **XIX°**)

Il Podestà

EDITRICE LUCANA - POTENZA

Eva's certificate of good conduct from Potenza.

"Here I am with a *Carta d'identita*," said Eva, showing the identification card she'd been issued during her time in Potenza. "And this certificate says I had good conduct while I was here."

Eva Lepehne Rosenfeld's ID card from Potenza.

I could hardly imagine Eva not having good conduct anywhere; she is such a sweet, gentle lady.

How all these people managed to keep their pictures and documents during the war—let alone still have them now, more than sixty years later—is simply phenomenal. (I cannot even count the number of times my own passport has gone missing from its file drawer.)

The officials in Potenza wanted to know more from these

former residents of their town. Talks began to arrange an event for Eva, Ruth, and Walter to return and speak directly to the people of Potenza. This was a wonderful idea, but we did not have the time to plan it at the moment. We were already expected in Tito, where Sindaco Pasquale Scavone was waiting for us.

I had to think of something to get the group moving. "There is so much more to be said. *Facciamo con calma*, let's do things calmly. Tomorrow night in Campagna, please join us for dinner. If we can fly across an ocean, you can drive on the *autostrada* to meet us to continue this conversation. As you know, we are headed to Tito, and it is getting late."

Everyone agreed with this plan, but before we could leave, it was decided that we would take a quick tour in *centro,* the center of town.

In Potenza, Sindaco (Mayor) Vito Santarsiero and other members of the town government present a gift to the group of Holocaust survivors who were interned in Potenza during WWII. (left to right) Walter Kleinmann, Ruth Goldman Tobias, and Eva Lepehne Rosenfeld.

Potenza was bustling on this Sunday evening, with people taking their *passeggiata*, stroll; vendors selling everything from jewelry to scarves; people stopping for coffee and greeting each other. Then there was our group. It was obvious that we were not natives, or so the local people thought. (Walter Kleinmann's birth certificate says Potenza!) Walter was so excited that he kept getting ahead of the group. He was on a mission to find a piece of his past—namely, the school he attended as a young boy, which he believed was attached to a church. At one point we lost him. There we were, a group of bewildered Americans standing in the middle of the *piazza* looking for Walter Kleinmann, who was nowhere to be found. Eventually, he came back, excited after having found the church he remembered.

Finally we headed to Tito, which was Eva's dream. In fact, Tito was more on her mind than Potenza. During World War II, Potenza was a fairly modern city, and Tito was an agricultural village, so the two were quite different. In Potenza, the homes had running water, while in Tito, residents had to get water from a well. Many of the farmers kept animals in their homes for warmth, as we saw in the agricultural museum in Benevento.

As mentioned earlier, Ruth's sister Cilla was born in Tito. Although Ruth had visited Tito in 2002 and spoke to the *carabiniere*, the people there still knew almost nothing about what had happened so long ago. Perhaps this visit with three former Jewish residents would change that.

The next day at 9:00 a.m., the "Pumpkin" started us out on a day trip to Ferramonti. We were all still weary from the events of the day before. This would be the group's last journey back to the past. It was about a two-and-a-half-hour drive to reach the former concentration camp, where many of our group's relatives had been interned.

Erwin Kleinmann's birth certificate.

COMUNE DI MILANO

CIO STATO CIVILE

CERTIFICATO DI NASCITA

Milano, _2 0 GEN 1951_

Goldmann

Rut

figli 2 di *Abraham Mores*

e di *Augarten Sheindel Rechel*

è nat 2 il giorno *12 giugno*

mille *novecentoquaranta* in Milano

come risulta dal Registro degli atti di nascita dell'anno 1940 al progressivo N. 1024 Registro 2 Parte 1 Serie

Rilasciato in carta libera per l'ammissione alle scuole materne, elementari e avviamento al lavoro.

Il Funzionario incaricato

L'Ufficiale dello Stato Civile

Progr. 3636 - 50000 - 1950   10-949 - TIPOGR. COMUNALE

Birth certificate for Ruth Goldman Tobias.

Birth certificate for Jeffrey Goldman.

Ruth, Eva, and Walter on the balcony of their apartment in Tito in 1943.

Sixty-five years later, the three former internees visit Tito. (left to right) Eva Lepehne Rosenfeld, Walter Kleinmann, Ruth Goldman Tobias, with the mayor of Tito, Pasquale Scavone. © 2008, Alec Pollack.

Gerda and Edith could see where Walter and Alfred were sent after Campagna.

Alec Pollak's maternal great-grandfather was in Ferramonti, and Herta, his grandmother, had visited Ferramonti from Vimercate (Milano) during the war.

Max Kempin's father was also there, and Max visited the camp from Milano and from Spezzano della Silla, where he stayed with his mother during her internment.

In addition, Ruth Goldman Tobias's father was in Ferramonti before joining the family in Potenza.

It was about noon when we arrived. Sindaco Francesco Scaglione was there to greet us, but unlike many of the other mayors, he did not wear a sash. Frankly, I think he was very surprised to see such a large group of people come to visit the former concentration camp of Ferramonti. Vince and I were certain that he had not seen that many survivors of the Holocaust at one time.

We entered the camp and, as before, there were just two barracks left. When we took the group through the small museum, Vince and I noticed that nothing had changed since our last visit in November. We watched the survivors walk the same grounds as their family members walked, each one saying there was no comparison between Ferramonti and the other camps in Europe.

Perhaps Edith Birns best describe the differences when she compared her experiences to those who were in Ferramonti. The Auschwitz survivor's words rendered everyone silent. "We were worked to death. We had no time to do anything but work and barely sleep. How could these people have had time to play sports? Look at these people, they look like they are at a picnic. I was right when I told Fred he had a picnic in Italy! Children! Children in school. The head of the camp in Ferramonti took the Jewish children away in his truck—but they went to get ice cream. My little sisters were taken away from me immediately, not to go get ice cream but to go to an oven."

A picnic after a sports match. Photo from the book by M. Rende, Ferramonti di Tarsia *(2009, Mursia, Italy), used with permission.*

Campo di Concentramento Ferramonti. Jewish school children with their teachers in the camp. © Fondazione Museo Internazionale della Memoria Ferramonti di Tarsia. See copyright page.

"Look here," said Walter, calling us over to a photo. "This is the same rabbi who married my parents in Genoa. Can you imagine, a wedding in a camp?"

And so it went. Eva looked on, and I could tell she was thinking of her father, who had perished in Auschwitz. In Ferramonti, people did not perish.

After another emotional day, everyone looked forward to returning to Campagna and having our quiet farewell dinner with friends from Potenza and Campagna. Little did we know the evening would not be nearly as quiet as we thought.

Edith Birns viewing pictures of internees in Ferramonti at picnic.
© Alec Pollak, 2008.

Concentration Camp, Ferramonti di Tarsia. "The September Group" Alec
Pollak, Vince Marmorale, Teddy Tobias, Ruth Goldman Tobias, Edith Birns,
Walter Kleinmann, Ursula Korn Selig, Eric Rosenfeld, Eva Lepehne Rosenfeld,
Helen Kempin, Max Kempin, Gerda Mammon, Elizabeth Bettina.
© Alec Pollak, 2008.

53

FRATELLO DE LATTE: THE MILK BROTHER

That evening, a miracle would occur before our very eyes. I expected the dinner conversation to focus on planning *Giorno Della Memoria* events to include Walter, Ruth, and Eva in Campagna and Potenza. I did not expect all the noise and hand gestures that greeted me when the elevator door opened.

"Come, you have to hear this," urged Ruth, her eyes wide and glistening with tears as she grabbed me by the arm and pulled me into a group of people who were all talking at once.

In the middle of the crowd, Walter Kleinmann was speaking with a man I had not seen before. *The man must be from Potenza*, I thought. And he was—Potenza from more than sixty years ago!

The man standing with Walter, Rocco Giacomino, was in his early seventies. "*Ho trovato mio fratello dopo tutti questi anni*," he said. I found my brother after all these years.

I was confused. At about five foot four with dark features and almost no hair, Rocco looked nothing like Walter, who is six feet tall with blond gray hair and blue eyes. So for him to say he found his "brother" seemed unlikely.

Cinzia and Rocco Giacomino, Walter Kleinmann, and Giuliana Giacomino.
© Alec Pollack, 2008.

The truth was that they *shared* the same mother. Rocco's mother was the long-lost "wet nurse" who saved Walter's life. Rocco had been searching for Walter and the Kleinmann family for more than fifty years.

I stopped dead in my tracks. How did this happen? How did Rocco find us? No one even knew his or his mother's name twenty-four hours ago in Potenza.

Where was Vince? If there was ever something to capture on film, this was it. Vince was upstairs in the breakfast room filming Eva Rosenfeld. I ran upstairs.

"Stop filming—now. You both need to see what is happening, and it needs to be filmed—we can continue with Eva later."

Vince's camera had been in use for a while and the batteries were low. Enter Alec, stage right, with a laptop and Web cam. Thank goodness for those who understand technology. I brought everyone to the breakfast room to capture what had taken place.

It turned out that Rocco had never forgotten his mother breast-feeding baby Walter Kleinmann and Rocco's younger brother, Mario, who was born around the same time. Rocco had searched for him for years without success, including asking the Italian Consulate in New York for assistance. Walter and his family had *also* tried to find Rocco and his family, but the Giacominos had moved and the families lost touch. Although they had not seen each other since 1948, they always fondly remembered each other.

Walter and Rocco both hoped that one day their paths would cross again. They had almost given up hope.

On the previous evening, a lazy Sunday, Rocco was sitting in his armchair, dozing after dinner. The late-evening news played in the background, when he heard two words: "Walter Kleinmann." He jumped. "*È lui!*" It is him! Rocco pointed to the TV where the news story from our meeting in Potenza was airing. He began screaming for his wife to come to the room; his daughter, Giuliana, raced out of bed to find what the commotion was all about.

"Walter Kleinmann," Rocco said, screaming at the television. With two words, a dream had come true—almost. Now, how to find "*il mio fratello di latte*"? Where was Walter Kleinmann?

Rocco and his family spent the night calling all the hotels in Potenza, to no avail—Walter Kleinmann was not registered at any of them. Now what? Early the next morning, after a sleepless night, they continued. First, the local television station, RAI 2; then the *Comune*. After a series of phone calls, Rocco finally reached Dottoressa De Marca, who told him that Walter was staying in Campagna. She knew we were in Ferramonti for the day and would be back for dinner at eight PM when she and the others would join us. Thank heavens we had made those plans.

Rocco could not wait and drove immediately to the hotel in Campagna, where he waited. Fifty years of time and only *one* hour separated them.

Walter Kleinmann had gone for a *passeggiata* before dinner. He had no idea what awaited him in the lobby.

For Rocco, the final minutes seemed endless. Finally, there he was. "*È proprio come suo padre.*" He is just like his father.

Minutes later, Walter sat in silence, listening to how this had unfolded. What was the likelihood that Rocco would be home, barely awake, with the TV playing the evening news rather than a soccer match, and hear *one* meaningful name?

Out came the pictures from Rocco's pocket: Walter as a toddler with his parents; Max and Lizi Kleinmann; Rocco's mother, Giulia Ruggeri. Rocco then took out a letter written December 20, 1948, by Mrs. Kleinmann and a young Walter. After that letter was sent, the families moved and lost touch.

Eva looked at the pictures and said in her soft voice,

"Rocco, I can see your mother holding this baby. Walter." As she said the words, she cradled her arms as if holding a baby, imitating Rocco's mother. Eva looked at the adult Walter and said, "I remember her coming three to four times a day to feed you." By then, we all needed tissues.

To think: in Potenza, Italy, in 1941, a Catholic woman gave life to both her son *and* a son of another religion, a Jewish boy.

Walter listened with happy tears in his eyes, and glanced at his wife, Elaine. Fate had united the families that meant so much to each other. The two "milk brothers" kept smiling, and Walter said, over and over again, "This is unbelievable. It is a dream come true."

By this time, our guests from Campagna and Potenza had arrived, and our so-called quiet little going-away dinner became a loud and loving celebration that lasted into the night, capped off with beautiful music by Sandro, our favorite trumpeter.

You just never know what will happen—or what *did* happen in Italy.

Campagna 2008. Elaine Kleinmann, Walter Kleinmann, Cinzia Giacomino, Giuliana Giacomino, Eve Lepehne Rosenfeld. The "Milk Brother" reunion.

A young Walter with his parents in Potenza.

Walter's wet nurse, Giulia Ruggeri, the "milk mother" holding her grandson.

Epilogue

"Never forget that the war will be over and that the entire historical side will fade away. Try to create as much as possible: Things, debates . . . that will interest people in 1952 or 2052."

—Irène Némirovsky's note to herself, June 2, 1942.
(from a special exhibit, "Woman of Letters: Irène Némirovsky & Suite Française" at the Museum of Jewish Heritage)

Walter Wolff had it right. During bad times, there were good people, and without them, he and the other Jews would not have survived.

And as Adriana Ottolenghi firmly stated, "For each one of us who is here now who survived, there is someone who risked his or her life to help us. For everyone who was deported, there was someone who betrayed them and turned them in."

✦

Italy has many "Giovanni Palatuccis" who helped save Jews, as David Cohen stated. These Italians made sure that Hitler did not achieve his Final Solution, There are 52 survivors in this book who had 54 children, 78 grandchildren and 10 great-grandchildren—194 people total.

It has been a privilege to be welcomed into the lives of witnesses to history and hear their intimate stories. In addition, in a very short period of time, an incredible bond has formed amongst us. It has been an honor to be called "another daughter."

After returning from our trip to Italy in September, Helen Kempin said, "We became a family on this trip." Some of the survivors really have discovered other "families," and new friends to add to the old, and what thrills me most is that the stories keep growing. They keep providing intertwining connections that span thousands of miles, many countries, more than seventy years, and many generations.

Walter and Elaine Kleinmann spent the 2008 Christmas holidays with Rocco and his family in Potenza. Imagine the "milk brothers" together again for this festive season, sharing religions, cultures, and traditions. And many old friendships have new memories added to the old to share.

Eva Rosenfeld is working to improve the Jewish cemetery in Genoa, where her mother's final resting place is located, so that it honors those who are buried there. They are the lucky ones, to have graves when so many others who were murdered do not.

Many dreams came true on our journeys, including having the Potenza group return together to the city that saved them. The picture of these survivors as children sixty-five years ago is priceless. (The city of Potenza is now working with us on an exchange program for their students, and students here in the United States.)

When I look back, I almost can't believe any of this happened. But it did. I could not invent this if I tried. As I have said before, truth is stranger than fiction.

If I have learned one thing, it is that one never knows when an event can completely change your life, or at least add a very unexpected twist. Sometimes all it takes is a picture or a name flashing across on the television screen and bingo, you have a new "family."

I have also learned that almost *nothing* is impossible. Simply believe in something and then take action to make it happen. So often we stop ourselves before we start. I have done that many times in the past, but this time was different. An almost inexplicable force guided me to make these dreams come true. Somehow we took four trips to Italy, and extraordinary things happened on each trip.

Working with Vince Marmorale, Mr. Search Engine Holocaust, has been an adventure of its own. His knowledge and years of dedication to this subject are extraordinary. Not only has his guidance been exceptional, but he made me laugh when things didn't always go according to plan.

Finally, as many of the survivors have remarked, the most educated group of people in the world at the time created the Holocaust and the "Final Solution." Yet in many cases, it was the simple people, the "uneducated" people who saved the Jews. Simple goodness triumphed over sophisticated evil.

This unexpected journey of discovery is not over—not by a long shot. I just know there are many more stories to be heard. Perhaps one of you reading this sees a name or a picture of a relative—maybe even yourself. I can be reached at www.elizabethbettina.com, so please contact me. I can't wait to hear what stories you have to share.

The "Milk Brothers" Family Reunion. December 25, 2008. The Kleinmann and Giacomino families in Potenza.

A letter from Lizi Kleinmann (Walter's mother) to Giula Ruggeri, (Rocco's mother) on December 20, 1948. Walter arrived in Potenza on December 20, 2008—exactly 60 years later to celebrate Christmas with his "Milk Brother"

Appendix A

LIST OF 272 INTERNEES IN CAMPAGNA ON SEPTEMBER 16, 1940

	Cognome	Nome	Paternità	Età	Professione	Cittadinanza
1.	Adler	Leo	Giacobbe	1887	orefice	germ.
2.	Barta	Maurizio	Simone	1881	commerc.	slov.
3.	Beder	Abramo	Szyja	1913	medico	pol.
4.	Berg	Rodolfo	Luigi	1890	albergatore	germ.
5.	Berger	Alberto	Maurizio	1914	tappezziere	apol.ex boemo
6.	Bestàndig	Samuele	Leone	1902	pelliciaio	apol.ex pol.
7.	Blaufeld	Wolf	Markus	1904	rabbino	apol.ex pol.
8.	Blej	Giulio	Leone	1910	insegnante	rumeno
9.	Borensztajn	Lajbus	Mosè	1901	commerc.	pol.
10.	Brandweiner	Enrico	Salomone	1889	macellaio	germ.
11.	Buchsbaum	Maurizio	Pinkas	1906	commerc.	pol.
12.	Carenni	Giovanni	Nicola	1899	impiegato	apol.ex ital.
13.	Cingolani	Ruggero	Riccardo	1904	maniscalco	ital.
14.	Danzig	Giovanni	Bertoldo	1920	meccanico	boemo
15.	David	Sigfrido	Alberto	1908	prof.in filos.	germ.
16.	Degai	Alessandro	Nicola	1890	pittore	apol.ex russo
17.	Donath	Edoardo	Bernardo	1905	ingegnere	slov.
18.	Ehrmann	Giuseppe	Emanuele	1897	commerc.	pol.
19.	Eisen	Mosè	Chaim	1887	viaggiatore	germ.
20.	Elsner	Rodolfo	Bernardo	1900	impiegato	germ.
21.	Engel	Guglielmo	Giulio	1906	architetto	slov.
22.	Epstein	Bernardo	Mosè	1913	rabbino	slov.
23.	Ernst	Arturo	Massimiliano	1885	scrittore	germ.
24.	Fabbris	Girolamo	Francesco	1920	falegname	jugosl.
25.	Feith	Guglielmo	Michele	1899	avvocato	boemo
26.	Finkelstein	Mosè	Enrico	1897	commerc.	germ.
27.	Förster	Ugo	Ernesto	1915	chimico	germ.
28.	Fränkel	Bernardo	Saul	1889	commerc.	apol.ex pol.
29.	Freudmann	Massimil.	Carlo	1892	orologiaio	boemo
30.	Friedjung	Giovanni	Ernesto	1913	possidente	germ.
31.	Gaffiers	Walter Alb.	Alberto	1869	prof.giornal.	ingl.
32.	Gewürz	Szyja	Henoch	1895	libraio	pol.
33.	Grott	Bela	Giacobbe	1916	tipografo	slov.
34.	Grünfeld	Massimil.	Vojtech	1900	commerc.	slàv.
35.	Habib	Eliezer	Giuseppe	1903	commerc.	apol.ex turco
36.	Hammerschmidt	Daniele	Leopoldo	1884	commerc.	germ.
37.	Hammerschmidt	Guglielmo	Leopoldo	1889	commerc.	germ.
38.	Hauser	Maurizio	Ermanno	1898	commerc.	apol.ex pol.

*Elenco, composto di sette pagine, degli internati presenti a Campagna in data 16 settembre 1940.

Cognome	Nome	Paternità	Età	Professione	Cittadinanza
39. Heger	Davide	Simone	1890	commerc.	germ.
40. Heger	Isacco	Giuseppe	1910	medico	apol.ex pol.
41. Hirsch	Bernardo	Sigismondo	1914	commerc.	apol.ex ital.
42. Hirsch	Giulio	Sigismondo	1915	commerc.	apol.ex ital..
43. Hirsch	Sigismondo	Isaja	1882	commerc.	apol.ex ital.
44. Hoffmann	Alessandro	Enrico	1883	commerc.	germ.
45. Hönigsfeld	Marco	Maurizio	1887	commerc.	apol.ex ital.
46. Horowitz	Arturo	Isidoro	1905	medico	pol.
47. Igel	Adolfo	Giacobbe	1885	commerc.	germ.
48. Iwanicki	Antonio	Stefano	1918	agronomo	pol.
49. Jacob	Alfredo	Luigi	1905	commerc.	germ.
50. Jacob	Erberto	Luigi	1904	agricoltore	germ.
51. Jeithner	Rodolfo	Riccardo	1901	commerc.	germ.
52. Jellinek	Oscar	Bernardo	1904	commerc.	germ.
53. Jellinek	Teodoro	Leopoldo	1885	commerc.	germ.
54. Jockl	Giorgio	Edmondo	1903	impiegato	germ.
55. Juchwid	MassimilianoHirsch		1908	contabile	apol.ex russo
56. Jungleib	Giuseppe	Mosè	1915	dentista	germ.
57. Kahn	Luigi	Maurizio	1873	possidente	apol.ex germ.
58. Kalika	Bernardo	Maurizio	1908	infermiere	apol.ex ital.
59.Karp	Ernesto	Baruch	1899	commerc.	germ.
60. Klein	Giuseppe	Leopoldo	1896	ingegnere	germ.
61. Klein	Isacco	Salomone	1912	medico	germ.
62. Klein	Maurizio	Isidoro	1893	autista mec.	germ.
63. Kleinmann	MassimilianoWolf		1909	medico	apol.ex germ.
64. Klüger	Gustavo	Gerson	1892	impiegato	germ.
65. Kniebel	Leopoldo	Simone	1882	chimico	germ.
66. Kniebel	Erich	Leopoldo	1921	saldatore tecn.germ.	
67. Knirscha	Andrea	Ippolito	1887	artista lirico,apol.ex russo	
68. Koblitz	Francesco	Adolfo	1885	chimico	boemo
69. Köhler	Leone	Massimiliano1897		commercw	germ.
70. Kohn	Giuseppe	Giovanni	1903	commerc.	germ.
71. Kohn	Guglielmo	Lodovico	1888	commerc.	germ.
72. Kohn	Samuele	Isacco	1889	commerc.	apol.ex pol.
73. Kohn	Ugo	Bernardo	1913	parucchiere	germ.
74. Komin	Ignazio	Giacomo	1905	commerc.	germ.
75. Königsberg	Isacco	Joel	1891	pittore	germ.
76. Kopp	Guglielmo	Ermanno	1900	segr.d'albergo,slov	
77. Koppelmann	Feibisdh	Salomone	1888	impiegato	germ.

	Cognome	Nome	Paternità	Età	Professione	Citadinanza
78.	Korn	Bruno	Israele	1911	sarto	germ.
79.	Korn	Paolo	Davide	1895	commerc.	germ.
80.	Körner	Szloma	Feibisch	1880	maestro	germ.
81.	Krausz	Arturo	Guglielmo	1898	vetraio	germ.
82.	Krausz	Massimiliano	Ermanno	1890	commerc.	germ.
83.	Krohn	Martino	Adolfo	1883	commerc.	germ.
84.	Ksinski	Ugo	Israele	1890	commerc.	germ.
85.	Kuttner	Sigfrido	Davide	1903	scenografo	germ.
86.	Labischinski	Federico	Guglielmo	1891	impiegato	germ.
87.	Lampl	Maurizio	Alois	1900	impiegato	germ.
88.	Landau	Naftali Hersch	Isacco	19	medico	pol.
89.	Landau	Samuele	Carlo	1882	fotografo	germ.
90.	Lande	Isidoro	Mosè	1904	medico	apol.ex pol.
91.	Langnas	Ignazio	Nadhmann	1899	commerc.	germ.
92.	Lauterbach	Alberto	Davide	1897	dentista	apol.ex ital.
93.	Lederer	Giorgio	Giacobbe	1888	farmacista	germ.
94.	Lehmann	Gerardo	Massimiliano	1914	decoratore	germ.
95.	Lehmann	Giovanni	Emilio	1901	commerc.	germ.
96.	Lehmann	Kurt	Emilio	1907	commerc.	germ.
97.	Lehmann	Massimiliano	Giacomo	1886	pittore imbianch.	germ.
98.	Levinger	Sigfrido	Giacomo	1881	benestante	apol.ex germ.
99.	Lewin	Alfredo	Gilio	1911	commerc.	germ.
100.	Lion	Paolo	Edoardo	1889	benestante	germ.
101.	Lipenholc	Giuseppe	Szmujlo	1910	medico	pol.
102.	Lipschitz	Eugenio	Ignazio	1883	commerc.	apol.ex ital.
103.	Lovese	Giulio	Paolo	1898	manovale	franc.
104.	Löwinger	Sigismondo	Ignazio	1889	commerc.	germ.
105.	Löwy	Giorgio	Giacobbe	1894	impiegato	boemo
106.	Löwy	Guglielmo	Carlo	1893	cuoco	germ.
107.	Ludmer	Enrico	Leopoldo	1908	professore	boemo
108.	Lustig	Walter	Lodovico	1894	impiegato	germ.
109.	Maier	Arnoldo	Leopoldo	1890	caffettiere	germ.
110.	Marcovivi	Alessandro	Giuseppe	1894	dott.in legge	apol.ex rumeno
111.	Marcus	Benno	Leopoldo	1899	giornalista	germ.
112.	Marder	Pinkas	Aurell	1892	commerc.	germ.
113.	Margulius	Kurt	Sigismondo	1912	decoratore	germ.
114.	Markus	Desiderio	Maurizio	1895	commerc.	apol.ex ital.
115.	Meyer	Giuseppe	Bertoldo	1882	commerc.	germ.
116.	Meyerhof	Giovanni	Gustavo	1881	commerc.	apol.ex germ.

Cognome	Nome	Paternità	Età	Professione	Cittadinanza
117. Münster	Ladislao	Massimiliano	1900	medico	apol.ex ital
118. Nachmann Chaim Mayer		Mendel	1887	commerciante	pol.
119. Nachmann	Juda	Giuseppe	1892	viaggiatore	pol.
120. Nadel	Heinz Marco	Maurizio	1911	ragioniere	germ.
121. Nasch	Alberto	Federico	1899	commerc.	germ.
122. Nathan	Bernardo	Giuseppe	1881	commerc.	spñh.ex ital.
123. Neisser	Arturo	Alberto	1875	dott.in fil.	germ.
124. Neumann	Emilio	Ermanno	1889	impiegato	germ.
125. Neumann	Eugenio	Francesco	1881	commerc.	apol.ex ital.
126. Neumann	Felice	Enrico	1887	impiegato	germ.
127. Neustetl	Elia	Marco	1884	commerc.	germ.
128. Nunes	Franco Giorgio	Isacco	1893	assicuratore	ital.
129. Orbach	Ernesto	Sigismondo	1882	dentista	germ.
130. Osmund	Otto Teodoro	Giulio	1873	cons.di stato	germ.
131. Pape	Szapse	Arone Isacco	1913	medico	pol.
132. Pechner	Enrico	Giuseppe	1896	commerc.	germ.
133. Peringer	Naftali	Giacomo	1881	commerc.	germ.
134. Pfingst	Arnoldo	Adolfo	1888	mecanico	apol.ex germ.
135. Pinell	Otto	Emilio	1892	commerc.	germ.
136. Pintschuk	Giuseppe	Massimiliano	1886	industriale	germ.
137. Piombo	Elia	G.Battista	1908	casalinga	franc.
138. Pionkowski	Giorgio	Adolfo	1919	commerc.	boemo
139. Piskorski	Giuseppe	Casimiro	1910	impiegato	pol.
140. Platzner	Arturo	Marco	1883	commerc.	apol.ex ital.
141. Pohorilles	Noah	Lion	1885	scrittore	germ.
142. Polak	Arnost(Ernesto)	Alois	1895	industriale	boemo
143. Pollak	Arturo Roberto	Gustavo	1904	impiegato	germ.
144. Pollak	Carlo	Enrico	1891	commerc.	germ.
145. Pollak	Emilio	Massimiliano	1885	caffettiere	germ.
146. Pollak	Ernesto	Lodovico	1893	editore	boemo
147. Pollak	Ervino	Samuele	1899	amministratore, germ.
148. Pollak	Kurt	Eugenio	1897	rappresentante, germ.
149. Pollak	Vojtech	Ignazio	1900	impiegato	slov.
150. Popper	Federico	Ignazio	1892	possidente	germ.
151. Porjesz	Giacobbe	Nathan	1880	commerc.	germ.
152. Poznanski	Conrad	Otto	1915	studente	germ.
153. Präger	Elia	Mayer	1888	calzolaio	germ.
154. Prager	Federico	Sigismondo	1894	commerc.	germ.
155. Presser	Ottone	Giuseppe	1902	attore comico	germ.

Cognome	Nome	Paternità	Età	Professione	Cittadinanza
156. Prohaska	Francesco	Giuseppe	1891	tecnico	boemo
157. Propst	Rodolfo	Michele	1914	medico	pol.
158. Ramras	Enrico	Emanuele	1887	commerc.	germ.
159. Rawitz	Kurt	Massimiliano	1912	medico	germ.
160. Redler	Fischel	Vittorio	1908	prof.in fil.	pol.
161. Reinharz	Markus	Simone	1896	fabbricante	germ.
162. Rieser	Helmut	Gustavo	1914	chimico	germ.
163. Romano	Samuele	Giuseppe	1899	vend.ambul.	apol.ex ital.
164. Rosen	Samuele	Elia	1872	possidente	apol.ex russo
165. Rosensteàn	Paolo	Leo	1894	commerc.	germ.
166. Rosenzweig	Mosè	Giacobbe	1911	medico	apol.ex pol.
167. Rubel	Maurizio	Simone	1891	architetto	germ.
168. Rubel	Walter	Maurizio	1922	stud.chimico	germ.
169. Russ	Arturo	Abramo	1896	commerc.	germ.
170. Russ	Martino	Abramo	1898	medico	germ.
171. Sagi	Nicola	Giulio	1896	impiegato	apol.ex ital.
172. Salomon	Ernesto	Giacobbe	1893	industriale	germ.
173. Salza	Andrea	Vittorio	1905	commerc.	apol.ex russo
174. Salzer	Massimiliano	Alessandro	1885	cuoco	germ.
175. Sander	Ugo	Emilio	1866	commerc.	germ.
176. Schaffer	Israele	Marco	1905	commerc.	apol.ex rumeno
177. Schargel	Alfredo	Pinkas	1908	autista	germ.
178. Schatz	Harry Bernardo	Giacobbe	1920	sarto	apol.ex pol.
179. Schaufeld	Davide	Giacobbe	1894	commerc.	apol.ex germ.
180. Schechter	Arigo	Davide	1915	commerc.	germ.
181. Scheer	Guglielmo Arnoldo	Massim.	1905	medico	apol.ex pol.
182. Schick	Walter	Adolfo	1901	ingegnere	germ.
183. Schiffer	Ermanno	Samuele	1886	dirett.teatro	germ.
184. Schloss	Ermanno	Bernardo	1884	commerc.	germ.
185. Schloss	Hans Werner	Ermanno	1921	elettricista	germ.
186. Schlosser	Leonardo	Emanuele	1899	galvanista	germ.
187. Schnaymann	Sally	Israele	1888	commerc.	germ.
188. Schneiberg	Mosè	Bahamin	1907	ambulante	apol.ex turco
189. Schneider	Teodoro	Mandel	1900	impiegato	germ.
190. Schnitzler	Roberto	Federico	1894	commerc.	germ.
191. Schotten	Giacobbe	Enrico	1896	saponiere	germ.
192. Schreier	Ervino	Salomone	1899	dentista	germ.
193. Schröter	Rodolfo	Bernardo	1908	impiegato	germ.
194. Schwammenthal	Leiser	Davide	1900	commerc.	apol.ex rumeno

Cognome	Nome	Paternità	Età	Professione	Cittadinanza
195. Schwarz	Ferdinando	Lazzaro	1912	cantore	germ.
196. Schwarz	Davide	Hersch Wolf	1910	medico	pol.
197. Schwarz	Paolo	Vojtech	1912	avvocato	germ.
198. Schwarz	Salomone	Herz	1885	magazziniere	germ.
199. Seidmann	Michele	Isacco	1905	musicista	germ.
200. Seif	Rachmiel	Efraim	1893	commerc.	germ.
201. Semel	Rodolfo	Leone	1895	commerc.	germ.
202. Silberbusch	Massimiliano	Davide	1890	rappresent.	germ.
203. Silberstein	Augusto	Emilio	1903	chimico farm.	germ.
204. Singer	Emilio	Leopoldo	1886	ortopedico	germ.
205. Skall	Enrico	Ottone	1914	dott.econ.	boemo
206. Smulevich	Leone	Aronne	1916	sarto	apol.ex pol.
207. Smulevich	Sigismondo	Emanuele	1890	sarto	apol.ex ital.
208. Sobek	Rodolfo	Emanuele	1894	industriale	germ.
209. Spiegel	Meyer	Hersch	1912	commerc.	germ.
210. Spiegler	Gustavo	Sigismondo	1882	dirett.banca	germ.
211. Spitzer	Leo	Samuele	1895	impiegato	germ.
212. Spitzer	Riccardo	Giuseppe	1881	piazzista	germ.
213. Stein	Leopoldo	Rodolfo	1892	commerc.	apol.ex germ.
214. Steinberg	Massimiliano	Berhardo	1890	privato	apol.ex lettone
215. Steiner	Federico	Riccardo	1919	macellaio	germ.
216. Steiner	Isidoro	Adolfo	1895	falegname	apol.ex ital.
217. Steiner	Giov.Giorgio	Alberto	1884	impiegato	germ.
218. Steinweis	Enrico	Giacobbe	1890	commerc.	germ.
219. Sterk	Andrea	Francesco	1903	albergatore	apol.ex ital.
220. Stern	Ermanno	Marco	1892	albergatore	apol.ex ital.
221. Stern	Paolo	Emilio	1914	commerc.	germ.
222. Stern	Riccardo	Giacobbe	1881	fachino	germ.
223. Sternberg	Enrico	Bernardo	1890	commerc.	germ.
224. Stricker	Federico	Filippo	1898	autista	germ.
225. Striffler	Enrico	Luciano	1894	benestante	franc.
226. Süsskind	Gustavo	Alberto	1881	avvocato	germ.
227. Tänzer	Massimiliano	Chaim	1909	medico	pol.
228. Teichner	Bertoldo	Adolfo	1903	commerc.	germ.
229. Tiefenthal	Guglielmo	Carlo	1898	impiegato	germ.
230. Toch	Carlo	Bernardo	1892	commerc.	germ.
231. Trichter	Davide	Guglielmo	1882	avvocato	germ.
232. Tüchler	Leopoldo	Sigismondo	1898	commerc.	germ.
233. Uhryn	Zenobius Bohdan	Demetrio	1912	veterinario	pol.

Cognome	Nome	Paternità	Età	Professione	Cittadinanza
234. Urich	Lodovico	Bernardo	1884	filatelista	germ.
235. Villa	Samuele	Guglielmo	1876	fabbricante	ungherese
236. Vogelfänger	Davide	Giacobbe	1882	rigattiere	germ.
237. Wachsberger	Davide	Isacco	1881	rabbino	apol.ex ital.
238. Wahl	Federico	Israele	1895	commerc.	germ.
239. Mallentin	Paolo	Adolfo	1896	commerc.	germ.
240. Walter	Paolo	Marco	1906	avvocato	boemo
241. Warzé	Emilio	Alfonso	1877	ingegnere	belgo
242. Wechselberg	Davide	Giacobbe	1902	impiegato	apol.ex germ.
243. Weil	Carlo	Rodolfo	1913	impiegato	boemo
244. Weil	Guglielmo	Rodolfo	1916	impiegato	tecn.boemo
245. Weiner	Eugenio	Adolfo	1904	rappresentante	germ.
246. Weininger	Ugo	Guglielmo	1887	architetto	germ.
247. Weinstein	Samuele	Maurizio	1881	calzolaio	germ.
248. Weinstock	Giovanni Ulisse	Sigfrido	1910	avvocato	apol.ex ital.
249. Weintraub	Emanuele	Israele	1886	commerc.	apol.ex ital.
250. Weiss	Giovanni	Adolfo	1891	viaggiatore	germ.
251. Weiss	Giuseppe	Giacobbe	1894	libraio	germ.
252. Weisz	Alfredo	Emanuele	1898	impiegato	germ.
253. Weitzmann	Kurt	Edmondo	1911	impiegato	germ.
254. Weitzmann	Guglielmo	Giacobbe	1896	fotografo	germ.
255. Weprik	Demetrio	Giorgio	1895	contadino	pol.
256. Werndorfer	Eugenio	Guglielmo	1893	commerc.	apol.ex ital.
257. Wertheim	Walter Feder.	Giuseppe	1900	chimico	germ.
258. Wiener	Ugo	Isidoro	1892	commerc.	germ.
259. Windwehr	Aronne	Simone	1903	pelliciaio	apol.ex pol.
260. Witkowski	Kurt	Aronne	1914	medico	germ.
261. Wolff	Horst	Kurt	1911	commerc.	germ.
262. Wolff	Walter	Giuseppe	1917	studente	germ.
263. Wolfsohn	Victor	Emanuele	1882	giogelliere	germ.
264. Woodcock	Henry Hugh	Davide	1880	pensionato	ingl.
265. Wulfin	Samuele	Isacco	1912	medico	lituano
266. Zeisler	Giuseppe	Michele	1881	esportatore	germ.
267. Zezmer	Bruno	Giacomo	1914	medico	apol.ex pol.
268. Zindweh	Nathan	Marco	1883	rappresent.	germ.
269. Zins	Bogdan Daniele	Carlo	1905	impieg.e music.	pol.
270. Zipser	Francesco	Lazzaro	1895	avvocato	germ.
271. Zuckerbäcker	Riccardo	Sigismondo	1887	elettricista	germ.
272. Zwirn	Salomone	Mosè	1884	commerc.	germ.

Appendix B

LIST OF SURVIVORS INTERVIEWED FOR THIS BOOK

Bold font indicates the person was interviewed
for this book or the documentary.

NAME	COUNTRY OF ORIGIN	LOCATION IN ITALY DURING WWII
Alfred Birns	**Germany**	**Campagna Ferramonti**
Mother Birns	Germany	Milano
Father Birns	Germany	Campagna Ferramonti
Eva Deutsch Costabel	**Yugoslavia**	**Northern Italian Camp**
Max Kempin	**Germany**	**Milano**
Father	Germany	Ferramonti
Mother	Germany	Spezzano della Silla
Brother Felix	Germany	Milano
Sister Erma	Germany	Rome
Herta Mingelgrün Pollak	**Germany**	**Vimercate (Milano)**
Father	Germany	Ferramonti
Mother	Germany	Vimercate
Mr. Branko Pollak	Germany	Emilia Romana

NAME	COUNTRY OF ORIGIN	LOCATION IN ITALY DURING WWII
Eva Lephene Rosenfeld	Germany	Potenza/Tito
Doris Blumenkranz Schechter	**Austria**	**Guardiagrele**
Sister	Italy	Guardiagrele
Mother	Austria	Guardiagrele
Father	Austria	Guardiagrele
Ursula Korn Selig	**Germany**	**Città di Castello**
Mother	Germany	Città di Castello
Father	Germany	Campagna / Città di Castello
Horst Stein	**Germany**	**Civitella del Tronto**
Father	Germany	Ferramonti
Mother	Germany	Milano
Ruth Goldman Tobias	**Italy**	**Potenza/Tito**
Sister Cilla	Italy	Potenza/Tito
Brother Jeffrey	Italy	Potenza/Tito
Mother	Poland	Potenza/Tito
Father	Poland	Potenza/Tito
Gloria Virey	**Italy**	**Arezzo**
Mother	Austria	Campagna/Arezzo
Father	Austria	Campagna/Arezzo
Giorgina Vitale	**Italy**	**Piea**
Sister Michelina	Italy	Piea
Sister Emilia	Italy	Piea
Mother	Italy	Piea
Father	Italy	Piea
Grandfather	Italy	Piea

NAME	COUNTRY OF ORIGIN	LOCATION IN ITALY DURING WWII
Walter Wolff	**Germany**	**Campagna** **Ferramonti** **Casale Monferrato**
Bruno Wolff	Germany	Ferramonti Casale Monferrato
Mother Wolff	Germany	Cosenza Ferramonti Casale Monferrato

Appendix C

HISTORICAL DOCUMENTS

(translation follows)

C O M U N E   D I   G U A R D I A G R E L E

(Provincia di Chieti)

==

ATTO DI PRESCRIZIONI

L'anno millenovecentoquaranta, anno XIX, il giorno ventitre del mese di novembre, nella Casa Comunale di Guardiagrele.

Avanti di Noi Dott. LUCIANO DE MATTEO, Commissario Prefettizio del Comune suddetto, Autorità Locale di P.S., in seguito ad invito, é personalmente comparso il nominato Blumenkranz Efroin Fischel di David e di Ettel Blasser, nato a Rozwxadow il 2 novembre 1903, ebreo apolide, internato in questo Comune il giorno 18 corrente, proveniente dal campo di concentramento di Agnone.

NOI COMMISSARIO PREFETTIZIO

in applicazione delle istruzioni pervenute dalle Superiori Autorità: Vista la vigente legge di P.S. ed il relativo Regolamento:

ABBIAMO OBBLIGATO ALL'INTERNATO SUDDETTO

di osservare scrupolosamente le seguenti prescrizioni:

1) Non allontanarsi assolutamente da questo Comune;

2) Presentarsi una volta al giorno al locale Comando di Stazione CC.RR.

3) Non cambiare l'abitaziobe scelta senza il preventivo permesso dell'Autorità di P.S.

4) Non ritirarsi alla sera più tardi delle ore 20 e non uscire al mattino più presto delle ore 7.;

5) Non detenere e portare armi od altri strumenti atti ad offendere;

6) Non frequentare prostiboli, osterie ed altri pubblici esercizi;

7) Non frequentare riunioni, spettacoli o trattenimenti pubblici;

8) Tenere buona condotta; non dar luogo a sospetti ed astenersi dal frequentare compagnie comunque sospette.

9) Darsi a stabile occupazione nei modi che saranno stabiliti dal sottoscritto.

L'internato dichiara di essere bene edotto di quanto sopra e delle altre disposizioni contenute nel vigente Regolamento per l'esecuzione della Legge di P.S., assicurando la scrupolosa osservanza delle prescrizioni che precedono e delle altre che, eventualmente, comunque, possa essere impartite.

This document is an Order that laid out the rules for interned Jews in Chieti. A translation follows.

la signora ᴾrimavera ᴰomenichella posta in Via delle Murene N.9 .
di questo capoluogo.

ᴰel che si é redatto il presente verbale, in quattro esemplari
di cui:

- uno viene consegnato all'internato Blumenkranz Efroin Fischel,
- uno viene conservato negli atti di questo ᵁfficio;
- Uno viene spedito alla R.Prefettura di Chieti;
- uno viene spedito al Comando Stazione dei CC.RR. di ᴳuardiagrele.

L'INTERNATO

[signature]

IL COMMISSARIO PREFETTIZIO
Autorità ᴸocale di P.S.

[signature]

REGIA QUESTURA DI CHIETI   IᴼΞ luglio
======= Gabinetto =======   F..   Chieti ΞΞΞΞΞΞΞΞ 1940 XVIII
Nᵒ C8809
OGGETTO: Blumenkraunz Bertha di Lazar nata Goldstein,di anni 32, ebrea
         Tedesca.

                     Signor PODESTA'   GUARDIAGRELE   1§
                 e per conoscenza   1§
                      Comando Stazione Ma.CC.   2
                                          GUARDIAGRELE

    All'internata sopra indicato è stata fissata la residenza in codesto comune.
    Essa,pertanto,munita di foglio di via,deve presentarsi in codesto
Ufficio che è pregato di provvedere a sistemarlo in una economica pen=
sione,a spese proprie,tenendo presente che le verranno corrisposte lire
6=50 giornaliere,più £.50 mensili per l'alloggio.
    Al la predetta _____ codesto Ufficio,con apposito verbale, pre=
scriverà l'obbligo di non allontanarsi assolutamente da codesto Comune
e di presentarsi una volta al giorno a codesto Comando di Stazione RR.CC.
    Prego assicurare.
                                          IL QUESTORE
                                       (F.Enrico Cavallo)

Province of Chieti
ORDER

The following documents are examples of rules governing Foreign Jewish Internees in the Comune of Guardiagrele in the Province of Chieti.

On the twenty third day of the month of November in nineteen forty, in the nineteenth year of the Fascist era, in the City Hall of Guardiagrele

Before me, Doctor LUCIANO DE MATTEO, Commissioner of the Prefecture of the above mentioned city, local authority of the State Police, and by invitation, has personally appeared Blumenkranz Efroin Fischel of Davide and Ethel Blaser, born in Rozwxadow on November 2nd 1903, stateless Jew, detained in this Comune on the 18th of this month, having come from the concentration camp of Agnone.

I, AS COMMISSIONER of the PREFECTURE

in application of the instructions given by Superior Authority:

Given the current law of the State Police and the relative Regulation:

HAVE OBLIGATED
THE ABOVE MENTIONED INTERNEE

to scrupulously observe the following regulations:

1) Must not in an absolute sense leave this City;

2) Must go to the local Command Post of the Royal Carabinieri on a daily basis;

3) Must not change designated address without first seeking permission from the Police Authority;

4) Must not return home later than 8 in the evening and not to leave earlier than 7 in the morning;

5) Must not carry or hold arms or other instruments that may be harmful;

6) Must not patronize brothels, saloons, or other public gathering places;

7) Must not attend meetings, events, or any type of entertainment;

8) Must have good conduct; not act in a suspicious fashion and must refrain from keeping the company of suspicious individuals;

9) must take up stable residence in the manner established by myself.

The internee declares having been informed of the above-mentioned regulations and of other regulations contained in the current regulation for the execution of the law of the Police Authority, and guarantees the scrupulous observance of the regulations mentioned and of others that may eventually, in any case, be imparted.

{line missing}

Ms. Domenichella Primavera located in Via delle Murene n 9, of this province.

Wrote the present summary in four copies of which

- One is given to the internee Blumenkranz Efroin Fischel;
- One is reserved in the files of this office
- One is to be sent to the Prefecture of Chieti
- One is to be sent to the Command Post of the Royal Carabinieri of Guardiagrele

Internee
(Signature)

The Prefecture Commissioner
(Signature)
Local Authority

The following document shows the stipend that Bertha Blumenkranz received from the Italian government while she was interned in Guardiagrele. The Italian government provided the internees with money for housing and food.

REGIA QUESTURA DI CHIETI   Chieti, 10 July 1940 XVII
---Cabinet------
N 08809
SUBJECT: Blumenkraunz Bertha of Lazar born Goldstein, 32 years of age, German Jew

Mr. Podesta` of GUARDIAGRIELE
For your information
Command Post Guardiagrele

A residence has been established in your city for the above-mentioned internee.

She must come to this office, with a travel document, and your office should kindly provide lodging for her in an inexpensive hostel, at her expense considering that she will receive 6.50 lira a day in addition to the 50 lira per month for housing.

To the above-mentioned person, your office will mandate, with a written deed, the obligation not to leave the city and to check in on a daily basis at your Command Post. Please guarantee.

The Officer
(Dr. Enrico Cavallo)

Translation courtesy of the Consulate General of Italy New York

Appendix D

BOOK TIME LINE

October 31, 1922	Benito Mussolini becomes Prime Minister of Italy
January 30, 1933	Adolf Hitler becomes Chancellor of Germany
September 15, 1935	Nuremberg Laws passed in Germany. Limit Jewish rights
March 11, 1938	Aunchluss. Germany annexes Austria
Summer 1938	Racial Laws begin to be passed in Italy. Limit Jewish Rights
November 9, 1938	*Kristallnacht* begins
November 10, 1938	Deportation of Jews to concentration camps begin
May 22, 1939	Germany and Italy sign "The Pact of Steel" which is a military alliance between the two countries

June 10, 1940	Italy announces that it has entered the war as junior ally to Germany
June 10, 1940	Foreign Jews begin to be arrested in Italy and sent to Italian Concentration Camps
Mid–June 1940	Foreign Jews in Italy transferred to concentration camps (i.e. Ferramonti, Campagna, small towns)
January 20, 1942	"Wannsee Conference [Berlin]. Coordinate full implementation of the Final Solution
Mid- 1942	Six killing centers became operational. At each of those places, gas chambers destroyed Jewish lives
July 10, 1943	Allies land in Sicily
July 25, 1943	Mussolini ousted from Power in Italy
September 3, 1943	Battle in Salerno begins (28 miles from Campagna)
September 8, 1943	Italy joins Allies

September 8, 1943	Germany (now Italy's enemy) invades Italy and begins round ups of Jews for deportation
September 23, 1943	Mussolini forms a new Government in Northern Italy and is the Duce of the "Italian Social Republic" (Salò)
October 16, 1943	1,259 Jews arrested in Rome
July 1944	Henry Gibbons leaves Naples with 982 Jews for Fort Ontario, Oswego, New York
September 13, 1944	Giovanni Palatucci arrested and sent to Dachau
January 27, 1945	Auschwitz liberated
February 10, 1945	Giovanni Palatucci dies in Dachau
April 29, 1945	Dachau liberated
May 8, 1945	World War II ends in Europe

Appendix E

NUMBERS OF JEWS LIVING IN EACH EUROPEAN COUNTRY PRIOR TO WWII AND WHO WERE MURDERED

JEWISH LOSSES IN THE HOLOCAUST

COUNTRY	Jewish Pre-War Population	Murdered
Austria	185,000	50,000
Belgium	65,700	28,900
Czechslovakia	207,260	149,150
Estonia	4,500	2,000
France	350,000	77,320
Germany (as of August 1939)	185,000	141,500
Greece	77,380	67,000
Hungary	825,000	569,000
Latvia	91,500	71,500
Lithuania	168,000	143,000
Luxembourg	3,500	1,950
Netherlands	140,000	100,000
Norway	1,700	762

COUNTRY	Jewish Pre-War Population	Murdered
Poland	3,300,000	3,000,000
Romania	609,000	287,000
Russia	3,020,000	1,100,000
Yugoslavia	78,000	63,300
Europe	9,796,840	5,860,129

Pre-War Total World Jewish Population	**16,500,000**
Total World Jewish Population, 1945	**11,125,000**

Source: Museum of Jewish Heritage, New York (as of November 7, 2008)
Core Collection: "The War Against the Jews"

Lucy Dawidowicz, in *The War Against the Jews,* has studied the Holocaust and the percentage of Jews killed.

For example, in Poland, before World War II, there were 3,300,000 Jews, and 3,000,000 (90 percent) were killed; in Germany/Austria there were 240,000 Jews before World War II, and 210,000 (90 percent) were killed; in Belgium there were 65,000 Jews before World War II, and 40,000 (60 percent) were killed; and in Italy there were 40,000 Jews before World War II, and 8,000 (20 percent) were killed.

Source: Lucy S. Dawidowicz, *The War Against the Jews: 1933-1945*
(Bantam,1986)

Appendix F

LETTERS FROM VINCE MARMORALE AND SOME SURVIVORS AND FAMILY MEMBERS INTERVIEWED FOR THIS BOOK

The Life-Changing Phone Calls

Little did I know back in June of 1995 that a phone call from a complete stranger named Walter Wolff would forever change my life. I asked Walter about his experiences during World War II. Walter responded, "I survived in Italy, but I don't have much of a story."

After listening to Walter for two hours, I realized that he had a story that needed to be told because so little is known about the saving of Jews by the Italian people during World War II. It was apparent to me that Walter had a lifelong desire to share his story in order to give thanks to the Italian people for saving his life and the lives of his brother and mother.

Since that telephone call, so many years ago, Walter and I traveled an incredible journey with the mission to tell his story about the Italian people and bring a different Italy to light. When we began, we never envisioned how large this story would become and how many Jews with similar stories of salvation would cross our paths.

We toured the country presenting the story of the ordinary Italian people who had the courage to care during the Holocaust. We spoke at many schools, universities, civic groups, synagogues, and Italian organizations. We appeared on television and were interviewed on radio, but even with all that, we had hit a brick wall. I could not take this story to another level—having the world learn about this little known aspect of the Holocaust.

Then, one day, Walter called me and told me he had met Elizabeth Bettina, and she arranged a visit back to his past. When I met Elizabeth, I was impressed with her tenacity and power of positive thinking. Thus began a journey that brought such joy to a nice elderly gentleman I had grown to love and admire, and this journey *did* take this story to another level.

We did go to Italy. Walter was honored in Campagna and was reunited with some of his rescuers. We were fortunate to have audiences with Cardinal Kasper, president of the Pontifical Council for Promoting Christian Unity, and Cardinal Ruini, Vicar General of the Diocese of Rome.

What even I didn't know then was that that trip was only the beginning. We found so many "Walters" with similar stories and took more unbelievable trips to Italy. In retrospect, I never thought the events of the past two years could ever happen. On a personal note, I'm so happy that my dear friend

Walter's story and those like him were told in this book. I feel a debt of gratitude to Elizabeth for telling these stories. The world needs stories like this—stories of goodness and hope.

—Vincent Marmorale

✦

Life has lots of surprises, and I think some of them are miracles. Our little story is amazing.

My good friend Walter Wolff was asked to speak at Queens College about his life and the years he spent in Italy during the war. After he was released from Dachau, he was lucky to get to Italy, where his life was saved, and he had pictures to show the years from Germany and how he got to Italy.

On the special day when he spoke at Queens College, suddenly a voice came from the audience. "My family comes from there . . ." It was like a miracle. Elizabeth came over to us, and we talked and talked. It was unbelievable.

After that she arranged a trip for us to go to Italy and made our trip(s) unbelievable—we love her and thank her and are very happy she wrote a book all about it. Not only were trips arranged, but a wonderful lasting friendship was born.

Unfortunately, Walter is no longer with us, but he was delighted to know that Elizabeth was working on a book that would include his story.

—Thank you Elizabeth.

Gerda Mammon

✦

Dear Elizabeth,

I would have never thought when I met you that I would travel back to where Fred was in Italy—Campagna and Ferramonti. I always knew why Fred survived for so long in Italy with Walter: it was because they were treated well, and I was able to see where they were and walk the town and the camp. Where they were was nothing like where I was—Auschwitz. Like I have said all these years, they did have a picnic in Italy, and I saw the pictures to prove it. What can I say but thank you for an experience of a lifetime.

—LOVE,

EDITH BIRNS

✦

When I first met Vincent with Walter Wolff, I certainly had no idea that I would start a relationship of this sort.

And I was not aware of the scope of the project that they were involved in. It grew, and we had a taping in New York with many people present, and it culminated with a trip to Italy and having a private audience with the Pope.

I feel privileged that my story will be included in Elizabeth's book and grateful for the efforts in putting all this together.

—GIORGINA DE LEON VITALE

✦

We are proud of my mom, and she has spoken to school groups and adult groups about her unique situation, but not until a book like this has it been known that the Italians were really different. I thank God that they are the way they are, and they still go on strike. It shows that they can be conscientious objectors and not just run with the herd.

It was wonderful to meet Elizabeth because she is a dynamo and very passionate about telling this story, and I was surprised to find out that she wasn't Jewish.

I feel fortunate that I met her, and that my mom met her, and I am excited that other people will be able to hear our story.

—Miriam Vitale (Giorgina's daughter)

✦

Dear Elizabeth,

Thank you so much for what you are doing—helping bring the story of Gandino and its people to others. If it was not for those people, I would not be here today, and if it were not for so many other good people in Italy, my other friends, Horst, Herta and Max would also not be here today. It is still unbelievable to me to think that I knew them in Italy before, during and after the war, and you have put our stories together. Thank you.

—Marina Lowi Zinn

✦

Dear Elizabeth,

Who said that dreams don't become reality? I can prove that, because my dream became reality through your help. And here is why!

When, about 13 years ago, Walter Wolff and Vince Marmorale interviewed me about my Holocaust experience in Italy and made it public to help set the record straight and inform the world of the great unrecognized part Italy and the Italian people played in serving the Jews, I was delighted.

Later when you joined our team effort, and gave it the "lightening" push it needed and this is why I love you (carbon copy of my daughter's personality). I mentioned to you that my dream was to visit and thank the people of Civitella (the camp I was interned) for the warm, friendly and courteous treatment.

I don't know how, but you made my dream come through with an additional unbelievable bonus, which I still think I am dreaming, to see and shake hands with the Holy Father.

The unforgettable memories experienced with my wife and children are now eternally embedded in my heart.

This would not have been possible if it were not for the hard work, persistence and planning by you and Vince, for which I and my family are tremendously thankful.

And last—we need the truth. Thank you for telling the stories of how I and others survived in Italy.

—HORST STEIN

✦

Dear Elizabeth,

I was very happy to contribute to the documentary by telling the story of my life in Italy during the Holocaust, and explaining how the Italian people saved my life. I also think it is very important to write a book, and it is wonderful that my life in Italy is being told, and I hope a lot of people will read it and will see the goodness of the Italian people. I am very proud to serve as a witness to those terrible times and be able to explain the difference between the German and Italian people of the time, because the world does not know how the Italian people treated us. When I speak to people, they always say that "Italy was a fascist country" and believe that the Italians must have been just like the Germans. It hurts me to hear this.

Even when he [Mussolini] became an ally with Hitler, he did the best he could for the Jews, under the circumstances, by opening internment camps, which were not at all like the German death camps. Mussolini interned the Jews under humane conditions where they were treated well. I went to one of these camps, Ferramonti di Tarsia, to visit my father who was interned there. I am very proud of being able to tell how good the Italians were with us and how they helped us, risking their lives. I'm also happy that I can be a witness to history and be able to tell how Italians are the best people in the world with the greatest hearts.

—Herta Mingelgrün Pollak

✦

To Elizabeth—with Love from Ursula,

My emotions and impressions about the three trips I took to Italy with your help, you worked so hard to put it all together.

Here are my thoughts:

Trip #1:

I was invited by the President of Italy to be present on January 24th at the Quirinale to honor Righteous Gentiles who saved Jewish lives during the Holocaust. My savior, Monsignor Benjamino Schivo is 98 years old and my best friend, like a father since I was 12 years old. To be honored after so many years by the President was such a great emotion, I cannot describe here I was received with such honor when as a child and teenage, I was hidden, poor and fighting for survival.

Trip #2:

June 14th—Back to Rome again with the help of Elizabeth in Piazza San Pietro, I had a private audience with the Pope, and he gave me his benediction, emotion took over again. Now I had an emotion to surpass the one of January. I did not think that could be possible.

Trip # 3:

In September another emotional trip in to the past. This time we visited two so-called concentration camps in the south of Italy. We went to Campagna, where Elizabeth's family comes from. I discussed this connection between Elizabeth and me, my father was interned in Campagna from 1940–1941. We went to this camp—now a museum—and I found a huge poster of my father shaking hands with the local bishop, and I just stood there in tears and, again, I thought which emotion leaves the deepest scar in me. I do not have the answer; each event was so personal and each is so different but I know I shall never forget as long as I live all the experience I had this year. And yes, all this is due to the efforts of Elizabeth,

I am forever grateful,

—URSULA KORN SELIG

✦

Dear Elizabeth,

Thank you for taking me back to my geographical and sentimental roots. On this eventful and emotional sojourn, I was able not only to retrace my parents' internment in Campagna, Potenza, and Tito, but also to validate the many testimonies that I had heard about the humane treatment of interned foreign Jews by the local people of this area during 1940–45. This trip went back into my personal memory of time, during which I found that some of characters were still very much alive.

Seeing my father's image on a poster of the convent of San Bartolomeo in Campagna, along with other interned men; meeting a woman in Potenza's main square, who per chance was visiting from Naples and who knew my mother during the war; and unexpectedly meeting, after more than sixty years, my "milk brother" whose mother had nursed me in 1941 when my own mother was unable to breast feed me, helped me frame the images of goodness guided by the hand of God during these perilous years.

The interned Jews residing in Potenza and the surrounding towns during 1940–45 in what was known then as "confino libero" were indeed very lucky to have lived among people who, for the most part, did not embrace the racial laws of their own country, and who acted decently and ethically toward the foreigners among them.

—WALTER KLEINMANN

✦

Dear Elizabeth,

When we first met, I did not quite get how important this mission was nor why you were so personally involved. Now I get it! Thanks for your efforts, determination, your amazing connections, your can do attitude. This experience was beyond amazing.

AFFETTUOSAMENTE, (AFFECTIONATELY)

—ELAINE (KLEINMANN)

✦

Elizabeth,

Your ability to make things happen and engage people in your world and your adventures is truly an amazing thing. Thanks so much for giving me the chance to tell my family's story and be a part of these adventures and more to come!

—ALEC POLLAK

✦

Dear Elizabeth,

It was all you said and more, I'll never forget it.

—HELEN KEMPIN

✦

Dear Elizabeth,

Thank you for everything you did for us, especially for me. With all my affection.

—MAX KEMPIN

✦

Dear Elizabeth,

We want to thank you for all the hard work and endless hours you put in to make our trip possible and such an awesome experience. We will never forget it.

—FONDLY,
RUTH AND TED (TOBIAS)

✦

Dear Elizabeth,

We still don't believe that trip really happened, but it did and you made it happen. It was the most memorable trip we ever had, all thanks to you and your persistence. You didn't just give of yourself, but also of your very precious time.

Hope to see you soon in Nashville and consider our home yours.

—FONDLY,
EVA AND ERIC (ROSENFELD)

✦

Thoughts,

It seems like yesterday that Mr. Walter Wolff returned to Campagna after he was interned in Campagna during the 1940's. He stayed with us for a few days, telling us about his ups and downs, telling us about his gratitude to the people of Campagna, "Good People" during "Bad Times". This could have been a place that was one of suffering, but was instead, it was a place that was civil and humane.

The visit of Mr. Wolff and those of others; children, grandchildren, and other family members of those interned in the camp of Campagna was incredibly moving. To see Ursula Korn Selig, Walter Kleinmann, Edith Birns and Gerda Mammon view the images of that period when their family members were interned in Campagna was very emotional.

Thanks to Vincent Marmorale and Elizabeth Nicolosi, we hope that we will continue to have visits in the future, so that people will know what was and more importantly, that it should not be forgotten.

—Michele Aiello
President of the
"Comitato Palatucci"

✦

Thoughts.

If I go back in my memory to 1996, the year I began my research on the Jews who were interned in Campagna, I could never have imagined in those days that this research would contribute to various, significant events.

I could have never thought that a list of Jewish names, who were interned in Campagna in 1940 that was included in my book, would land in the hands of Elizabeth Bettina, a woman whose family roots are from Campagna, but lives on the other side of the world in New York. I could have never thought that her passion for this story and her collaboration with Vincent Marmorale, would bring them to Campagna with Walter Wolff, who was interned in Campagna. I could also never have imagined that she would even bring a large group of American Jews to Campagna, some who had relatives interned here.

The height of my astonishment was when Walter Kleinmann recognized his father in a photo in the Museum of Memory and Peace—and the next day, he even met his "milk brother" who lived in Potenza! Who could have imagined this!

To think that because of my work and the determination demonstrated by Elizabeth Bettina and Vincent Marmorale, the two "milk brothers" would meet again after 60 year—and embrace—in front of my eyes! I was extremely moved when Walter Kleinmann said with tears in his eyes, "I have waited for this moment for 60 years."

Certainly, so many things have happened since 1996 and continue to happen; I can't but help to think what else can happen.

—SINCERELY,
GIANLUCA PETRONI
CAMPAGNA, ITALY

✦

Dear Elizabeth,

We applaud you for what you are doing so that what Happened is not forgotten. It is also important to remember who saved human life. In the name of the Comunità Ebraica di Casale, (Jewish Community of Casale) we thank you for what you are doing. We are close to you in thoughts.

—ARRIVEDERCI A PRESTO,

GIORGIO OTTOLENGHI

Bibliography

Suggested reading to further explore the Holocaust and Italy

Bassani, Giorgio. *The Garden of the Finzi-Continis*. Translated by William Weaver. New York: Everyman's Library, 2005.

Caracciolo, Nicola. *The Uncertain Refuge: Italy and the Jews During the Holocaust*. Edited by Richard Koffler. Translated by Florette Rechnitz Koffler. Chicago: University of Illinois Press, 1995.

Carpi, Daniel. *Between Mussolini and Hitler: The Jews and the Italian Authorities in France and Tunisia*. New York: Brandeis University Press, 1994.

Cornwell, John. *Hitler's Pope: The Secret History of Pius XII*. New York: Viking Press, 1999.

Dalin, David G. *The Myth of Hitler's Pope: How Pope Pius XII Rescued Jews from the Nazis*. Washington, DC: Regnery Publishing, 2005.

Diamand, Salim. *Dottore! Internment in Italy, 1940–1945*. Oakville, ON: Mosaic Press, 1987.

Folino, Francesco. *Ferramonti, un lager di Mussolini*. Cosenza, Italy: Brenner, 1985.

Gentry, Jimmy. *An American Life*. Franklin, TN: Pleasantview Press, 2002.

Gilbert, Martin. *The Holocaust: A History of the Jews of Europe During the Second World War*. New York: Holt, Rinehart & Winston, 1981.

Gilbert, Martin. *The Righteous: The Unsung Heroes of the Holocaust*. Henry Holt and Company, LLC, 2003–-2004.

Gruber, Ruth. *Haven: The Dramatic Story of 1,000 World War II Refugees and How They Came to America*. New York: Crown Publishing, 2000.

Herzer, Ivo, James Burgwyn, and Klaus Voigt, eds. *The Italian Refuge: Rescue of Jews During the Holocaust*. Washington, DC: Catholic University of America Press, 1989.

Hughes, H. Stuart. *Prisoners of Hope: The Silver Age of the Italian Jews, 1924–1974*. Cambridge, MA: Harvard University Press, 1996.

Kurzman, Dan. *A Special Mission: Hitler's Secret Plot to Seize the Vatican and Kidnap Pope Pius XII*. Cambridge, MA: Da Capo Press, 2007.

Lapide, Pinchas. *Three Popes and the Jews*. New York: Hawthorn Books, 1967.

Levi, Primo. *If This is a Man*. Translated by S. J. Woolf. New York: Everyman's Library, 2000.

McGrory, Mary. "Italy's Heroes of the Holocaust," *Washington Post*, December 2, 1993.

Marchione, Margherita. *Yours is a Precious Witness: Memoirs of Jews and Catholics in Wartime Italy*. New York: Paulist Press, 1997.

Melzer, Milton. *Rescue: The Story of How Gentiles Saved Jews in the Holocaust*. New York: Harper & Row, 1988.

Michaelis, Meir. *Mussolini and the Jews: German–Italian Relations and the Jewish Question, 1992–1945*. New York: Oxford University Press, 1978.

Petroni, Gianluca. *Gli ebrei a campagna durante il secondo conflitto mondiale: Giovanni Palatucci*. Campagna, Italy: Edizione Comitato, "Giovanni Palatucci," Campagna, Italy 2001.

Rabinowitz, Dorothy. "An Army of Schindlers from Italy," *Wall Street Journal*, December 22, 1993.

Raimo, Goffredo. *A Dachau, per amore: Giovanni Palatucci*. Montella, Italy: Litotipografia Dragonetti, 1992.

Roth, John. *The Holocaust Chronicle: A History in Words and Pictures*. Lincolnwood, IL: Publications International, 2000.

Rychlak, Ronald J. *Hitler, the War, and the Pope*. Columbus, MS: Genesis Press, 2000.

Sarfatti, Michele. *The Jews in Mussolini's Italy: From Equality to Persecution*. Madison, WI: University of Wisconsin Press, 2006.

Wiesel, Elie. *Night*. New York: Bantam Books, 1984.

Wolff, Walter. *Bad Times, Good People: A Holocaust Survivor Recounts His Life in Italy During World War II*, 1999. Long Beach, New York, Walter Wolff

Wyman, David S. *Abandonment of the Jews: America and the Holocaust, 1941–1945.* New York: Pantheon Books, 1984.

Zimmerman, Joshua D.. *Jews in Italy under Fascist and Nazi Rule 1922–1945.* Cambridge University Press, 2005.

Zuccotti, Susan. *The Italians and the Holocaust: Persecution, Rescue, and Survival.* Lincoln, NE: University of Nebraska Press, 1996.

Zuccotti, Susan. *Under His Very Windows: The Vatican and the Holocaust in Italy.* New Haven, CT: Yale University Press, 2002.

Suggested documentaries

Rochlitz, Joseph. *The Righteous Enemy.* DVD. Waltham, MA: Parstel Ltd. Films, 1987.

Rotter, Sy. *A Debt to Honor.* DVD. Washington, DC: Documentaries International, 1995.

Suggested films

The Assisi Underground. VHS. Directed by Alexander Ramati. Santa Monica, CA: MGM/UA Home Entertainment, 1985.

The Garden of the Finzi-Continis. DVD. Directed by Vittorio de Sica. Culver City, CA: Columbia TriStar Home Video, 2001.

Life is Beautiful. DVD. Directed by Roberto Benigni. New York: Miramax Films, 1997.

The Secret of Santa Vittoria. DVD. Directed by Stanley Kramer. Century City, CA: United Artists, 2008.

Suggested Web sites

Simon Wiesenthal Center. http://www.wiesnethal.com.

United States Holocaust Memorial Museum. http://www.USHmm.org.

Yad Vashem: The Holocaust Martyrs' and Heroes' Remembrance Authority. http://www.yadvashem.org.

About the Author

Elizabeth Bettina is a native New Yorker who lived in Italy. Elizabeth graduated from Smith College, in Northampton, Massachusetts. Presently, she works in marketing in New York.

Acknowledgments

As Walter Wolff once said, it took at least fifty people to help him survive—it has certainly taken more than fifty people to have this all come together. At the risk of inadvertently omitting some, I list here but a few of the people to whom I wish to give special thanks:

To all the survivors who welcomed me into their lives—I can never thank you enough for sharing your stories and generously providing me with so many extraordinary memories and photographs.

To all the people who risked their lives helping Jews during World War II—without you, the Jews in this book and many others would not have survived. Your actions are lessons in humanity, of the triumph of good over evil.

To Vincent Marmorale—

For imparting his extraordinary knowledge of the history of this time and place, and for his immeasurable guidance in reviewing the book in all stages. Words are insufficient to describe Vince's knowledge about this period in history and the years he dedicated lecturing with Walter Wolff.

And to Vince's family, for embracing me as one of their own.

To Vince De Giaimo, who recognized the importance of preserving these stories for future generations to learn about a little-known piece of history directly from those who were there at the time.

To Amy Roth—our angel.

To Cardinal Kasper, Cardinal Ruini, Monsignor Caccia, Monsignor Filippi and Dottoressa Savoia for recognizing the importance of this story and the need for it to be told.

To Gary Krupp who helped arrange our meeting with the pope.

To my many friends, who encouraged me over the years and listened to these stories. Without you, this book would not exist: Lisa Anderson, Jeff Baker, Jenn Bidner, Ira Braunschweig, Danielle Carbone, Jane Conway, Katie Engustian, Paula Flatow, Maryanne Foglia, Loretta Goldberg, Lisa Fried Grodin, Daniella Hildisch, Bruno Manduca, Kayalyn Marafioti, Ann Marchesano, David Marshall, Tracy McLure, Ginny Yost Mumm, Kate Naughton, Rose Riggins, Ellie Sommers, Ellen Barre Spiegel, Cullen Stanley, J'nn Sullivan; the Bennett, Brause, Hess, Lowry, Misthal, Posner, Scanlan, Shacnow, Silver, Valli, Wactlar and Zide Families.

Special thanks go to Ellen Auwarter, for years of love and friendship that began at our church on Long Island, and for her thoughtful guidance and suggestions throughout; Gail Greenwald for reviewing many of the stories and teaching me Yoga as a way to balance the journey as it unfolded; Michele Marwill for listening to these stories and offering her unique perspective; Anita Parker, who visited Campagna with me long before I understood the complexity of this story, and participated in the "Walter Wolff" and "September Trips." She made sure that the book captured the extraordinary events and coincidences she experienced; Stuart Gezelter, my techno guru—I'd be lost without you.

For my Nashville friends—

The Martin/Orland Family, who invited to me to Eli's Bar Mitzvah. Because of you, I met Eva Lepehne Rosenfeld—who connected me to the Kleinmann and Goldman stories;

The Jamison Family, who introduced me to John and Mary Love Patton, who in turn connected me to Jimmy Gentry;

Jimmy Gentry, for his heroism so long ago in liberating Dachau. His reaction to the stories and photos was priceless and affirmed the significance of these collected memories; and Theresa McCoy, a wonderful friend and supporter with a heart of gold.

To my friends at Cushman & Wakefield Sonnenblick Goldman—Elizabeth Dhimoshi, Cynthia Rodriguez, David Schaiman, Barbara Szurlej and Maureen Wlodarczyk. Special thanks go to Maria Spalt who read some of the very first drafts and encouraged me to learn more, and Alicja Kubit, who just knew that things would happen the way they did, and to the scanner, for helping reproduce the photos you see in the book.

To my friends at Farragut Capital, especially Tom Boytinck and Anja Wahlscheidt. Thank you for giving me time and resources to research this story.

The wonderful people at Thomas Nelson, who believed that this story needed to be told and that I could tell it—especially:

David Dunham, whom I met while researching this story; neither of us knew exactly what I would find, but he believed in it from the start;

Joel Miller, my current publisher, who absorbed David's commitment and carried this through to completion;

My editors—Lisa Wysocky, who worked tirelessly weaving the diverse pieces of cloth into a coherent and beautiful quilt, and

Kristen Parrish, who joined the "September Trip" to Italy and saw some of the stories unfold before her very eyes. Her dedication to this book and the people in it are extraordinary. (Kristen, I apologize for how the winding roads made you feel!) To Kristen Vaasgard, who designed a book jacket that truly conveys the story; and to the team, especially Walter, who typeset the book and designed the photo layout. All of you handled with grace and patience a book that continued to evolve as it was being written. Thanks to the rest of the team, especially Jason Jones, who worked on making sure this book reached your hands.

To Alec Pollak, for the many amazing photos you captured on our "September Trip"—you are so very talented.

To Ben Asen, for the wonderful photo you took for the cover of this book. Thank you.

To my lawyers at Reavis Parent Lehrer LLP, especially Heidi Reavis, Deena Merlen, and Nicole Page for guiding me through the publishing industry process.

To Engel Entertainment, especially Steve Engel, Susan Lee and Adrian Heinzelman for filming the survivors' stories.

To the Italian Consulate, Consul General Francesco Maria Taló, former Consul General Antonio Bandini and Consuelo Bandini, Deputy Consul Giovanni Favilli, who has watched this from the start.

Special thanks to Matilde Adabbo and Elizabeth Calello for the many laughs and tears we shared.

To Rosario Mariani and Deborah Baracena of Eurofly S.p.A.—Thank you for your unflappable patience with numerous reservations and many requests for wheelchairs;

To the Mencucci Family and the staff at the Atlante Star

Hotel—Thank you for making our visits so comfortable and for treating us like family;

To everyone at the *Ristorante/Hotel Avigliano*, especially Zio Peppe for sharing his book with me and hosting us several times;

To Gianluca Petroni, who researched Campagna's history and wrote the doctoral thesis that was the catalyst to this incredible journey.

To Michele Aiello, Carmine Granito, Sandro Scannapieco and the other members of the Comitato Palatucci for all their work;

The people of Benevento, who—understood the significance of Giovanni Palatucci's legacy and supported us during this project and our visits;

To the people of the Hotel Capital who took care of us and watched in awe with us when the "Milk Brothers" reunited.

To Dott. Rende and Dott. Panebianco of Ferramonti for providing me with extraordinary pictures that contributed to the story.

Special thanks to all my relatives too numerous to mention individually—especially those in Italy, the Granito, Insalata, Izzo and Del Giorno families— for decades of shared memories here and abroad.

To my friends in Italy—Lalla Ardino, Gilda Bassano, Maurizio and Antonietta Cammerano, Andrea and Syliva Fanfani, Horace Gibson, Anna LaGaipa, Laura and Donald Malcom, Mario and Vittorio Vescovi and the group from Borgo San Lorenzo.

To my teachers—from elementary school through college— you taught me that knowledge is power.

To my Godmother Isabel McLoughlin and family, Zia

Antonetta Nicolosi, Rochetta and Joe Caringella—who loved and supported me throughout my life, Bob and Connie Korrow and Rika and John Wimer—you are like family.

Aunt Ida Granito Caligara and her family—especially my cousin Patricia, who was as surprised as I was to learn about Campagna's story.

To my immediate family:

Mom and Dad, my brother and sister for lovingly teaching me my first lessons in humanity and service to others and for always being there.

And my dear niece Nanci—I wrote this for you and all the descendants of the people in these stories, so that you and they know the history created by your family and theirs.

And . . . all those mentioned in the book and so many others who have always championed and inspired me, I cannot possibly name each of you, but your influence will be felt always. Thank you all.

"Do you know what it is like to know that someone risked their life to save yours?"

—URSULA KORN SELIG